Restoring Respect for Justice

A SYMPOSIUM

SECOND EDITION

Martin Wright has been Director of the Howard League for Penal Reform, Policy Officer of Victim Support, and Librarian of the Cambridge Institute of Criminology. He is a Senior Research Fellow at the Faculty of Health and Life Sciences, De Montfort University, Leicester. Besides having spoken at many international symposia, he is the author of *Making Good: Prisons, Punishment and Beyond* (originally written in 1976 and to be re-issued with some new materials by Waterside Press in 2008) and *Justice for Victims and Offenders: A Restorative Response to Crime.* He is joint editor, with Burt Galaway, of *Mediation and Criminal Justice: Victims, Offenders and Community.* He was a founder member of the Restorative Justice Consortium and of the European Forum for Restorative Justice. He is a voluntary mediator with the Lambeth Mediation Service, London.

Restoring Respect for Justice
A SYMPOSIUM
SECOND EDITION

Published by
WATERSIDE PRESS
Sherfield Gables
Sherfield on Loddon
Hook
Hampshire RG27 0JG

Telephone 01256 882250 UK Landline low-cost calls 0845 2300 744
E-mail enquiries@watersidepress.co.uk
Online catalogue and bookstore www.WatersidePress.co.uk

ISBN Paperback 978 1 904380 38 2

First edition Waterside Press, 1999 (ISBN Paperback 978 1 872870 78 6)

Restoring Respect For Justice has been translated into Russian and Polish.

Cataloguing-In-Publication Data A catalogue record for this book can be
obtained from the British Library.

Cover design © 2007 Waterside Press.

Printing and binding Biddles Ltd., King's Lynn, Norfolk, UK

North American distributor International Specialised Book Services
(ISBS), 920 NE 58th Ave, Suite 300, Portland, Oregon, 97213-3786, USA
Telephone 1 800 944 6190 Fax 1 503 280 8832 orders@isbs.com
www.isbs.com

Restoring Respect for Justice

A SYMPOSIUM

SECOND EDITION

Martin Wright

With a Foreword by Howard Zehr

❦ **WATERSIDE** PRESS

Acknowledgements

I am extremely grateful to Guy Masters, who agreed to act as research assistant but has contributed much more than that implies; also to Joanna Adler, for kindly sending the extract from her PhD thesis, to Lisa Wright, for reading the text as a lay person and making helpful stylistic comments, to Hendrik Kaptein and John Stephenson, who read and commented on individual chapters, and to Marian Liebmann for doing the same for the *Update*. Responsibility, as ever, remains mine. Like most authors I am deeply indebted to all the librarians who have helped to track down information, as well as to the many colleagues on whose ideas the contributors to the Symposium have liberally drawn; without them this volume would be a very thin one. Particular thanks also to Roger Graef for writing the *Foreword* to the original edition, and to Howard Zehr for likewise contributing to this one.

Martin Wright
January 2008

Restoring Respect for Justice
A SYMPOSIUM

CONTENTS

Foreword

This book is entitled *Restoring Respect for Justice* but it could also be entitled *Restoring Respect in Justice.*
Like Roger Graef in his *Foreword* to the original edition, I am convinced that much offending is driven by issues of respect and disrespect, honour and dishonour. James Gilligan, in his book *Violence: Reflections on a National Epidemic,* argues that violence is motivated by an effort to remove, avoid or discharge shame. I am also convinced that one reason the criminal justice system so dismally backfires is that it treats offenders disrespectfully. If violence begets violence, so does disrespect beget disrespect.

Working with crime victims, I have also come to understand that part of their trauma is the disrespect they experience not only from their offender but all too often from their communities and families. Their trauma is compounded by the disrespect they so often experience from justice.

What victims and offenders most need from justice is respect. And this is precisely what restorative justice seeks to deliver.

In this refreshing book, Martin Wright — a leading thinker in the restorative justice field — looks at the existing criminal justice system from the differing viewpoints of people working within it. From those perspectives, he suggests ways that restorative justice might address some of the faults and contradictions: ways that it might make justice more respectful and more respected. A growing body of research confirms that he is on the right track. A 2007 examination of 36 studies of restorative justice programmes from around the world, by Lawrence Sherman and Heather Strang, found high degrees of victim satisfaction, reduced victim trauma, generally lower recidivism rates by offenders and projected lowered overall costs for healthcare and justice. They conclude, 'The evidence on RJ is far more extensive, and positive, than it has been for many other policies that have been rolled out nationally'.

Restorative justice has spread widely throughout the world in the past two decades. It has not only spread geographically, but it has entered new arenas: many schools, for example, are adapting restorative approaches to discipline and problem solving. This gives reason for much optimism. Yet Wright is also aware of the limits and dangers. In too many cases, practice falls short of the ideal. Many interventions that are being termed 'restorative' are not restorative at all.

It is timely, then, that a new edition of this book—originally published in 1999—is being released. In an *Update*, Wright provides a brief overview of changes that have taken place since that time. He also expands his examination of the psychological effects of punishment, showing that the results are often less or even the opposite of what is intended, and explores how the stated aims of sentencing often counteract each other. He suggests ways that restorative justice might point a way out of this dilemma.

Restoring Respect for Justice shows how justice might be made a more respectful and healing experience for those impacted—victims, offenders, communities. In doing so, it has the potential to restore confidence and respect for justice as a whole. By restoring respect in justice, respect can be restored for justice.

Howard Zehr
October 2007

Howard Zehr is Professor of Restorative Justice at the Center for Justice and Peacebuilding, Eastern Mennonite University, Harrisonburg, Virginia, USA

Extracts from the Foreword to the first edition

Respect is the operative word in this important book. Much violent crime happens in the name of responding to real or imagined disrespect—young black people call it 'dissing'. Many a head has been cracked on the same grounds as the Montagues' and Capulets' quarrel in sixteenth century Verona, over who bit whose thumb at whom. The simple 'offence' of wearing the wrong football or gang colours in a rival part of town can be considered enough of an insult to provoke violence.

Respect for 'violence done in the name of justice' is essential for the criminal justice system itself to work. The panoply of the criminal justice system—the high bench, the dock, wigs and robes in the Crown Court, the demand to 'be upstanding', the whispering and incomprehensible Latinate rhetoric, the whole theatre of the court is designed to engender respect for the law. Yet the persistent re-offending by those who pass through the system suggests that such respect is not being paid. Victims too often feel revictimised by the experience of adversarial trials.

How is it that a system that fails so badly—and so publicly—for victims, offenders and the general public nevertheless continues to command a major share of public spending? Worse still, its primary remedy for its failure is more of the same—more coppers, more courts, and more prisons.

The justice system manages to escape self-criticism, and radical overhaul by outsiders. With rare exceptions, like this book and others by Martin Wright and like-minded reformers—we seem incapable of the kind of rational and radical thought about justice which has been applied to make progress in other fields of endeavour.

It's not that many of us are actually pleased with the justice system. As the Politician shrewdly admits in this excellent 'Symposium', much of the posturing about tougher penalties and more prisons is done by people who actually know better, to satisfy the uncritical instincts of voters and those in the media ... The various speakers in the author's Symposium go on to reinforce this conclusion from their diverse perspectives. Their arguments may differ, but the message is crystal clear—that punishment alone is a hopelessly inadequate means to bring about constructive changes in behaviour. They acknowledge a place for some punishment, but crucially, only in connection with incentives and other forms of more positive encouragement ...

Can anything be done with the system we have? ... the Symposium rightly, in my view, holds up victim-offender mediation as the model of another approach to crime, justice, and rehabilitation both for offenders and for victims—and the communities in which they live. Although many victims choose not to accept the chance to meet their offender, others find it a liberating experience in which they can tell the offender about the impact of the whole experience—not just those things allowed in court, if they are called as a witness at all.

This makes it possible for the victim to feel involved in a way the justice system precludes. And it gives the offender a chance not just to suffer the humiliation which those who see mediation as punishment want it to be, but also to learn—constructively—of the impact of their actions on other people. In Lipsey's terms, this is a key to their rehabilitation. John Braithwaite calls it 'reintegrative shaming', which it can be, especially if other friends and members of their own and the victim's family are present.

That theme runs through this vitally important book. It makes clear that we cannot leave these issues to professionals, who—at least in this Symposium—are well aware of their limitations. Change will only come when we accept that *all* of us are involved, and must play our part if the elusive goal of the reduction of offending is to be realised.

Roger Graef
August 1999

Roger Graef is a criminologist, author, broadcaster, documentary-maker and the founder of Films of Record

Introduction

The need for restorative justice is as great today as when this book was first published in 1999. Concern about crime remains high, despite the fact that over that period the level of many crimes has gone down. The new Labour government that came to power in the UK in 1997 has emphasised deterrence in its attempt to control crime. It has introduced over 50 Acts on criminal justice, creating over 3,000 new offences. Offenders are not so much encouraged and assisted to do better; the aim is rather to manage and control them. The prison population in England and Wales has broken new records. New sentences, including minimum and indeterminate ones, have been introduced, with a Sentencing Guidelines Council to try to make sense of them. In a word, more of the same.

But there is another way. Restorative justice has also been developing during this time. Although the practice is lagging behind the theory, the phrase is heard more often in everyday speech, and a number of projects are implementing it, even if only in a limited way. The Government has produced a statement of strategy on restorative justice, and the Youth Justice Board has encouraged more use of restorative methods.[1] Research findings are building up, and the idea is being developed in other countries, encouraged by the Council of Europe,[2] the European Union,[3] and the United Nations.[4] A European Forum on Restorative Justice has been formed, which holds conferences and other events, publishes a newsletter, promotes research and maintains a website.[5] Before we can conclude that restorative justice offers a better model than criminal justice, however, some important questions need to be answered: does the practice fully implement the theory of restorative justice; can it be applied to the most serious violent and 'white-collar' crimes; and what can be done when a fully restorative process appears to be inadvisable or impossible?

If there is one major obstacle to the spread of this philosophy, despite its overwhelmingly favourable evaluations,[6] this symposium points to the persistent belief in the use of punishment as a deterrent and in the possibility of applying it in a way that is both fair and logically defensible. At one time it was widely believed that bleeding patients was good medical practice, but with greater understanding it came to be recognised that this was misconceived and counterproductive. It is time to re-evaluate the effects of punishment in a comparable way.

Progress needs to be made by a range of people who work in, or think about, the criminal justice system. This book therefore approaches the subject from the point of view of some of the key practitioners, as if they were speaking at a symposium. It is hoped that this will present the issues in a more multi-faceted way than the standard academic format, although sources are cited in the usual way. I have tried to use non-technical language, so that people from each discipline can understand the others. To avoid overloading the presentations with statistics, a 'civil servant' is on hand to produce these at the end of each session; and some controversial questions are dealt with in discussion.

In the opening session the political context is given by the Politician, who is willing to base policy on research findings, and suggests a politically acceptable way of presenting the idea while appearing suitably hard-nosed. She proposes giving a financial incentive not to individuals but to the system, to develop non-custodial measures, including restorative ones. Secondly, the Psychologist looks at a neglected subject: the actual psychological effects of punishment. So many people, including lawyers, take deterrence for granted, with a disregard for evidence which in any other context they would find unthinkable. The Psychologist points to its unwanted side-effects, including efforts to escape it by any means, even the killing of witnesses; and gives examples of projects which have effectively encouraged people to behave well.

The main alternative to punishment, for more than a century, has been rehabilitation, and in the third session the Probation Officer explores the strengths and weaknesses of this concept; the government is bent on replacing it, but is control a good or even workable replacement? He points to evidence that public opinion is not as punitive as is commonly supposed, and that deterrence can actually increase recidivism. The fourth speaker is a Victim Assistance Worker, who considers recent moves to make the criminal process less of an ordeal for victims, and questions whether reforms such as victim impact statements can ever be adequate while the basis of the system remains the same.

The fifth and sixth contributors are the Judge and the Philosopher, both looking at aspects of sentencing. The Judge explains the dilemmas created for her by the theory of general deterrence, and the conflict between the demands of retribution, mercy and proportionality. She suggests that the way forward could lie in using reparation rather than punishment as a basis. But she recognises that there is no way of devising 'key performance indicators' for the assessment of judges. The Philosopher draws a distinction between punishments and sanctions. He looks at the ethics of punishment, and agrees with the judge that there is no objective way of determining the right amount to inflict; and proposes some principles which could form the basis for future development

Finally the Mediator describes in practical terms a system based on a new philosophical approach, and tries to answer some of the questions which may arise in people's minds. Two particular points are the way in which restorative justice could contribute to prevention, and the fact that it aims not merely at an outcome but an out-of-court process which—unlike many aspects of the adversarial process—will be helpful to those who take part in it, especially victims.

I would like to explain a couple of stylistic notes. To avoid the clumsiness of repeating 'himself or herself' or using plurals referring to single individuals, the masculine has generally been used for offenders and victims, but with 'he or she' from time to time as a reminder of gender differences. Secondly, the word 'judge' has been used as a generic term for judges and magistrates.

The symposium takes the institutions and legislation of England and Wales as its reference point; this will in many cases also be applicable to Scotland and Northern Ireland, which have different systems, and sometimes to other countries; as evidence of this, *Restoring Respect* has already been translated into Polish and Russian.

Martin Wright September 2007

---

1 Youth Justice Board (2006) *Developing Restorative Justice: An Action Plan*. London: YJB. www.yjb.gov.uk.
2 Council of Europe (1999) *Recommendation no. R(99)19 of the Committee of Ministers to Member States Concerning Mediation in Penal Matters*. Strasbourg: Council of Europe; Ivo Aertsen *et al.* (2004) *Rebuilding Community Connections: Mediation and Restorative Justice in Europe*. Strasbourg: Council of Europe.
3 European Union Council (2001) *Framework Decision of 15 March 2001 on the Standing of Victims in Criminal Proceedings*.

[4] United Nations (2002) *Basic Principles on the Use of Restorative Justice Programmes in Criminal Matters*. UN Economic and Social Council; United Nations. Office on Drugs and Crime (2006) *Handbook on Restorative Justice Programmes*. New York: United Nations.

[5] www.euforumrj.org

[6] For example, L Sherman and H Strang (2007) *Restorative Justice: the Evidence*. London: Smith Institute. www.smith-institute.org.uk

The Politician

As a politician one of the things I should most like to achieve is a harmonious society. We shall never eliminate conflict, and life would be a little dull without it (which is why some of us are a bit ambivalent about Utopias!). But we do want to try to prevent people taking advantage of each other in an unfair way which, when you think about it, is part of the definition of crime. In other contexts it is a description of some of the pressures which lead to crime: many crimes, though by no means all, are committed by people who have themselves been badly treated, whether by receiving less than their share of parental care, educational and other opportunities, or by suffering economic exploitation or actual abuse. They try to get what they think they are entitled to, in any way they can. That does not *excuse* them, if we believe in free will, but it helps to *explain* the behaviour of some lawbreakers — a distinction which politicians are not always very good at making — and it is therefore a factor we have to consider if we want to reduce the amount of crime that is committed.

However, that takes us into the realm of general social policy. As a spokeswoman on Home Affairs, I have to focus specifically on crime. I want to reduce crime if I can, as we all do, and, let's be honest, I want to be *seen* to be tackling the problem: to reduce the crime figures, especially the kinds that cause public fear and indignation. Secondly, I want the small proportion that are cleared up to be dealt with in a satisfactory way. In the current climate we have also to keep within spending limits; and naturally we want to keep within limits of humanity set by international conventions on human rights, especially now that the European Convention is part of British law.

Reducing crime

To start with the most talked-about sanction, imprisonment does have some advantages for politicians, although it is also generally the most expensive, except in the United States, where the legal processes of Death Row make capital punishment even more costly (five to ten times as expensive as a 40-year prison sentence, according to one expert (Hodgkinson, 1996)). Prison sentences give the appearance that we are 'doing something'. When Michael Howard was Home Secretary he won support in some quarters with slogans like 'Prison works' and 'If you won't do the time, don't do the crime'; in the United States many judges and prosecutors (district attorneys) are elected, and it is easier for them to attract votes if they take a similar simplistic stance than if they try to educate the electorate. This is especially true if the opposing party is ruthless in portraying humaneness as weakness, as the governor of Massachusetts Michael Dukakis found in 1988 when he became a Democratic presidential candidate: he was blamed by his Republican opponents for the release on furlough of Willie Horton who had been convicted of rape and then committed another rape while on parole. Bill Clinton did not make the same mistake; although he began as a liberal governor of Arkansas and exercised clemency, when he was a candidate for the presidency he returned to his home state to sign the death warrant of Ricky Ray Rector, who was clearly *non compos mentis*.

Home Secretaries like to see newspaper headlines such as 'Baker acts to curb menace of dangerous dogs', and their two main methods are creating new offences and increasing the penalties for existing ones. But these are risky strategies: more offences on the Statute Book usually mean more offences in the Criminal Statistics, and locking up more people provides only a temporary respite. As a Conservative Home Secretary famously said, 'Prisons are an expensive way of making bad people worse' (Home Office, 1990). (It's a shame to spoil the epigram, but I think he should have said 'making people behave worse', because I don't think we fallible humans should condemn our fellows as 'bad', but only their behaviour.)

The folk wisdom is that the way we deal with convicted offenders is an important part of keeping the amount of crime in check, and that toughness works—especially prison. Privately, I have my doubts about this, and the research gives little support to the idea. At the end of this talk I will ask the Civil Servant to summarise some of it. Politicians ought to be able to promise that they will base their policies on research; but I can't openly support replacing imprisonment with controversial measures which don't sound 'tough' unless I can make them acceptable to the general public. They also have to be reasonably proof against rubbishing by hard-line politicians and the tabloid newspapers, unscrupulously pursuing debating points and ideas that conform to, and reinforce, the preconceptions of their voters and readers, who therefore continue, respectively, to vote for them and to buy those newspapers.

The procedure for dealing with accused persons is also important. It is easy to demand rough justice, and to caricature concern for due process as 'soft', but agents of justice who flout the rules are hypocritical and lead, literally, to contempt of courts; and wrongful convictions do not protect the public because they leave the real perpetrators at large.

There is another piece of folk wisdom—and this one does have criminological support: that the fear of being caught is much greater than the fear of what might come after being caught. Only three per cent of offences result in a caution or conviction, and frequent offenders know better than anyone how often they get away with it. Stepping up the punishment is like revving up the engine of a car stuck in soggy ground: when the wheels are slipping, they throw up a lot of mud but the car sinks deeper and goes nowhere.

That is what will happen to those who imagine that the courts have 'power' to make much difference to the crime rate. They can impose sanctions, but can do little to control the attitudes and behaviour of the recipients.

Trying to control crime waves by means of sentences imposed by the courts puts me in mind of King Canute.

Everybody knows one thing about King Canute, and most of them have got it wrong The popular version is that he had his throne placed on the shore, commanded the incoming tide to turn back, and was made to look foolish when it didn't. The more authentic version is different. He did not believe that he could control the tide. He was a shrewd and popular administrator, but when his flattering courtiers told him that he was omnipotent, it was precisely to prove them wrong that when the tide was rising he made them take his throne to the shore, sat in it, ordered the unruly sea to turn back, and made sure that when the tide disobeyed him they, too, got their feet wet.

The lesson of King Canute does not seem to have been learnt, however, as far as today's courts are concerned, and there are still demands for 'tough' policies — partly because of retributive attitudes, but partly because people really do seem to believe that they would work, and politicians wish to appear to be in tune with public opinion.

Prison as containment

But to be fair to us politicians (and if I'm not, who will be?), it is not all about appearances. Even the most liberal penal reformers admit that some people cannot be left at liberty, when there is a substantial risk that they will commit another very serious crime. And for less serious but persistent offenders prison does, as judges sometimes say, 'give the public a rest from their activities', even if this is only a short term respite because they come out again or others emerge to seize their perch in the underworld hierarchy. So I honestly don't think it is tenable to be a total abolitionist with regard to prison, as it is with capital punishment — which could not have been abolished if prisons were not an alternative.

Paying the price

We are all subject to cash limits these days, although Home Secretaries can often use the fear of crime and disorder to find more; Jack Straw, for example, obtained an extra £43 million for prisons soon after becoming Home Secretary in May 1997, and a further £100 million early in 1998, despite the new Labour government's policy of keeping strictly within the spending plans of the previous Conservative administration. The threat of prison riots is a potent bargaining counter. As far as cash limits are concerned, prisons are obviously very expensive—the Civil Servant will tell you just how expensive a little later. The prison service employs two members of staff for every three prisoners (Home Office, 1998a), so you can work out roughly how much 65,000 prisoners cost for staff alone. So the cost could be one of the strongest arguments for reformers, if they could get round the punitive attitudes I was just talking about. One of the answers is to overcome bureaucratic obstacles to the transfer of funds from one budget to another. I know the Home Office has been looking at restructuring (Home Office, 1998b), and I should like to put before you a practical version of payment by results which could be used to achieve this.

Criminal justice system: cost transfer
It is worth looking at this question of cost, because it is important not only for criminal justice but for other aspects of policy such as looking after ex-hospital patients in the community. The principle is simple. If you find that patients or prisoners are being kept in restrictive (and costly) institutions, and you want to transfer some of them to less restrictive (and less expensive) supervision in the community which is funded by a different budget, it will not work unless part of the money saved is transferred from the former to the latter, and the Treasury agrees to accept less than 100 per cent of the saving.

Let us see how this applies to criminal justice. A survey of the prison population shows that by generally acceptable criteria many people are in prison who by most objective standards do not need to be there: their offences are not very serious, nor dangerous, and they do not have long criminal records. In 1996, 94,500 people were sentenced to immediate imprisonment in England and Wales, only 15,400 (16 per cent) of them for violent or sexual crimes (Home Office, 1997: *Table 7.6*). Often their needs could be better (and less expensively) met in the community, and they need support if they are to make a new start.

Although courts decide about imprisonment, they are influenced by probation officers' pre-sentence reports (PSRs). But if these make a case for community sentences in borderline (i.e. difficult) cases, the probation officers know they will have to deal with them, without extra resources, while the prison service reaps the benefit of reduced pressure of numbers. However, if community sentences are to be used in place of imprisonment, the public has to be reassured that they are likely to be effective. This is how the proposal would operate:

1. Identify categories of offender for whom the probation service could create constructive community programmes offering a better hope than prison of providing the support they need, for example vocational skills, literacy, numeracy, anger management, accommodation, and help in finding employment. Further options include reparation to the victim or the community and, where both victim and offender are willing, victim/offender mediation.

2. A fund would be set up to which the probation service could apply for grants. For every reduction in the prison population below its level at the start of the scheme there would be a *per capita* contribution to the fund of, say, 50 per cent of the cost of a prison place, with the balance going to the Treasury to increase the budget for crime prevention in the widest sense, including pastoral care for school children, parenting education, and other long-term investments. The probation funds would have to be used for specific projects, not just be absorbed into routine work.

3. Able probation officers would thus have an incentive to look for ways of providing effective services for which there was local need: besides benefiting their clients, it would give them job satisfaction and would be a useful addition to their CVs.

4. The programmes would have defined admission criteria and independent evaluation, to ensure that they were correctly used. The knowledge that the regimes were strictly controlled should make them acceptable to courts and the public, especially if they contained an element of reparation.

The proposal is based on a system operated in California in the 1960s. In five years it cost $60 million, but saved $180 million in the closure of old prisons and the cancellation of new ones—huge sums at that time. In the end it lapsed, not because of inherent flaws, but for reasons which could be put right—for example, it should be based on prison population rather than on numbers received into prison, and the funding must keep pace with inflation.

The first cases sentenced to these programmes instead of prison would reduce prison overcrowding, and would thus produce only small savings; but further substantial savings would allow cuts in the prison building programme, and after that closure of wings and even whole prisons (Wright, 1982: 152-6).

Even offenders have rights

The question of human rights is not as high among the priorities of politicians and the public as it should be, particularly in the context of the penal system. Even the British public rebels against some excesses, such as the chaining of a pregnant women prisoner to a bed in 1995 when she was allowed out to hospital to give birth, for which she was awarded £20,000 (*Guardian*, 10 June 1998), and the shackling of a man dying of cancer, after which his family was offered £25,000 (*The Times*, 18 June 1998). Despite these cases, another woman prisoner, with multiple sclerosis, was shackled to a hospital bed for 13 days after suffering a stroke (*Guardian*, 10 July 1998). The European Court of Human Rights has shown over the past three decades that its standards are more stringent, and a government which has some pretensions to upholding law and humanity is well advised to avoid practices that risk yet another rebuff from our European colleagues.

But even though I do not agree that prisons can be abolished, I concede that they are not the answer, nor even a substantial part of it. We must look in other directions if we are to make a serious attempt to reduce the number of crimes.

A POLITICAL STRATEGY

In the light of all this, I have a five-point strategy.

Rhetoric

1. I shall continue to use the language of toughness, because whether you like it or not that is what much of the public wants, and it is necessary if I am going to get the votes of supporters of my own party, let alone attract people from other parties. As I have said, our main political opponents, and the popular press, have no compunction about ridiculing anything that smacks (if I may use that word) of 'softness'. But I shall choose my words. I shall speak of firm *action* rather than *punishment,* and if I use expressions like 'zero tolerance' I shall mean only that misdemeanours are not ignored, without implying that the response will be a harsh one. But I shall also stress the importance of preventing crime, and the fact that it doesn't just need government action, or money, or security devices, but action by all sorts of people, from helping to run youth activities to refraining from buying second-hand goods with 'no questions asked'.

Prison

2. In the same vein, I shall not claim to be a prison abolitionist. There is a place for prisons—and not only for serial killers. I will remind liberal

reformers of an awkward fact. One of their examples of the inefficacy of deterrence harks back to the epidemic of garotting in late 1862. The standard version goes like this: there was an epidemic of robberies using the unpleasant technique of garotting, or choking, the victim (which incidentally shows that you can have copycat crimes without the assistance of mass media). At first there was an increase in *recorded* crime, which fuelled the alarm of *The Times*, *Punch* and their affluent readers; but this was probably because the police had been spurred into action by the moral panic, and did not reflect any increase in criminal activity on the streets. The government, as governments do, reacted by rushing through an Act, the hopefully named Security from Violence Act, or 'Garotter's Act', re-introducing flogging which had been abolished as recently as 1861 (Pearson, 1983: 142-155). But then the number of garottings went down, say the reformers triumphantly, *before* the Act became law on 13 July 1863; there are fashions in crime as in other things, and this one had run its course before the deterrent was in use. But *why* had the numbers gone down? Because the gangs had been rounded up by the police. So the episode may not be an argument for deterrence, but it is one for containment. A short-term advantage perhaps, and I don't deny that in those days of solitary confinement and no after-care many of the offenders probably returned, perforce, to their way of life; but in the immediate situation the police action was necessary and effective, even if the Garotter's Act wasn't.

So if deterrence doesn't work very well, what about containment? There are some who, even liberal reformers agree, have to be locked up for a very long time, even forever; and as for the less serious offenders, while they are locked up, the public has a rest from their activities. That is the line which, politicians find, goes down well in public; but those of us who have done our homework know of the Home Office estimate that if the prison population increases by a substantial percentage, crime begins to go down by a much smaller percentage. The Civil Servant will give details. In any case, as the reformers are quick to tell us, nearly all of them will come out sometime, often more anti-social than before. The tough policy might add an element of deterrence to the containment effect, but this would not increase the reduction (so to speak) by very much.

The logic of this is clearly to make less use of prison, with more community programmes to try to change offenders' behaviour. Reformers claim that making offenders face reality is actually tougher than letting them sit mindlessly in prison; but this doesn't cut much ice with Joe Public — sorry, with ordinary, hard-working, tax-paying, centre-right-minded people like my constituents. It is too easy for the Opposition and the tabloids to caricature community sentences as 'soft', and they are quick to pick on examples that seem to go over the top, like sending a young offender on safari which is supposed to increase his self-awareness and self-esteem, especially if he then re-offends. And however carefully thought-through decisions are, it is hard to defend them publicly in individual cases because of the requirements of confidentiality. So it seems as if our Black Maria is in a hole, but we are under tremendous pressure to keep spinning the wheels. 'Tough versus lenient' is a sterile argument; I hope the Symposium will come up with a third direction, which can be put across as firm and effective.

I have said that a community safety policy must include an element of containment, that is, the use of coercion to limit unacceptable behaviour. I agree that this has to be kept to a minimum (in this respect the interests of justice and thrift coincide). It is also worth remembering that for many purposes measures such as disqualification (from driving, managing a company, working with children, and so on) could be an adequate form of containment.

Prevention

3. My third strategy will be to put far more resources into crime prevention — although it affects many departments and much of the cost will come from them. They will however reap the benefits. I have given reasons why general deterrence will no longer be the cornerstone of crime control policy, although the prospect of entering the criminal justice system at all will still be a deterrent for many. Deterrence, although it sounds so simple, is an oblique approach; the straightforward way to try to prevent crime is to have a crime prevention policy.

Crimes broadly speaking have three elements, a subject, a verb and an object, in other words an offender, a criminal act, and a target or victim. If we look first at the 'verb', the act, it is only a crime because the Parliament (or other lawmaker) has defined it as such, and it is worth considering whether certain acts still need to be on the list, especially when there is no victim other than the person himself or herself (possession of small quantities of drugs), or another person who is willing (homosexual acts in private). Drugs are a huge question; for the present I will just say that serious questions are being asked about whether the war against drugs causes more harm than drug abuse itself (see for example the letter from the Lindesmith Centre in New York and many prominent people to the United Nations Secretary-General (*Guardian*, 11 June 1998)). Similarly with activities whose undesirability has only just been recognised: if society has realised the dangers of alcohol or tobacco or beef-on-the-bone, prohibition may not be the most effective way of reducing their consumption.

Secondly there is the 'object' of the crime. There has been considerable study of 'target hardening' and 'situational crime prevention'. Bolts and locks, and more sophisticated methods, have their place, but (as usual) at a price—not only the monetary cost, but the potential displacement of criminal activity to another area (from impregnable banks to cash in transit, or from cash theft to credit card fraud—the latter, perhaps, the lesser of two evils). There are also psychological costs. Grilles are a barrier to a friendly relationship between staff and customer, so some banks have gone to the further expense of installing screens which remain hidden until they pop up in a fraction of a second at the touch of an alarm button. Fortifying one's home is expensive, inconvenient, and a constant reminder of one's fear. There is a constant balance to be struck between making life easier for the customer and/or more profitable for the trader, through for example self-service supermarkets with reduced staff, and making it easier for the thief or fraudster. I propose to commission an analysis of the cost/benefit of increasing ordinary staff (bus conductors, railway station and on-board staff, park keepers, concierges, and so on) as against security staff, closed-circuit television surveillance, and the cost (police, courts and sometimes imprisonment) of the extra crimes attributable to the lack of 'natural' supervision. I am studying a proposal that organizations which do not employ enough main-grade staff to provide reasonable supervision of their premises or vehicles would have to bear the costs of prosecution of, for example, vandals or shoplifters.

Last but not least there is the 'subject': the perpetrator. The best restraint is self-restraint; the internal police constable is always on duty (well, almost). I am enough of an optimist to believe that most of us behave with consideration for others most of the time, for all sorts of reasons: because we care about them or value them, because we realise that we depend on each other, because we take pride in behaving well, because we are sensitive to other people's disapproval, or because we fear official punishment or unofficial retaliation. Only the last two, disapproval and punishment, are dependent on being found out; the others we—usually—enforce on ourselves (though we sometimes want to make sure we are found out if we have done something virtuous when no one was looking). Even when we behave in a way that harms others, we often have to overcome considerate feelings first, by persuading ourselves that no one will really suffer (shoplifting, dodging fares or taxes), the victim can afford it (burglary), the victim deserved it (some forms of violence), or that the victim enjoyed it (paedophilia). But there are also some who do not care what they do to others because they feel that others do not care about them; the results may be anything from vandalism, committed by bored young people left to their own devices, to extreme violence.

The implications for crime prevention are clear: 'Give me a child until it is seven years old and its mind is mine for life', as the Jesuits say. Many studies have confirmed the truth of this intuitive principle. One of the best known is the method of the High/Scope Educational Research Foundation in Michigan, USA, where pre-school children are encouraged to make positive choices about the play activities they wish to pursue. Working with a staff ratio of at least one teacher to ten children, and a maximum class size of 20, the staff use methods such as small group activities, tidying-up time, outside play time, snack time and story time, and close contact with parents. The Perry Pre-school Program, in a disadvantaged, black neighbourhood of Ypsilanti, Michigan, has been researched over a period of 30 years, and by the age of 19 the children were found to be more likely to have completed their schooling, less likely to have needed special educational support, more likely to have found a job, and 40 per cent less likely to have been arrested. By the age of 27 they were still less likely to have been arrested, and specifically to have been arrested five or more times or for drug-related offences. It was calculated that every $1 spent on the programme produced a return of $7 to the taxpayer in reduced crime, lower demand for special education, welfare and other public services.

The Home Office survey from which this summary is taken (Utting, 1996: 37-40) warned that results in 1990s Britain might not be so dramatic as in 1960s America, and that this is not the *only* model to follow; but four 'Young children first' projects are being funded by the Home Office (but for only three years) and evaluated, and a whole range of programmes has been started in many places (Goldblatt and Lewis, 1998). In mid-1998 a £540 million initiative called Sure Start was announced for children from conception to the age of three. Initially it will focus on 250 deprived areas, using health visitors and other outreach workers to introduce parents to basic parenting, health and life skills. It is the result of co-operation between several government departments, and will have built-in evaluation (*Observer*, 19 July; *Guardian*, 24 July 1998). We need to build the foundations of a society in which every child is valued and feels respected, so that no one wants to say, like the Miller of the Dee in the old song:

I care for nobody, no, not I,
And nobody cares for me.

Obviously there is a lot more to be said and done about crime prevention — even some of the High/Scope children went on to offend — but for the moment I am talking about fundamentals.

A most important aspect of prevention is the prevention of violence. This is a huge subject which I cannot discuss in detail here, but I take very seriously the comprehensive review of the causes and prevention of violence by the Gulbenkian Foundation (1995). This Commission considered violence *by* and *against* children, the effects of parental example, physical punishment and humiliation, sexual abuse, television, pornography, violence in sport, and many other factors with proven or suspected links to violence. It recommends general and specific measures to reduce violence and promote non-violent values, especially conflict resolution; a long-term strategy, it is true, but a vital one.

My party cannot ignore the target-hardening approach to crime prevention, but I want to assure you that we will take 'social crime prevention' seriously: job creation, welfare to work, skills training must all be part of any integrated strategy both for primary crime reduction and for the reduction of re-offending, in addition to the basics of education, housing and recreation.

Restorative justice
4. I shall be following the restorative justice initiatives about which we have been hearing a lot recently with interest – and the public reaction to them. Several of the features of restorative justice intuitively make good sense. Many people will be attracted by the idea of putting the victim's recovery first, and enabling him or her to take part outside the conventional criminal justice process. I think my constituents also appreciate the fact that offenders are held to account, but in a constructive way that requires them to do something to put right the wrong. The liberal-minded penal reformers should like the fact that the rehabilitation of disadvantaged offenders has a place in the restorative concept. And I have taken note of public opinion polls which have found that when you ask people, a very high percentage of them think that offenders should have to make good the consequences of their crime wherever possible, or do community service instead of going to prison; we shall probably hear more about that from other speakers.

There are however some questions in my mind, and I look forward to hearing what the Mediator has to say about them. One is the measurement of effectiveness; I want, and I think the public wants, to know that the measures that we are taking reduce crime. Another is the question of fairness: is it acceptable that different offenders make different reparation for similar offences, because their victims responded differently? And this leads to the more general question of how restorative justice can fit in with the conventional way of doing things.

Research

5. As I said earlier, I am a believer in research-based policy, which I take as a test of a politician's good faith (especially in the Home Office). I am therefore committed to allocating resources to research and taking account of it in policy formulation. Politicians are not often willing to admit it, except on occasions like this when we are under Chatham House rules, but we have mixed feelings about research. Sometimes it has advantages: like a Royal Commission it can give us a breathing space before we have to make a decision. But once we have the results, they sometimes point to solutions that are counter-intuitive, and we know that to explain them to the electorate will be an uphill struggle, especially if the tabloid newspapers decide to sell more copies by ridiculing the findings. There is the added complication that findings do not always point in the same direction; and of course research, like everything else, is (dare I say it in the presence of several distinguished academics) variable in quality. Nevertheless I do believe that social initiatives, like chemical or engineering ones, should be systematically evaluated, and I will encourage the Home Office and other funders to include a research component in new projects, both to assess their achievements, if any, and to devise feasible systems of record-keeping so that their management, and providers of funds, can monitor them year by year to ensure that they are fulfilling their promise. The Home Office and the Youth Justice Board have shown an encouraging awareness of the value of research.

I should like to finish by saying that I often feel frustrated at being unable to talk as openly and as realistically as I have here. It is a great shame that it is so difficult to escape the dogma of 'boot camps', 'prison works', and so on. Politicians must take their share of the blame (especially those in the other parties, as I would claim!), but it will not surprise you if I also blame the media. Two examples of many. When the European Court of Human Rights found that a father had been inhumane when caning his 12-year-old son, *The Sun*'s headline was 'EU meddlers ready to outlaw smacking' (*The Sun*, 16 June 1998); and when the Home Secretary, Jack Straw, made the reasonable proposal that young offenders should be allowed out of institutions to take part in community activities to assist their reintegration, the *Daily Mail*'s summary was 'Straw lets young criminals out to play to cut crime' (*Daily Mail*, 23 July 1998). Progress will be difficult until journalism becomes more responsible.

I am not just making the trite (but justified) accusation that they are pandering to popular prejudices in the pursuit of increased sales. My allegation is of lazy-mindedness. All too often what happens is something like this. An event related to criminal justice takes place, such as a judge imposing a short or non-custodial sentence when something more severe might have been expected. Journalists either have no information about the offender's background or other circumstances which influenced the judge's decision, or if they do they treat it as 'making excuses' for the offender rather than as an attempt to find a sentence which is fair and reduces the chances that the offender will re-offend. The journalists telephone a relative of a victim or a hard-line MP and ask if they regard the sentence as ridiculously lenient; often the victim assents because to do less would seem to undervalue the seriousness of the harm done to them or their relative, and the politician agrees for his own reasons. Then they telephone a penal reform organization and try to get them to defend the sentence; if they do, the 'bleeding heart' stereotype is confirmed, but if the spokesperson does not follow the 'script', and tries to give a reasoned answer, this is likely to be simply not reported.

I wish I could get some of these journalists to see that there are some other questions that would interest their readers, such as 'Do you think it is right to keep 90 people in prison unnecessarily because of a likelihood that ten will re-offend?' 'Would you feel differently about Notorious Prisoner A's eventual release on parole if he were allowed to show his regret for his act by working for the good of the community during his sentence?' or 'Given that the tragic past cannot be undone, do you feel it is appropriate for Notorious Prisoner B to write a book about how she came to commit her offence and to use the proceeds to give her child a better start in life than she had?' The popular papers might actually gain popularity by being a bit less predictable, providing new subjects for conversation in pubs and clubs.

I support what the former Law Lord, Lord Ackner, said in the second reading debate on the Crime and Disorder Bill (*Hansard*, [HL], 19 March 1998):

> For the past three or four years the public have been misled into thinking that prison really works. They must be re-educated. That is not easy. I do not expect that the press are keen on so doing because it will not sell more papers, it will sell fewer.

I am not sure I agree with him about that, but still. Lord Ackner went on:

> I have suggested that there should be a Royal Commission or the resuscitation of the Council on Penal Policy to look in depth at why we send more people to prison than any other country in Europe . . . .

This proposal was endorsed by the former Home Secretary Lord Hurd (*Guardian Society*, 18 March 1998). Television also has a part to play. At one extreme it has confrontational chat-show programmes like *Kilroy!*

which sensationalise issues to a point where sensible debate is impossible, and often exploit their participants' trauma in the process. But it can also promote thoughtful discussion, and I believe that it has a duty to do so more often.

FACTS AND STATISTICS

The Civil Servant
The Politician mentioned that large-scale imprisonment does have a small effect on crime levels. In fact Home Office research estimated that a drop of one per cent in the level of recorded crime could be achieved at the cost of a 25 per cent increase in the prison population, and that is what appears to have happened over the last five years in England and Wales. The prison population in England and Wales was 40,606 at the end of 1992, and rose to a peak of 66,517 on 31 July 1998, an increase of 63 per cent (Howard League, 1998c).

There are three questions: has crime been increasing, has the use of prison been increasing, and are the two linked?

We have two sets of crime figures. The official *Criminal Statistics* (Home Office, 1997) give the number of notifiable offences recorded by the police. That number increased from 1986 to 1992 (except in 1988), from 3.8 million to 5.6 million. In the next four years it fell by 11 per cent, to 5.0 million in 1996. But the fall was mainly due to a fall in the largest category, property crimes; violent and sexual offences rose almost every year.

The *British Crime Survey* (BCS) asks a sample of about 15,000 people every two years if they have been victims during the past year. This means that many crimes which were not reported to the police, or which the police did not record, are included, but others, such as those with no individual victim, are not. Here the picture is of a steady rise from 11 million in 1981 to 19.2 million in 1995; not until 1997 was there a drop, to 16.4 million, and this figure shows a drop in violence as well (Mirrlees-Black *et al*, 1998).

Meanwhile in the years 1993 to 1996 when recorded crime was going down by 11 per cent, the prison population increased by 24 per cent from 44,565 to 55,281.

So on the surface it looks as if the Home Office estimate was too cautious; increasing the prison population by 25 per cent reduces crime by much more than 1 per cent. But like most statistics, these should be treated with great caution. Firstly, the BCS, unlike the official statistics, continued to show a rise until its latest survey. Secondly, if we take a different time span the picture changes: from 1986 to 1996 the recorded notifiable offences increased by 31 per cent, from 3.8 to 5.0 million, despite a rise of 18 per cent in the prison population from 46,889 to 55,281. Thirdly, the level of recorded violent offences against the person rose every year except 1995, from 125,500 in 1986 to 239,300 in 1996, and the BCS similarly showed an increase in violence from 2.2 million in 1981 to 3.4 million in 1997. Finally, as always, there have been many other influences at work in society, notably changes in the economic climate, unemployment, police campaigns against burglary, and the numbers of young males aged 15 to 25; compared with these, many people argue, even an increase of 20,000 in the prison population could at best have only a marginal effect—and no doubt penal reformers, looking at the re-conviction rates for ex-prisoners, would argue that it is counterproductive.

'Prison works'

Michael Howard, when Conservative Home Secretary, used the 'incapacitation' argument: he said that 197 burglars given community service orders went on to commit between three and 13 further offences, so that between 591 and 2,561 burglaries would have been prevented if all burglars were sent to prison for a year. But the 197 were taken from a sample of 3,900; the remaining 3,703 committed fewer than three offences, and there is no way of knowing in advance *which* offenders will commit further offences. Therefore the number of offences prevented for every 100 offenders locked up would have been far less, even without taking account of the harmful effects of prison (*Guardian 2,* 14 September 1994). This approach is simply not cost-effective.

In 1997 the Home Office published figures for reconviction rates, indicating that 53 per cent of prisoners released in 1993 were reconvicted within two years; the figures for other measures were: community service orders 52 per cent, probation 60 per cent, and combination orders (probation plus community service) 61 per cent. The then Minister of State, David Maclean, claimed that this showed that 'prison works' better than probation. But Paul Cavadino, chair of the Penal Affairs Consortium, describes this as a 'flagrant misuse of statistics'. He points out that the figures include 'pseudo-reconvictions', that is, convictions after the order was made for offences committed earlier. When these are eliminated, the figure for probation and community service falls by seven percentage points, and the figure for prison by only two per cent. Many of those given community sentences are young offenders, whose reconviction rates are normally higher than those of adults; but for custodial sentences they are higher still: 75 per cent for males under 21 and 89 per cent of those under 17 are reconvicted within two years of leaving penal establishments. Most importantly, Cavadino says, specialised community programmes have been shown to reduce reconviction rates by teaching offenders to restrain impulsive and aggressive actions, tackling alcohol and drug problems, and providing skills training leading to employment. There are also effective programmes for those convicted of sexual offences, firesetting and other offences (*Guardian 2*, 2 April 1997).

The other claim for the 'prison works' argument is simply that it takes offenders out of circulation. This is hard to prove or disprove. Incapacitation studies are unreliable, because they depend on unverifiable assumptions: no one knows how many unsolved crimes were committed by people with previous convictions which would have led to their being incapacitated by a prison sentence. Moreover, since prediction will certainly be inaccurate, and probably very inaccurate, a policy of incapacitation will result in many 'false positives', that is, people locked up for long periods who would not have re-offended, as well as false negatives—cases where offenders re-offend though not classified as dangerous. One Home Office study found that, of 700 men released from prison, 52 were considered 'dangerous'; but of the 77 offences against persons committed within two years of release, only 13 were by men who had been classified as dangerous. So a policy of locking up the 'dangerous' would have failed to prevent 64 of the offences. Conversely, 18 of these 77 offences were considered serious, and only nine of them were committed by the 52 'dangerous' offenders; thus 43 prisoners were wrongly classed as dangerous, a false positive rate of over 80 per cent (Pease and Wolfson, 1979; Ainsworth and Pease, 1981). Incarceration on this basis would be both unjust and expensive.

Cost

Home Office expenditure on prisons in 1996-97 was £217m (capital) and £1,388m (current); for probation £698.4m (Home Office, 1998a).

The average current expenditure was £24,233 per prison place per year (Prison Service, 1997: 17, 29), and for adult males the average prison sentence in 1996 was 23.6 months (Home Office, 1997: *Table 7.16*), so that the average sentence for men cost nearly £50,000. For community measures, the targets for 1998-99 are: £1,750 per probation order, £1,300 per community service order, and £3,350 per combination order (probation plus community service) (Home Office, 1998a).

The cost of the police was £10,354m; the amount specifically allocated to crime prevention £156.8m.

For victims, the cost of Victim Support was £11.7m, and of the Criminal Injuries Compensation Authority £230.4m.

The reconviction rates for community penalties have been within two percentage points of the figures for prison throughout the period 1987-1995 (Goldblatt and Lewis, 1998: 90); and in September 1998 the all-

A. I should very much like to, but unfortunately I don't believe that the public is ready for it, especially given the cynical enthusiasm with which the tabloids caricature any well-thought-out policy.

Q. With respect, I really don't think that answer is good enough. As for the tabloids, we know that 'good news isn't news' for them, but they do print success stories in their features sections. And quite apart from the reasoned arguments, don't you accept that there is a tremendous political bonus to be earned, since prisons are so disproportionately more expensive than more constructive measures? You yourself outlined a way of transferring expenditure to community sanctions; to make it work, don't you have to work to gain community acceptance?

A. Yes, and it won't be easy, especially in high-crime areas.

Q. The public (apparently including yourself, if I may say so) are unaware of the strength of feeling in favour of reparation, because politicians and the media keep telling them how punitive they are. Why don't you act in the spirit of the survey which the Civil Servant mentioned? Don't you think that it might actually be a politically smart move to tap into this strength of feeling in favour of bringing good out of harm?

A. I remain to be persuaded. Most of those surveys are a bit dated, and the recent international crime survey found that British and American respondents were the strongest supporters of prison, and this proportion had increased over time.

Q. If public opinion surveys pointed one way, and research into 'what works' the other, which would you base your policies on?

A. Fortunately there is no evidence that they do point in different directions.

Q. With reference to your ingenious scheme for cost transfer, do you think you can persuade the Treasury to let you organize it so that alternative measures also receive funding when they save work for prosecutors, probation officers, and other 'gatekeepers'?

A. The Treasury is always suspicious of the 'Spend now to save later' argument, but I hope they see that with this one they don't have to pay until the conditions have actually been met. In transport the principle has been established that the proceeds of road pricing should be reserved for public transport; similarly the proceeds of savings on prisons should go to develop community sanctions and, better still, crime prevention initiatives.

Q. Has it occurred to you to challenge the 'Prison works' slogan head on? Don't you think the public knows more about the reality of prison than the tabloids and some of your Parliamentary colleagues give them credit for?

A. As I said, it is difficult to challenge if the other side plays dirty and makes you out to be 'soft' if you take anything but a simplistic, populist line.

Q. On the question of 'Prison works', what would you say in response to the experience of Western Australia? It is quoted by Tony Doob, whom the Civil Servant mentioned. Incapacitation was suggested as a solution to the unusually high number of road deaths resulting from police chases of cars stolen by young offenders. A detailed study by the Crime Research Centre of the University of Western Australia concluded that not only the policy had not worked, but that, in the words of Richard Harding, director of the Centre,

> such responses will always fail. Selective incapacitation will never work; court dispositions, coming at the very end of the delinquency continuum, will never significantly affect what happens at the beginning or in the middle of that continuum; flagrant breaches of international standards, which represent hard-won universal wisdom as to optimum strategies in the less than optimal world of juvenile dislocation and dysfunction, will always backfire.
>
> The only philosophy that consistently offers hope is one that attempts to draw multi-problem youth into society rather than drive them out.

Harding goes on to point out that 'In applying that philosophy, of course, it will continue to be necessary to identify and isolate some youths for some periods. But that must be done with compassion and understanding, not rage and revenge' (quoted in Doob *et al*, 1995: 97).

A. I wouldn't disagree with that. The Civil Servant has passed me a copy of the Canadian review, and elsewhere it quotes a report by a committee in Ontario:

> By giving *all* children and youth a better start in life and better chances for healthy development, we create a more equitable and healthy society . . . People are concerned about violence in schools, for example, but that sort of

behaviour does not suddenly appear out of nowhere. Law enforcement, after the behaviour has appeared, will not substantially lower the rate of these behaviours. [We will help] more young people to have the sense of belonging and self-esteem they need to become effective, participating members of society (quoted in Doob *et al*, 1995: 100-101).

That is the policy of my party, and when you put it like that it sounds fine. But you have to remember that these policies are never going to be 100 per cent effective, and it would be a pretty repressive society if they were. In spite of our best efforts (which are always subject to financial and other constraints) some people – few, we hope – are going to do unacceptable things, and we have to be seen to be doing something about it. It has to be enough to make the public feel protected, but without being counter-productive. That is quite a balancing act.

SESSION 2

The Psychologist

It is generally assumed that if you punish someone for doing something, they are likely to stop doing it, and that if you threaten punishment they will be discouraged from doing it at all; but as usual, things aren't so simple. In psychological terms, punishment is the delivery of a (painful) stimulus in response to an action with the intention of reducing the future probability of that action, and that is what I mainly wish to talk about; specifically, what psychological research tells us about the effects of punishment, and whether this suggests that punishment as meted out by the criminal justice system is likely to modify people's behaviour in the way intended. It should be remembered that the psychological experiments were only about individual conditioning, or in legal parlance individual deterrence, not general deterrence, which I will leave to the Judge to consider; no one is suggesting that any laboratory rat or pigeon knew or cared what was happening to others. In the context of criminal justice, punishment refers specifically to punitive sanctions: the deliberate legal infliction of pain, or at least inconvenience, on someone convicted of a legally defined crime, and not to primarily rehabilitative sanctions, such as probation.

If punishment has to be used, there should be strict safeguards. It must never be used in a humiliating or degrading manner — a condition often disregarded in penal systems, especially prisons. Everyone should always be treated with respect as a human being and therefore, as psychologists, we recommend that punishment should be applied only in conjunction with positive reinforcement for desirable behaviour, and only for the purpose of eliminating undesirable behaviours that cannot be reduced in other ways (for example G Martin and J Pear, 1992: 176-7). As a further safeguard, in all programmes involving punishment, careful data should be collected to monitor the effects of the programme. The conditions under which the programme should be applied must be stated clearly, written down, and adhered to (p.178 of that work). Already we can see that the criminal justice system does not measure up to the required standards.

It sometimes seems, depressingly, that people are much more inventive in devising punishments than in finding ways to guide offenders back into the community; it is easier to destroy than to build. There are still demands for punishments that humiliate. The objection to these is not merely that they contravene international statements on

Human Rights, which prohibit cruel, inhuman and degrading punishment, but that like other punishments they are counter-productive. Youth workers know that, despite bravado, troubled and troublesome young people often have a very low opinion of themselves; they need to be built up, not put down still further. As one writer has put it,

> we must not give the child the idea of being degraded. Once put into [this] inferior position, . . . cast out from the honest and decent society of "good" children, [a young person is] also freed from their morality, their prohibitions, and the duty of being honest. "Now that I am a thief, I am allowed to steal" (quoted by Nixon, 1974).

The way to influence how they *do* behave is through incentives, and other methods in which an understanding of psychology can help. If we can minimise the pressures towards undesirable behaviour and maximise conditions for a desirable alternative response, punishment may not be required (Martin and Pear, 1992: 172). These strategies are not normally used in the criminal justice system, where there is a tendency to punish whether or not it is necessary; but as I expect the Mediator will describe, they are found in victim/offender mediation, where for example an offender may agree to avoid his former companions (minimising the pressure) and to apologise and make reparation (desirable response). Let us compare these psychological insights with what happens in the criminal justice process.

PUNISHMENT

For many years psychological research has consistently told us four things about punishment. Firstly, it tells people what not to do, but not what to do. Secondly, it can have undesirable and even counter-productive side-effects. Thirdly, it can only influence behaviour to a certain extent, under certain conditions and often only temporarily. Fourthly, rewards for desirable behaviour are generally more effective than punishments for unwanted behaviour. May I just say that, like so many people who talk about criminal behaviour, I plead guilty in advance to devoting most of this talk to offenders; but this is inevitable since I was asked to talk about punishment. I will conclude, however, by briefly considering a psychological attribute important for victims, forgiveness.

Punishment only says 'Thou shalt not'

In considering these five points, we have to remember that the effects of punishment are limited. It *does not establish any new behaviour, but only suppresses old behaviour.* There are other disadvantages, although there is less research evidence for them. It can make the person who receives it resentful of authority, so that if they do what the one who inflicts it wants, it is with reluctance, and probably only when there is a risk of being found out. As William Godwin put it, 'coercion cannot convince, cannot conciliate, but on the contrary alienates the mind of him against whom it is employed'. Punishment may appear to produce obedience, and even a change of opinion, but the conversion is the result of fear. Punishment leaves him a slave (Godwin, (1793) 1985: 644, 646, 668). In a word, punishment does not treat people with respect, and as a result it does not lead them to respect others.

Even if the conditions are met and the punishment checks a particular type of behaviour, the effects wear off: punishments have a short-lived effect unless they are consistently and promptly applied — again, these conditions are hardly met in the criminal justice system. In a well known experiment by B F Skinner in 1938, rats were taught to pull a bar to obtain the 'reward' of food. Skinner then tried to extinguish this behaviour. For one group of rats he merely cut off the food supply; they went on hopefully pulling the bar. The other group were punished with a mild slap on the paws the first few times they pulled the bar. They drastically reduced their bar pulling at first, but by the end of four hours after punishment had ceased they were doing it as much as the unpunished rats (summary from Varela, 1971: 225 and Munn *et al,* 1969). Another psychologist gives an everyday example: the mother who tries to stop her child from nail-biting simply by punishing him when she catches him doing it usually finds that when she lets up on her punishment, the child soon starts again (Kendler, 1963: 280). In this instance the behaviour of animals appears to be consistent with that of humans. Although the pain inflicted in the laboratory was far more prompt and more certain than that of criminal justice, its effects wore off very soon. It may, however, suppress the undesired response for long enough for the desired one to be reinforced (Munn *et al,* 1969), but this of course depends on such reinforcement being available — for example, recovering drug addicts need to be provided with something else that is, in psychological terms, rewarding.

Unwanted side-effects of punishment

What is likely to be going through a young prisoner's mind, and how much of it, if any, is encouraging him or her to be law-abiding in future?

Thoughts of a young prisoner

Blaming self, others, circumstances:
If only I'd been luckier, cleverer, quicker — perhaps I will next time
My lawyer/probation officer was useless

Fear
You have to be tough in here or you really get hurt — or kill yourself

Aggression
I'll get the person who grassed on me

Defiance
Next time I'll use a weapon, bribe a witness
Next time will be bigger and better
Next time if I'm caught I'll get a prison sentence instead of youth custody — that'll show I'm a hard man
I got a good headline in the local newspaper
I'll show them I'm not afraid
They can stuff their job-seeking — the first thing I'm going to do when I come out is have a good holiday. I deserve it after this

Break-up of family relationships
I don't suppose my girlfriend will wait for me
I don't want her and the children to visit, it would be too painful for all of us
If she goes out with anyone else, I'll get both of them when I come out

Neutralisation, self-justification
The person I robbed can afford it; or,
I would have paid back what I took from the till if they hadn't locked me up; or
She was asking for it; or
I'm sorry he got hurt, but it was him or me
Everyone here says the same.
We are the victims and there is no justice

Deterrence
I'd better not do it again

Table 1

Table 1 shows some of the thoughts many young prisoners have; the only one that is in line with society's intentions is the last, and it is often far outweighed by the others. Punishment produces a range of unwanted side-effects; I will list seven of them. (Here I will stick to the mainly psychological ones; the Judge is going to consider effects on the legal process.) These unintended consequences at best make it less desirable as a means of social control, and at worst outweigh any advantages it may offer. They should not be left out of any calculations about deterrence. Some of them are based on theory, others on psychological research. Then I will look at the psychological effects of two specific punishments, imprisonment and physical punishment.

1. *Strong punishment tends to elicit aggressive behaviour.*
The person punished imitates the aggressive behaviour inflicted on him, which may be more serious than the original behaviour (Atkinson *et al,* 1987: 233; Dember and Jenkins, 1970: 362). A survey of the way in which mothers handled their children's aggressive behaviour towards themselves and their husbands found that the most severely punitive mothers had the most aggressive children (Kendler, 1963: 400). Animals subjected to pain become aggressive if there is another animal, or an inanimate object, against which to direct the aggression (Azrin, quoted by Dember and Jenkins, 1970: 361-2).

It can, paradoxically, be a 'badge of courage', enhancing the offender's status among his delinquent peers; some prisoners' autobiographies, for example, tell how it felt demeaning to be sent to a young offenders' institution, and when they were sent to an adult prison it was a sign of having 'arrived' in the criminal world.

2. *Strong punishment can produce other undesirable emotional side-effects* such as general fearfulness, which are unpleasant for all concerned, and frequently interfere with desirable behaviour. Conversely, it can destroy a person's self-esteem, so that he thinks of himself as unable to be anything but a criminal. It may make the offender dislike the person or system inflicting the punishment, and reject the values they profess to uphold; or offenders may react with violence to the violence that has been inflicted on them.

Under certain circumstances punishment may sustain or fixate behaviour rather than eliminate it, or it may make a child rigid and inflexible (Dember and Jenkins, 1970: 362), and for some, attention even in the form of severe punishment may be gratifying.

A comprehensive review of psychological research on punishment concludes that:

> The primary disadvantage of punishment for humans may well be the social disruption that results. The existence of the human animal is completely dependent upon the assistance of other humans during the first few years of life . . . To the extent to which punishment eliminates or disrupts social interaction, it can be expected to make the individual incapable of existing in human society (Azrin and Holz, 1966: 442).

Elsewhere the same authors say that punishment may produce behavioural changes that lead to incapacity for effective life (Azrin and Holz, 1966: 439-40).

It has been suggested that young offenders could be 'scared straight' by being shown what prisons do to people; but this doesn't work, because when you are scared, you can't think straight. It is also immoral, because it depends for its effect on having barbaric prisons.

3. *Even at quite low intensities of punishment, people try to avoid being punished, but not necessarily by being good.* In psychological terms, this is called 'avoidance': it is action taken to avoid the 'aversive event'. Punishment of schoolchildren may lead to truancy rather than to good behaviour (Azrin and Holz, 1966: 383-384, 408, 439-440). Some offenders try to escape, hide, deny responsibility, attribute blame to others, tell lies, attack the police, threaten or kill witnesses (Bandura and Walters, 1963: 15, 186, 213). Little research appears to have been done on this, but one textbook gives an example in a psychological context: a man acquired a ten-month-old dog, which repeatedly brought home chickens from his neighbour's garden. Each time, the dog was punished. It continued to catch chickens, but stopped bringing them home (Kendler, 1963: 282). From the human, criminal world numerous examples are reported:

- A jeweller was killed during a robbery to prevent him identifying the bandits (*The Times*, 10 May 1988).
- A man who had served an eight-year sentence continued to offend but rather than face another prison term he carried a gun in order to resist arrest or kill himself; he shot a police officer who was arresting him (*Guardian*, 6 October 1983).
- A persistent drink-driver, already disqualified, and with a six-month suspended sentence hanging over him for a previous motoring offence, was determined to 'escape at all costs', and drove off at high speed, killing the young police officer who breathalysed him (*Guardian*, 7 May 1989).
- An armed robber, after a hold-up at a fast food place, herded the six members of staff into a walk-in deep freezer and 'just to make sure they could not identify him, he opened fire and delivered 21 bullets into their bodies' (*Guardian*, 4 May 1989).
- A sex attacker heard a voice inside his head saying 'You can't let her go. If you let her go she is only going to tell the police', and strangled her (*Guardian*, 4 July 1989).
- An immature young man forced a girl of seven to have sexual intercourse, and 'when he realised she would not stay silent, he murdered her' (*Guardian*, 16 May 1992).

- Airline pilots are reported as withholding information because they fear it will be used against them in prosecution. A near miss was not reported for fear of disciplinary action; pilots are providing only minimal information about problems such as engine failure, and some are illegally erasing voice tapes made in the cockpit. All this makes it difficult to expose errors, and safety will be impaired (*Independent on Sunday*, 22 September 1991). Similarly the pilot and navigator of an American jet which cut the cable of a ski lift and caused the death of 20 people have been convicted of concealing evidence (*Daily Mirror*, 2 September 1998; *Guardian*, 11 May 1999).
- A train driver refused to give evidence to an enquiry, after an incident in which passengers were killed, for similar reasons (*Guardian*, 22 February 1991).
- A boy who was being bullied by a teacher was deterred from telling anyone because he was scared that the teacher would hit him again if he did (*Guardian Education*, 18 June 1996).
- In schools where punishment is the main method of discipline, there is a 'Don't tell tales' culture, which makes it harder to find out what has happened; when the culprit or culprits cannot be identified some teachers respond by imposing collective punishments such as detention of the whole class, which are unfair on the innocent majority (see for example *Guardian*, 28 October 1986).

In some cases of child abuse, the threat of punishment leads each parent to blame the other, so that neither can be convicted (because they are the only witnesses) and no action can be taken to prevent them from abusing any other children they may have. Similarly, at present there is no encouragement for potential sexual offenders to come forward without fear of punishment or stigma, admit to desiring illegal behaviour, and request treatment. If society chooses punishment rather than prevention, can it claim to be serious about protecting children?

It is hard to avoid the conclusion that the threat of punishment is constantly making it harder to get at the truth, and leading to intimidation, assaults or murder of witnesses. That is not of course to say that the removal of the threat would cause everyone to own up; but it does show that deterrence is two-edged.

4. *Punishment may cause people to turn away from not only the aversive stimulus but the situation and people associated with it:* the child punished for making mistakes when reading a book will avoid books. Similarly, the effect can be to make the person punished dislike the one who inflicts

punishment (parent, teacher or employer) and authority in general, as well as the activity (school, work) with which the punishment is associated, especially if the punishment is felt to be inequitable (Bandura, 1977: 127) – and there are bound to be miscarriages of justice.

5. *Punishment (or the prospect of it) makes people think of themselves, not their victims:* they regret the penalty, not the crime. It can even make them think of themselves as victims, like Daniel Defoe's Moll Flanders, awaiting trial in Newgate in 1722:

> I seem'd not to Mourn that I had committed such Crimes, and for the Fact, as it was an Offence against God and my Neighbour; but I mourn'd that I was to be punish'd for it.

If a punishment is too severe, some people see the offender as a 'victim' of the system. An indication of this is the long tradition of concern for prisoners and penal reform; organized support for victims has developed only in the last three decades.

6. *Punishment has the wrong effects on the rest of us, the punishers.* Because it has quick short-term results in suppressing undesirable behaviour, it can tempt the user to rely heavily on it and neglect the use of positive reinforcement for desirable behaviour. However, the undesirable behaviour may return after only a temporary suppression; the person administering the punishment may then resort to progressively heavier doses thereby causing a vicious circle with disastrous side-effects (Martin and Pear, 1992: 176-177). When punishment is legitimised, it also encourages people to blame the offender, and to ignore the circumstances of the offence.

Why do humans continue to resort to such a problematic method to try to control each other? Part of the answer, it has been suggested, lies in the pattern of responses observed in Skinner's experiment. At first, the punishment produced a reduction in the behaviour which it was desired to suppress. This immediate result provides a 'positive reinforcement' to the inflictor of punishment. The other, more subtle after-effects, and the reversion to the original behaviour, are less obvious and hence are overlooked (Varela, 1971: 274), especially as a person is less likely to show aggression in the presence of the inflictor of punishment (Bandura and Walters, 1963: 129-130).

7. *Children often imitate adults: if adults apply punishment to children, the children are apt to do the same to others.* Punishment gives the wrong message. The threat 'Don't do it or else . . . ' teaches people that the way to persuade people to behave is by the use of force, whereas 'Don't do it

because . . . ' is educative, even if the explanation is '. . . because I shall be angry if you do'. This is especially seen in the upbringing of children, where it is widely viewed as acceptable to use force as long as the children are smaller than their parents. Children who are bullies, including those who are both bullies and victims, are significantly more likely to have authoritarian, punitive and unsupportive parents (Baldry and Farrington, 1998). The discussion is obscured by euphemisms such as 'spanking'; I will say more about physical punishment later on.

Locking up and hitting
There are two punishments which attract particular attention, one still in almost universal use, the other abolished in Western judicial systems though not in families, and I should like to consider them from a psychological point of view.

Psychological effects of imprisonment
It has become a truism that, as the English prison commissioner Alexander Paterson said, you cannot train people for freedom in conditions of captivity. In psychological terms, if the punishment physically prevents the subject from making the response, it is impossible to tell if the punishment has had an aversive effect (Azrin and Holz, 1966: 383-384).

The humourist Mark Steel has summed up the common effects of imprisonment:

> The prison system is based on punishment; but does the experience of prison make people less likely to commit crime? Well of course if you're going to survive it at all, the last thing you're going to do is to stand up in the prison canteen and say "I don't know about you, but I can see I've been a fool. I'm going to give up armed robbery and take up flower arranging".

> When someone does get sentenced to jail, the judge might as well say, "You are a common thief: I am condemning you to sit in a cell, 23 hours a day, with a man who's convinced he's a wolf, after which you will be released back into society with no money, no job and no prospects whatsoever. That will stop you from stealing again!" (*The Mark Steel Solution*, BBC Radio 4, 18 August 1995)

That could be described, in the current jargon, as 'honesty in sentencing'! Autobiographies of ex-prisoners commonly dwell on the conditions of imprisonment more than on the harm caused by the offences that led to it; their sympathy is with themselves and their fellow inmates, rather than with their victims. There is little clear evidence as to how many are deterred, are damaged, could have been persuaded to change their behaviour by less damaging means, or are turned into enemies of society.

I have tried to inform myself by reading both criminological studies and prisoners' autobiographies, as well as by visiting prisons, and this has confirmed the point I mentioned earlier: that punishment has side-effects, which people who theorise about punishment ignore. Other considerations have been or will be discussed by other speakers, such as whether other methods could be at least as effective (to be considered by the Probation Officer and the Mediator), and whether the deliberate infliction of pain by the state is ethical at all (by the Philosopher).

Some, like the recidivist 'Robert Allerton' whom Tony Parker interviewed, put the probability of being caught from their minds: 'You see, three days after you've come out of prison, you've forgotten all about it.' Or they regard it as 'an occupational risk, that's all—and one I'm quite prepared to take' (Parker and Allerton, 1962: 87, 88). Professional criminals who talked with Laurie Taylor also accepted prison or borstal as a straightforward 'cost', 'something you had to endure as part of your style of life'; but for some men aged 35 to 45 the prospect of another ten years in prison was becoming difficult to face (Taylor, 1984: 184).

As containment for the most serious offenders, prison can be defended; but as a punishment, it provides only temporary protection, and, since about 99 per cent of prisoners are released, it can often be counterproductive. One recent study showed that, whereas the problems caused by the imprisonment of mothers have often been pointed out, inmate fathers also experience frustration and helplessness because they cannot effectively perform their family roles; and the family itself can suffer, with mental deterioration in the parent (usually the mother) and behavioural problems in the children. Prison is supposed to coerce people into law-abiding behaviour, but it often establishes a degree of 'macho hardness' (Adler, 1997). Prisoners have to fight the system, and other prisoners, in order to survive (Stern, 1998: ch.6). They often experience hopelessness and despair, and feel that they have few reasons for living. Enforced unemployment in prisons can exacerbate this: prisoners are lucky if they have 15 hours' work a week; some have none, and little or no constructive activity to fill their enforced leisure time. Stress and anger are found especially among younger prisoners. The threat of violence is always to be expected in prisons; some, especially young prisoners, become 'predatory'; others lack the experience to cope with this, for example by becoming aggressive in self-defence, and are victimised. So it is not surprising that a substantial number of prisoners feel afraid (18 per cent in one study (Walmsley *et al*, 1992), half of whom had been assaulted by another prisoner in the past six months).

Problems of physical punishment

The second traditional punitive sanction is physical punishment. Experts on child law like Professor Michael Freeman of University College London have argued that children, like adults, have a right not to be hit (*Daily Telegraph, Guardian*, 10 October 1988). Caning children is considered 'inhuman or degrading' by the European Commission of Human Rights (*Guardian*, 8 November 1997). It is not only wrong but counter-productive, and in 16 cases led the British government to pay a total of £51,000 in compensation (*Independent*, 28 September 1988), although a 'slippering' is not severe enough for that (*Guardian*, 26 March 1993); half a century ago William Temple, a headmaster (from 1910 to 1914) and later to be Archbishop of Canterbury (during World War II), said 'I should certainly expect to find that a state-inflicted flogging tends to turn juvenile delinquents into definite criminals, because it makes the state appear as stern and hostile so that its inevitable consequence is to range the will of the offender in determined opposition to the state' (Temple, 1934: 38).

Temple's insight is confirmed by psychological research: a person or animal subjected to punishment may try to immobilise the punishing person, or direct aggression against others; in either case 'aggression would be expected as an elicited reaction to physical punishment' (Azrin and Holz, 1966: 440-441). Even verbal humiliation or castigation is likely to lead to verbal or physical aggression (Retzinger 1991; Nathanson 1992).

Long-term research on 700 children by John and Elizabeth Newson at the Child Development Research Unit, Nottingham, found that children smacked at least once a week were significantly more likely at the age of 11 to be 'always in hot water', truanting, or in trouble with neighbours, school or the police, and to have lower verbal reasoning quotients. At 16 they were significantly more likely to be involved in fights, to have friends who were a 'bad influence', to have been in *formal* trouble for truanting, not to be trusted by their mother to tell the truth, and to have a poor sense of right and wrong. And at 20 they were significantly more likely to have a criminal record (Newson and Newson, 1989).

In cases of cruelty to children it is often reported that the accused defended his violence on the grounds that he was disciplining the child; sometimes it turns out that violence was the only discipline he had experienced in his own childhood, and thus the abuse is carried on from one generation to the next. Peter Newell, co-ordinator of the campaigning group EPOCH (End Physical Punishment of Children) says that 'A significant proportion of these [child] murders comes about through an escalating discipline regime within the home' (*Night & Day*, 9

October 1994). A Cambridge researcher studied 65 homicide files and found that 'cultural acceptance for the use of *some* violence for the purposes of discipline, euphemistically called "corporal punishment", is an important factor to be considered in relation to these discipline filicides' (Wilczynski, 1997: 53, italics in original). The motive for striking the child was discipline in almost 1 in 7 of child homicides (p.101 of that work), but other factors were often also present, such as social isolation. The author concludes that all violence to children lies along a continuum, and by socially sanctioning the lower end of this continuum it becomes more likely that children will suffer from more extreme forms of violence; so 'corporal punishment should be strongly discouraged, and parents given advice on alternative methods of discipline' (p.216). People follow the state's example, for example by imprisoning children in rooms, attics or cupboards, sometimes for long periods; in one admittedly extreme case, in southern Italy, a family locked their daughter in a cupboard for 12 years because she had allegedly made eyes at a young man (*Badische Zeitung*, 11 October 1984, p.20).

Surveys in the 1980s and 1990s have found that the great majority of parents hit their children: in the USA 89 per cent of parents with children under 17 had hit their three-year-old child during the previous year, 84 per cent of parents in Romania regarded spanking as normal; in the United Kingdom 91 per cent of children had been hit, most of them in the past year. In Korea 97 per cent, and in India 91 per cent of males and 86 per cent of females, had been physically punished in their childhood. Some of this punishment amounted to battering. The United Kingdom was the last country in Western Europe to ban corporal punishment in state schools, in 1987, and in the USA only 27 of the 50 states had banned it by 1996 (EPOCH Worldwide and Rädda Barnen, [1996]: 6). Britain's 2,500 independent schools almost stopped using it (*Guardian*, 26 March 1993), and the prohibition has now been extended to them. As for parents, the former Prime Minister, John Major, is reported to be against any law restricting parents 'right' to slap their children (*Daily Mirror*, 10 September 1996); despite a ruling by the European Court of Human Rights (*A v UK*, 23 September 1998) that 'reasonable chastisement' can be inhuman or degrading, the new Labour government also defended 'a parent's right to discipline [note the euphemism] a child' (Paul Boateng, then health minister, *Guardian*, *Daily Telegraph*, 24 September 1998). It should be surprising, but perhaps it isn't, that the Archbishop of Canterbury, Dr George Carey, has said that it is acceptable to smack children 'gently', 'as long as it is done with love and discipline within the family set-up' (*Guardian*, 26 October 1996). Perhaps he was unaware of his predecessor's insights.

In spite of the widespread hitting of children, eight Western European countries have banned *all* such punishment (Sweden, in 1979, followed by Finland, Denmark, Norway, Austria, Cyprus, Latvia and Croatia, and the German government elected in October 1998 is planning to do the same (*Guardian*, 16 October 1998). Why? The Swedish Department of Justice explains: 'Because our democratic community needs children taught to think for themselves, who are used to making their own choices and to shouldering responsibility. It is impossible to beat a child into obedience and at the same time expect it to be able to think for itself' (Justice Department, n.d.). Apart from the question of the child's rights, there are three main reasons against hitting children: that it is ineffective, that there are better forms of discipline, and that when it is permitted, some parents will use it to excess.

It is ineffective because it loses the co-operation of the child and gives confusing messages (the classic example being the father who smacks his child for hitting other children). Better methods depend on the age of the child, but consist essentially of explaining to the child why the behaviour is not acceptable, rewarding good behaviour by attention or praise, and setting a good example. As regards 'escalation', of course many parents keep their smacking within limits (which indicates that they could manage without it altogether), but there is an intolerable amount of serious child abuse, and the violent parents often justify it to themselves in the name of discipline. In a survey of local authorities in the United Kingdom, three quarters of those responding had recorded that ten per cent or more (in some places 50 per cent or more) of parents gave physical punishment as the explanation of alleged abuse (EPOCH 1990: 6).

The Gulbenkian Commission (1995: 50-2, 133-6), after a wide-ranging review of the evidence, recommended that the idea of 'reasonable chastisement' should not be a legal justification for physical punishment or other humiliating treatment of children, not only because it is contrary to human rights but because it is counterproductive and can have tragic consequences.

- When three-year-old Heidi Koseda was starved to death, her step-father said that he had stopped giving her food as a punishment for taking sweets (and when she was skin and bone he didn't take her to the doctor because he thought he would get into trouble) (*The Times*, 25 September 1985).
- Doreen Mason died at the age of 16 months after her step-father punished her by hitting her, keeping her standing against the wall, and later held her under water for two minutes (*Guardian, The Times*, 6 December 1988).

- Another man punished his three-year-old son for crying by spinning him in a tumble-drier; he had also put the boy's hand on a hot-plate for ten seconds, and had locked him and his four-year-old sister in a cupboard for hours (*The Times*, 7 February 1989).
- Sukina Hammond, aged 6, refused to spell her name for her father; he thought she was being stubborn and began thrashing her with an electric flex, an assault which ended with his beating her to death (*Guardian*, 25 November 1989).

Cruelty to children can have repercussions far outside the family; Adolf Hitler's character was deformed by his authoritarian and violent-tempered father who ridiculed him, whistled for him as he did for his dog, and beat him (Waite 1977: 134, 137; Kubizek 1954: 32; Scheff 1994: 109-20), and Saddam Hussein was forced to work from the age of five by 'his stepfather, "Hassan the liar" as he was known locally, . . . a brutish man who used to amuse himself by humiliating Saddam. His common punishment was to beat the youth with an asphalt-covered stick, forcing him to dance around to dodge the blows'. Village boys often mocked him for being fatherless, and at eight he carried an iron bar to defend himself (Karsh and Rautsi, 1991: 10, 15; Darwish, 1998).

A method of discipline cannot be right which only works as long as the parent is stronger than the child. If the child is not cowed into submissiveness he will fight back, like 'Andy', who left home at 15: 'I took 15 year of getting beaten up off them, so I says "Right, my turn". I says, "If you hit me again I'm going to hit you back", so I did and I left' (Smith and Stewart, 1997: 103): one more homeless teenager.

Can punishment work? The research evidence

The third finding of psychological research is this. It is surprising that lawyers, whose professional life is centred on evidence when determining a person's guilt, pay so little regard to evidence when it comes to deciding what sanctions are likely to be effective. Since criminal sanctions are among other things an attempt to influence behaviour, one would expect lawyers to consult psychologists about sentencing. The consensus among psychologists was summed up by Professor Blackman at a conference of the Institute for the Study and Treatment of Delinquency (now the Centre for Crime and Justice Studies) in 1995:

> It is a matter of fact, in laboratories and in the real world, that making nasty events dependent on undesired behaviour does not necessarily reduce the future probability of that behaviour. Common-sense expectations about the dynamics of behaviour can be misleading. In fact the only effective way to produce behavioural change, in my view, is by trying not to suppress 'bad'

or undesirable behaviour but by attempting to shape up 'good' or desirable behaviour (Blackman, 1996).

I was encouraged to hear the Politician say that she would base her policies on research findings; here are some to start her off.

There are five main conditions in which punishment can lead to some of the desired effects: it should be immediate, certain, adequate but not excessive, there must be no reinforcement for the behaviour that is being checked, and, above all, *alternative behaviour* must be available. Some writers, however, do not support the use of punishment even to this limited extent. The social psychologist Jacobo Varela, for example, dismisses the findings as 'not very convincing', and says:

> The fact that punishment has an immediate effect but then a later reversal is . . . not known or understood by those who propose punishment as the means of controlling behavior . . . If we add to this the fact that punishment always creates a negative attitude in the punished person . . . , we should not be surprised that punishment, in the long run, only makes matters worse . . .

He adds that

> . . . even if punishment could be shown to be a possible means of behavior modification, the deleterious side-effects would still preclude its use. Finally, society's desire to use punishment as a tool is so strong, even when it has been understood that positive reinforcement is the best way of obtaining results, that the social scientist is obligated to re-emphasise the need for positive reinforcement and the abolition of punishment.

Later, he adds a further reason:

> By using punishment, we fail to eliminate the basic cause and add more complications, including an element of danger (Varela, 1971: 226)

Or to put it another way, if you put your faith in an ineffective safety measures you will not think it necessary to look for further protection, just as the builders of the *Titanic* thought that she was protected against icebergs and therefore failed to provide enough lifeboats (Wright, 1982).

Bearing these caveats in mind, it is worth looking briefly at the five pre-conditions for the effectiveness of punishment, and comparing them with what conventional criminal justice offers.

Immediate
Firstly, punishment should be immediate, otherwise the connection with the prohibited act is weakened, especially if the subject has been behaving well in the meantime; but everyone knows that criminal proceedings often take a long time to come to court. In early 1997 the

average delay in England was 131 days (Renshaw, 1998); the Home Secretary wants to halve this to 'only' ten weeks. American authors have said that 'our legal system utilises punishment for infractions of the law, yet punitive measures are applied not just days, weeks or months but often years after the alleged misbehavior' (Munn *et al*, 1969), and the same is true in many countries. Indeed, by the time the sentence is imposed, the offender may have settled into a non-delinquent lifestyle so that punishment has become inappropriate (Bandura and Walters, 1963: 196); to be fair, courts sometimes, but by no means always, take account of such circumstances. Consistency is also important if punishment is to be effective.

Certain
Secondly, punishment should be certain: the potential offender must believe that he or she is likely to be caught and punished. However criminologists are well aware how few offences are reported, recorded or cleared up, as the figures given by the Civil Servant show; and those who offend most often know at first hand how many chances there are of getting away with it. Sometimes they even *over*-estimate it, but are still not deterred. One study of 13 and 14-year-olds in high and low-delinquency areas in Australia found that more of those in the more delinquent areas thought that apprehension and painful punishment were likely; they also had a better (though not very complete) knowledge of penal measures used in children's courts. In each case the children with a higher expectation of being caught and harshly punished were those of low socio-economic status (Kraus, 1976).

Not excessive
Thirdly, there is the question of severity. Here research findings are complex. On the one hand, it has been found in laboratory experiments that gradually increasing punishments have little effect, because the animals become accustomed to them; a severe initial shock is necessary (Azrin and Holz, 1966: 393). Translated into criminal justice terms, this would suggest that a gradual progression through reprimands, warnings and so on is not as effective as a strong punishment on the first occasion. This appears at first sight an awkward fact for liberal reformers, who would prefer to believe the opposite. But as Munn and his colleagues point out, it is unsafe to generalise from findings based on laboratory experiments with animals where there is a simple punishment such as an electric shock, promptly and consistently administered, without the complicated side-effects of punishments on humans; and the animal is given only limited choices, whereas humans can respond in many different ways (Atkinson *et al*, 1987: 234). In any case ethical

considerations mean that we can't inflict severe punishments for minor offences, even if they would work.

Punishment must not be excessive, not only on ethical grounds, but because that generates anxiety and is counter-productive. A common response to the failure of punishment is to demand that it should be intensified, and there is some evidence that strong punishment suppresses behaviour – but it is likely to be harmful (Morgan and King, 1971) and can backfire. Punishment is less effective in restraining people who are angry (Baron *et al*, 1974: 303), and it often makes people angry. An extreme or painful punishment can result in aggressive behaviour more serious than before; it can cause physical harm which is unacceptable, or excessive anxiety, which makes the subject less able to learn, according to the authors of one standard psychological textbook, who say that they 'are not aware of any research which supports the use of severe punishment as a remedial measure', because of its adverse effects on the human being, but that numerous studies have indicated the generally greater effectiveness of praise (Munn *et al*, 1969: ch. 9).

Not rewarding
The fourth requirement is that the behaviour which we want to check should not be rewarding (in psychological language 'reinforcing' – Azrin and Holz, 1966: 419). But much criminal behaviour *is* rewarding, for example as a means of acquiring cash, or respect and 'street credibility' from peers, or excitement and a rush of adrenalin. 'If a strong state of deprivation exists, and a response, though punished, is maintained by frequent reinforcement, then even high intensities of punishment may be ineffective' (Azrin and Holz, 1966: 427). This is the one aspect of crimes against property which can be tackled by physical measures, 'extinguishing the stimulus' (Azrin and Holz, 1966: 431-432) by making it harder to commit the crime, through security devices, marking property so that it is harder to dispose of, and so on. For many types of crimes of violence, however, it offers little protection: the 'reward' is the violence itself and the use of power over another person. If an action, such as a robbery, is repeatedly 'rewarded', the habit may become too strong to be broken by punishment, even by long imprisonment: people adapt to the most unfavourable environments (Morgan and King, 1971, Ch. 3) and extended periods of punishment should be avoided, since the effect wears off (Azrin and Holz, 1966: 426-427).

An alternative must be available
The last condition is achievable, but not without effort on the part of the experimenter (in the case of animals) or of other members of society (in the case of humans). Some psychologists concede a place for mild

punishment, but they are unanimous that it *must be combined with positive reinforcement of desirable habits, providing the person immediately with an opportunity to do something for which he can be rewarded* (Azrin and Holz, 1966: 426-427; Kendler, 1963: 280-2; Morgan and King, 1971: ch. 3); indeed it is recommended that this should be designed *before* a punishment is inflicted (Martin and Pear, 1992: 171). This can work even when the alternative is a hard one, for example when a child is enabled to earn money by working instead of stealing (Skinner, 1958, quoted by Varela, 1971: 226-227). In this case the punishment can be described as 'informative' and more likely to lead to learning, whereas severe punishments cause excessive anxiety, or are regarded as retaliatory. Even the absence of any stimulus can be a punishment by comparison with an alternative action that is rewarded (Azrin and Holz, 1966: 391-392). The effects of punishment are not as predictable as those of reward: 'Reward essentially says, "Repeat what you have done"; punishment says "Stop it!" but fails to give an alternative. As a result, the organism may substitute an even less desirable response for the punished one' (Atkinson *et al*, 1987: 232). To quote Jacobo Varela again (1971: 226), 'even if punishment could be shown to be a possible means of behavior modification, the deleterious side-effects would still preclude its use'. To sum up, 'Punishment is most effective when it is used in combination with reward and when it is mild and informative. Unusually severe or unpredictable punishment may lead to unstable behavior or fixation [i.e. getting stuck in a pattern of behaviour]' (Munn *et al*, 1969).

The side-effects of any type of censure will be less serious if it is perceived as fair and followed by a gesture of re-acceptance — a smile, a hug, or something more formal — so that the child's *internal* controls are developed, as the Australian criminologist John Braithwaite has pointed out: 'Once established, conscience operates without external agents to enforce it' (Braithwaite, 1989: 178). To be perceived as fair, the process should include dialogue which the person understands. But even if families do this, some schools fail to maintain it. The aim, for both families and schools, should be discipline that is neither cold and firm, nor warm and permissive, but warm and firm (Braithwaite, 1989: 174-5).

THE USE OF INCENTIVES

The fouth conclusion from psychological research is that, all in all, behaviour can best be shaped by rewards. They can be sufficient to 'reinforce' the desired behaviour even when they are intermittent (Varela, 1971: 225), or when the action is only a small step in the direction of the desired behaviour (Skinner, 1958 quoted by Varela 1971: 226-227; Atkinson *et al*, 1987). However, delinquent behaviour also tends to provide intermittent rewards, which outweigh the inhibiting effects of punishment; a radical change in the offender's behaviour may cause him to lose social or material rewards without providing satisfying substitute ones (Bandura and Walters, 1963: 213). Thus it is essential that another form of behaviour should be available, which carries some form of 'reward'.

From a psychological point of view, therefore, I would recommend that general *incentive* would be a better basis for a well ordered society than general deterrence. I expect you know the fable of *The Sun and the North Wind*:

> The Sun and the North Wind were having a dispute about which of them was the stronger. As they argued, the North Wind saw a traveller riding down below on Earth, wrapped in his cloak against the autumn weather. 'I will show you who is stronger', said the North Wind: 'I will blow his cloak away'. The Sun agreed: the first one to remove the traveller's cloak would be the winner. The North Wind blew, and called the Hail and the Frost to help, but the harder he blew the more tightly the traveller pulled his cloak around him. Then it was the Sun's turn. He shone, the clouds evaporated, the traveller began to sweat—and took off his cloak before the Sun was even using all his strength.

The criminal justice system gives little attention to rewarding desired behaviour; a crude indication of this is that the relative amount of money allocated to pre-release and post-release supervision is less than one twenty-fifth of the cost of custody (£80 as against £2,190 in an average month in 1993/94: Home Office, 1995: 72). The stigma imposed by the system does little to encourage people to stop offending.

The responsibility for rewarding law-abiding behaviour lies with people in the community such as employers and landlords, and with government departments responsible for education, employment, housing, sport, the arts, and so on. We should take care that these normal incentives, together with respect and praise for achievement, are available to everyone. A reward in the form of praise can be effective in improving the achievement of tasks, particularly for children and for introverts.

When people want to change their behaviour, enabling them to do so can itself be a reward. But the criminal justice system, with the exception of some Probation Services, has little to do with initiatives of this kind; they are left to other agencies such as voluntary organizations and local authorities. There are large numbers of projects, national and local, designed to meet all kinds of needs. A national example (among many) is Home-Start, which uses trained volunteers to offer friendship, practical advice and support to families with pre-school children. It has 180 local services in the United Kingdom, supported by a national consultancy. It does not list crime reduction among its aims, but the problems for which it offers help include children's behavioural problems, parental conflict, domestic violence and suspected child abuse, and other factors which either are criminal or are associated with criminality. Researchers found substantial improvements in emotional well-being and ability to cope, although this could not be conclusively attributed to the volunteers' work. This and many other examples are described in *Reducing Criminality Among Young People*, a Home Office review by David Utting (1996), and in other publications, such as *Youth Crime Prevention*, a survey by the charity Crime Concern, which is funded by government and the private sector (Findlay *et al*, 1990), and the Waterville projects for children and young people in Tyne and Wear, a high-unemployment area of north-east England (Waterville Projects, 1997). Not all of these have been rigorously researched, and indeed there are limits to the amount of research that can be undertaken. What is needed is surely a system such as that described by the Politician, but not necessarily linked directly to crime, which would relieve them of the recurring headache caused by funding problems, provided they maintained agreed basic monitoring of their work. This could hardly fail to improve the quality of life for thousands of people, and would probably have spin-offs by improving their confidence, their employability, and their respect for other people.

The idea of a social order based entirely upon fear of punishment is unattractive, and as we have seen it would not even be very effective. This psychological finding is confirmed by history: repression, whether in a prison, an army or a whole country tends to lead to revolt. To base social control on reward is a more attractive idea. It might work as in the imaginary country described in the Utopian novel *Walden 2* by the behavioural psychologist B F Skinner, who conducted some of the pioneering experiments which pointed to the inefficacy of punishment and the advantages of reward as a means of controlling behaviour. But even this is not entirely satisfactory: it uses 'extrinsic' rewards which seem to reduce people to the status of very talented laboratory animals. Moreover, it is run as a benevolent autocracy, but there is no guarantee that the autocrats will go on being so benevolent. These are further reasons for sharing the Politician's scepticism about Utopias.

'Extrinsic' rewards are those which some person or persons has decided to attach to certain actions, to encourage them. This may have been done with great wisdom and sympathy, but it deprives people of their autonomy and tends to make people feel they are being manipulated, and to undermine self-determination and altruism. It also runs into the *Danegeld* problem: to obtain the required good behaviour, you have to keep providing the incentive (or to keep applying extrinsic punishments). So the ideal is to rely on 'intrinsic' incentives, although their power is not so obvious: a sense of achievement, job satisfaction, or enhanced self-esteem, self-respect and adequate wages (Braithwaite, 1998a: III J 2), and to make sure that these are greater than those offered by the nefarious alternatives (such as the proceeds of theft, the excitement of criminal activity, and underworld status).

COMING CLEAN

Even if we succeeded in providing a large array of incentives, harmful behaviour would not be eradicated; how should we respond to it when it occurs? One accepted starting point is to try to influence the attitudes and behaviour of offenders who have been caught. Part of it, as I have just suggested, could be based on *intrinsic* rewards, that is, benefits which flow from certain actions in themselves. This method uses 'cognitive' psychology, in which people are helped to recognise things as they are in the real world, and to *think*. Many people, after committing themselves to a questionable course of action, 'rationalise' their behaviour: they change their beliefs to bring them into line with what they have done. This does not help them to face reality. Sociologists like Gresham Sykes and David Matza call this 'neutralising': people persuade themselves, for example, that what they do does not really harm others, 'everybody does it', and so on. It has also been found that many of the people who become offenders have 'cognitive deficits' (McLennan-Murray, 1997: 17): often they are impulsive, their thinking is rigid, they are intolerant of others, egocentric, and not good at abstract thinking or critical reasoning. They do not recognise when they have a problem, they are not good at thinking up a variety of options, or thinking through the effects of their actions on themselves or others, and they tend to generate quick-fix solutions. (These qualities are by no means confined to offenders, of course; they are found in many others, including people who lay down the law about how offenders should be dealt with. Just as many offenders do not think ahead to the possibility of being caught, many politicians, and other advocates of incarceration, do not think ahead to what offenders will do on release from prison.)

So the way to change behaviour is not to threaten, cajole or manipulate (punish or reward), not to 'change' people (therapy or treatment), but to give them choice by enabling them to recognise that they can get satisfaction from different ways of handling situations. The emphasis is not on the content ('You must do this and not that') but on the process: firstly on thinking (problem solving, creative thinking and critical reasoning), and secondly on the use of skills (management of emotions, social skills, empathy, negotiation skills, and enhancement of values), to put together a pattern of behaviour which will bring intrinsic rewards. This of course requires a society where to behave with consideration for others is indeed rewarded (for example with employment, accommodation and relationships), and *is* therefore the rational choice. But even in present-day society, a researcher in Canada found that of 170 sex offenders (rapists and paedophiles) who had completed the Reasoning and Rehabilitation programme, the reconviction rate for *any* offence one year after release was 58 per cent lower than in a control group; for violent offenders and drug offenders the reductions were 35 and 36 per cent respectively (David Robinson, quoted by McLennan-Murray, 1997: 18).

The post-crime response can also determine the offender's acceptance into the community. This has been courageously demonstrated by the founders of the South African Truth and Reconciliation Commission, established under the post-*apartheid* Interim Constitution to 'promote national unity and reconciliation in a spirit of understanding' by:

- establishing as complete a picture as possible of the causes, nature and extent of the gross violations of human rights . . .
- facilitating the granting of amnesty to persons who make full disclosure of all the relevant facts relating to acts . . . which comply with the requirements of the Act (Promotion of National Unity and Reconciliation Act)
- . . . restoring the human and civil dignity of . . . . victims by granting them an opportunity to relate their own accounts of the violations . . . and recommending reparation measures in respect of them
- making recommendations . . . with regard to the creation of institutions conducive to a stable and fair society . . . .

Many of these acts were crimes by any standard; but many would have been difficult to prove. The government made a conscious choice. It could attempt to prosecute and punish as many people as possible, most of whom would deny the accusations, thereby clogging the courts and prisons, incurring huge expense, dividing the country, and seeing many offenders acquitted or not prosecuted at all for lack of evidence; or it could try to find the truth in a much larger number of cases, and encourage those who expressed contrition to be integrated into a relatively unified society. It chose the latter, and although of course it has not achieved full co-operation or universal support, it is generally regarded as being more in the public interest than the alternative.

In a small community in Canada the use of restorative methods allowed widespread sexual abuse of children to be brought to light: sexual offenders who plead guilty are placed on probation for three years, during which specially trained community members use an intensive, holistic approach to heal the victim, the victimiser and their families. In this way 'soft' restorative justice for 40 might prevent more crime than 'tough' justice for the few who could be detected and convicted by the conventional process (Church Council, 1996: 14-17, 31-33, 94-95, 154-156; Braithwaite, 1998a: III J 9).

The phrase 'coming clean' is apt. It means that a person acknowledges what he has done; it implies that he may feel ashamed of his 'dirty' actions but it does not dwell on this, emphasising instead that his confession has begun the cleansing process. The evidence suggests that we should at least consider what could be the result if the criminal justice system re-examined its priorities in a similar spirit: should we, too, look for 'reconciliation' rather than 'justice'?

Others have given more attention to the idea of shame. Some writers, like John Braithwaite, make a distinction between being humiliated by someone else, often an authority figure—an extrinsic process—and experiencing the intrinsic shame which comes from being required to talk about, and hence to understand, the offence and its effect on other people. The Mediator will no doubt have more to say about this. There is now a great deal of psychological evidence that shame is a very complex emotion, which pervades all aspects of social life. I will not review that research now, but it has been clearly shown how humiliation, perhaps best understood as shame that is considered excessive and undeserved, causes the humiliated person to react aggressively, whereas shame that is perceived as justified and deserved can form the basis of a valuable learning experience.

People who work with children have confirmed the insight of St Augustine, that we should 'hate the sin but love the sinner'. One head teacher has described how she encourages children to imagine that they carry a box containing different ways of behaving, from which they can choose the kinds which hurt other people, or those that do not; other children can then describe the effect of the behaviour without attaching a hurtful label to the owner of a particular 'box' (Alderson, 1997:20).

Conventional punishment depends for its effect on the offender having something to lose that he or she values (self-esteem, respect of family and friends, a home, liberty); if people have none of those things, then increasingly severe (not to say barbaric) punishments will be necessary to make an impact. There will also be greater impact if the punisher is someone the offender respects (which is not usually the case, especially if the offender's perception is, as one of them put it, that 'You steal in farthings and the boss steals in pounds' (Sprott *et al*, 1954: 293)). Anyone who doubts the corrosive effect of double standards in high places should read C H Rolph's account, still burning with indignation 50 years later, of the Commissioner of the City of London Police in the 1920s who sacked a police constable for handing half-a-crown to a colleague, but regularly claimed 'cab hire and stabling' and other unwarranted expenses, and had a personal servant paid from police funds (Rolph, 1974: 139-143).

But if the conditions are met, there is no need for punishment, nor even for deliberate humiliation, because the process itself leads the offender to experience shame, and this will be sufficient. Researchers who have studied the process say that reparation is the ostensible purpose for meetings between victims, offenders and their families, but that underneath it is a symbolic process involving 'the social rituals of respect, courtesy, apology and forgiveness, which seem to operate independently of the verbal agreements that are reached'. Such meetings provide an opportunity for this emotional exchange: although it may be brief, and may take place outside the actual meeting, it is 'the key to reconciliation, victim satisfaction, and decreasing recidivism' (Retzinger and Scheff, 1996). If shame is shared and communicated in this way, the damage to the bond between the offender and other participants may be repaired; the shame is then not stigmatising and rejecting, causing anger or depression, as in conventional courts, but reintegrative.

FORGIVENESS

As I mentioned at the beginning, I should not like to end without making a point of a different kind, even though I must do it very briefly. The psychological effects on victims, and ways of helping them, are a subject on their own, and I would need as much time again to begin to do justice to it. But one important aspect, relevant to the idea of repairing harm which we are discussing, is the question of forgiveness. Let me make it clear that I am approaching this from a psychological standpoint, not a moral or religious one, and I would never even suggest that anyone *ought* to forgive an offender, not least because I cannot be sure that, in their position, I would be capable of it.

Instead, what I should like to consider is whether the ability to forgive is helpful in overcoming hurt and anger, and if so whether people who want to forgive, but find it difficult, can be helped to do so. For some, the process is difficult because they experienced no parental modelling for it, or because they believe that anger gives them strength. It is important to recognise that it is a *process*. It starts with recognising the injury, often after an initial reaction of disbelief. This is often followed by anger. (The following draws on a paper by Richard P Fitzgibbons, 1986, and quotations by Howard Zehr from Flanigan's *Forgiving the Unforgivable*, 1992). At some stage the injured person has to decide how to respond. People who have been injured or unfairly treated often feel a desire for revenge; until it is recognised and released it can ruin relationships and aggravate psychosomatic illness. They may want to let the offender know the harm he did to them. As long ago as the first century AD the Greek and Roman philosophers Plutarch and Seneca advocated forgiveness for the control of anger. It helps people to put the painful experience behind them, facilitates the reconciliation of relationships, and makes it less likely that the anger will be misdirected into other relationships, which can be very self-destructive.

This was the experience of one British army officer, Eric Lomax, interrogated, tortured and imprisoned by Japanese soldiers in World War II. For years he was angry, difficult to live with, obsessed by his experiences and revengeful. Eventually he was able to contact one of his tormentors, Nagase Takashi, and discovered that he felt remorse and had set up a charitable foundation, as well as making personal atonement. They met and Lomax was able to express forgiveness. He wrote later:

> If I'd never been able to put a name to the face of one of the men who had harmed me, and never discovered that behind that face there was also a damaged life, the nightmares would always have come from the past without meaning. And I had proved for myself that remembering is not enough, if it simply hardens hate. Some time the hating has to stop (extract from Lomax, 1995).

It cannot of course be guaranteed that either party will react as these two did, and obviously no pressure should be placed on them to do so; but the system ought to make it *possible*, for both their sakes. Victims or victims' families should be given the opportunity, not to forget, but to regain peace of mind; and they might be helped in this if some of the murderers who are demonised by the popular press were in turn given the opportunity to repent and to show, by making amends, that their remorse was genuine.

Although forgiveness is an emotional process, it is often preceded by an intellectual decision to let go of anger (a phrase which some find less difficult than the word 'forgiveness'). In a cognitive forgiveness exercise patients may be asked to spend time trying to part with anger caused by past hurts in order to deal with present ones. As they begin to use such exercises, they feel relief from anger. Some feel guilty because the process takes so long; but those who are able to forgive, may in the process become aware of the person with whom they are angry, feel relief from emotional pain, and desire to express their forgiveness to others. People who can make these choices usually find them a step towards regaining their freedom and looking to the future.

FACTS AND STATISTICS

The Civil Servant

The speaker has given most of the research findings himself, but he did ask me to say how few offences are reported, recorded or cleared up. The *British Crime Survey* has consistently shown that only about half of crimes with individual victims are reported, and of those the police record not much more than half (Home Office, 1995: 25). There are however variations as between offences: nearly all thefts of motor vehicles are reported, for example, for insurance reasons, and a high proportion of burglaries where something was stolen, for the same reason—but reductions in the official statistics could mean that fewer people can afford insurance, and therefore if they are burgled they do not have the incentive to report it.

The other factor relevant to the point the Psychologist was making is of course the proportion of recorded crimes that are cleared up: about nine out of ten for homicides, three quarters of violent or sexual offences, and less than a quarter of thefts, robberies, burglaries and criminal damage—overall, about a quarter.

DISCUSSION

Q. Psychologists, as well as lawyers, have tended to focus on the individual who commits the crime; but as a sociologist, may I remind you that crimes are committed in a social context. What does psychology tell us about the 'crimes of the powerful' whose effects can be very serious both directly (such as damage to health through pollution, defrauding people of their life savings, and in some countries by being war-lords or tyrants), and indirectly, through the force of the example they set to people less fortunately placed? This is intangible, but I would argue that it is undeniable. These perpetrators are far from being driven by poverty, though it is possible that some of them suffer from maladjustment, psychopathy, and other disorders often attributed to 'common or garden' offenders. Like other people (some would say, more than other people) they have a tendency to hold on to what they have got, and are conscious that if a reduction of pressures towards crime meant a more equal distribution of assets, they would finish up with less.

A. Yes, neutralisation is probably one of the factors at work here too: 'Radiation occurs naturally, so adding to it does negligible harm', 'It's not my fault if they invested all their savings in my savings scheme', 'It's not illegal'. And no doubt it is convenient for captains of industry that crimes involving sex and violence attract more headlines, though I don't believe that they are such good manipulators as to have contrived this deliberately.

Q. If as you say certainty is a deterrent, shouldn't there be more prosecutions for crimes against health and safety legislation, environmental protection laws and tax cheating?

A. These offences should certainly not be ignored, but I believe that prosecution should be held in reserve as almost the ultimate sanction. The results show that the inspectors know what they are doing when they choose a restorative approach, that is, one based on putting right the harm rather than merely punishing the offenders. It gets results. When the Institute of Nuclear Power Operations changed from rulebook enforcement to a dialogue about how to achieve outcomes, the number of automatic emergency shutdowns in the United States declined from seven per unit in 1980 to one by 1993. The Mines Safety and Health Administration found that a 25 per cent increase in inspections was associated with a reduction in fatalities in the US of seven to 20 per cent; the level of penalties didn't lead to improvement in safety. In Australian nursing homes, where inspectors used a stigmatising approach there was a substantial *fall* in compliance with standards for the quality of care, accompanied by a business sub-culture of defiance and resistance to regulations; where inspectors were tolerant and understanding, there was a smaller fall; but compliance improved where inspectors followed a reintegrative shaming philosophy. The Mediator will say more about this, but briefly it means making clear to the managers that improvements are needed, but trusting them to co-operate, and praising them when they comply (Braithwaite, 1998a).

Q. Shouldn't white collar offenders be thrown into prison like common criminals?

A. On the contrary, I believe we should find ways of using restorative methods to keep other offenders out of prison too and reintegrate them into society.

Q. Would you agree that the rest of society salves its conscience for its own illegal or unethical deeds by taking it out on prisoners generally?

A. Yes, and curiously, as so often, prison is a microcosm of the outside world. One prisoner, a sex offender, said that offenders who regard themselves as the élite of the underworld harm their own families by behaving in a way which leads to their being imprisoned, and try to salve their consciences by taking it out on sex cases; but he shut them up by 'reminding them that (by getting themselves locked up for long periods) they have done their own children more harm than I ever could'—and by using his own 'fistic prowess' to defend himself (Letter to Howard League for Penal Reform, 10 February 1978).

Q. There would be a lot of people who agree with the Archbishop of Canterbury's remark, which you were so scathing about, that to smack children with love is acceptable. Surely a parent has a duty to smack a child if it runs into the road or puts its hand near an electric socket, to make sure it learns to avoid the danger?

A. Certainly a parent who does smack a child should show straight afterwards that they love the child, but the smack is not necessary: a child will immediately get the message from the parent's alarm when they grab it to pull it away from the danger. Anyway, many smacks are given in quite different situations. Similar arguments were used (by adults, of course) in Sweden when the law against assaulting children was introduced; but when children were invited on television, and spoke of the anger and frustration which they felt when they were hit by an adult, people began to understand their point of view.

SESSION 3

The Probation Officer

Let me begin by quoting a probation textbook of half a century ago, which said that the aims of probation were to help people to learn from their behaviour, build up their self-respect and have a sense of responsibility for other people's welfare, but that none of these can be done without 'the one great fundamental factor of love, or whatever other name is chosen for that warmth and strength of affection and fellow feeling . . . which alone makes life worth living for any human being' (Glover, 1949). The same author gives an example of the approach to probation at that time:

> Theresa was a wayward young woman of 16 who had been evicted from home by her stepmother, and from several hostels, on account of her behaviour. Her probation officer found lodgings for her, and all went well for a time; but one day Theresa stole a watch from her employer, left her lodgings, went to stay with a girlfriend who turned her out after a couple of days because Theresa stole and pawned her gloves to get money. The probation officer lent her the money to redeem them, and suggested that she might write and apologise to her landlady for leaving without notice. The landlady accepted her apology, Theresa paid back the probation officer in weekly instalments, and the magistrates decided that in view of her efforts to put matters right, no further action would be taken (Glover, 1949: 263-5).

Very different from to-day's talk of 'punishment in the community' and 'risk assessment'. (After hearing the Psychologist, you might think that emphasising punishment actually increases the risk, but that's another question.)

When the probation service began it was inspired by an ideal of rehabilitation, but it has always been overshadowed by the idea of punishment, and in the last quarter of this century it has been battered by waves of sceptics. Some of them said that it was unfair to offenders, because 'treatment' was forced on them and often didn't 'work', while others thought it was too indulgent, colluding with them by making excuses for their behaviour and shifting the blame to their upbringing or social deprivation. More recently, the rehabilitative ideal has been criticised for allowing offenders to ignore the effects of their actions on the victim, and for not enabling – or requiring – them to make amends.

Let me begin by outlining the traditional idea of rehabilitation, and three main criticisms of it, including the reversal of many of the original values in the 1990s. I want to consider some misconceptions about public opinion in relation to penal policy, which the Politician has already touched on. Then, looking at the future of probation, I will make the case that rehabilitation does work, and propose a way forward for the service in the twenty-first century, working with offenders, victims and the community.

THE ORIGINAL PROBATION IDEAL: REHABILITATION

The Probation Service had its origins in the church-based Police Court Mission in the late nineteenth century, and has traditionally seen offenders as human beings in difficulties, who should be given another chance. People argued about whether their behaviour originated in psychological flaws in their own characters (I am referring to the offenders, although probation officers sometimes asked these introspective questions about themselves too!). Should offenders be 'treated', or were they reacting to the injustices of society, which it was up to the rest of us to do something about?

When I use the word 'rehabilitation' I mean any measure intended to persuade and enable people to make more of their lives, rather than punishing them. Probation worked on the basis that many offenders started life with severe disadvantages, which led to their offending; so they needed help or treatment if they were to keep out of trouble in future. There were many success stories, like the one I began this talk with, and they owed much to probation officers. The service's 'mission statement', as we would call it to-day, was to 'advise, assist and befriend'.

But research did not always support probation officers' optimism. One study found that when offenders had problems, and had not committed serious offences, the support of probation officers halved the reconviction rate, but the results were considerably worse if the same methods were applied to people with a criminal life-style but few personal problems (Folkard *et al*, 1976: 20-21). Of course it is difficult to know which results follow from the individual's personality and circumstances, and which might be due to other people's efforts. What is certain is that many offenders do come from emotionally deprived backgrounds of unemployment or low incomes. One example among many:

A survey of 1,389 individuals on probation, aged 17, 20 and 23, found that two thirds of young offenders had a weekly income of less that £40 per week (in 1991), and for 37 per cent their position was aggravated by having to pay off fines (Smith and Stewart, 1997). For some, imprisonment of parents perpetuates parental deprivation into the next generation: 33 per cent of prisoners had dependent children living with them when imprisoned (Dodd and Hunter, 1992: 17).

This is confirmed by the Chief Inspector of Prisons, in a review of the treatment of young prisoners (Home Office. Chief Inspector, 1997: ch.3), which found that 'a staggering proportion of these young people had a *history of care or Social Services contact* (over half of under 18s)' (italics in original). The Civil Servant will give more details. It does not mean that deprivation 'causes' delinquency — if it did, 100 per cent of deprived youngsters would become delinquents — nor does it excuse it, but it is clearly a powerful combination of pressures which anyone would find difficult to withstand. As Smith and Stewart say, in accounts of many of these young people's lives 'there is a strong sense of one calamity being piled on another; one can imagine a young person somehow dealing with any one of these traumatic events, but not all of them' (1997:103).

One of the problems is confused thinking with regard to sentencing: courts are not always sure whether they are trying to punish or rehabilitate, and sometimes they try to persuade themselves that they can do both at once. It's true that people can benefit in some ways during imprisonment, for example if they are among the fortunate ones who receive appropriate training or therapy, but this is generally in spite of the prison regime, not because of it. It is still common for the working week in prisons to be less than 25 hours. There is a deep confusion about what the aims are; for example, one Home Office working party recommended imprisonment as a deterrent to vagrants and explained in the next paragraph how beneficial prison can be to them (Home Office, 1974: paras. 40, 41).

In another case, a young mother whose marriage was on the rocks, in desperation, resorted to robbery. She was sentenced to 18 months in prison, reduced on appeal to one year 'as an act of mercy'; but the sentence was not suspended or replaced by a non-custodial one because the court felt that 'Mrs L still needed discipline and training' (*The Times/Daily Telegraph/Guardian* 19 January 1978). The judge presumably believed that she would receive this in prison; even if she did, it is hard to see how he thought that separation from her family, and from any supportive friends she may have had, would affect her children or make it easier for her to cope. Twenty years later the same judicial contradictions were still around: parents who boarded up the windows and door of the filthy room where they kept their youngest daughter in appalling conditions were sent to prison; but the sentence was only six months because, the judge told them, 'you are intellectually limited and your other children need you' (the other children were well cared for)

(*Guardian*, 11 September 1998). A six-month sentence currently means three months in prison without compulsory supervision after release: enough to unsettle the other children, while teaching the parents nothing about parenting. As regards imprisonment, the arguments have been so often stated that I would not repeat them here, except that the public still does not seem to realise their significance. The charge list is long: for example that prisons are 'schools for crime', which bring together people who have little in common except that they have broken the law; they create an 'inmate sub-culture' whose values are at odds with those which the penal system is supposed to uphold; and that they '*de*-habilitate' people so that further effort is required to *re*habilitate them from the harm inflicted in the name of the state. (One experienced ex-prisoner told me that inmates don't spend their time plotting future villainy — they're fully occupied trying to have an easier time in prison. But that's no better: they are still not thinking about making it up to their victims, or leading law-abiding lives, which is what it's supposed to be about.) The government elected in Britain in May 1997 promised to tackle social exclusion, but pressed ahead with a penal policy which consigned hundreds more people each month to the most drastic social exclusion of all, and the numbers of people thus excluded rose to the highest level ever. The Civil Servant will give figures.

Some politicians, especially hard-line populists like the Conservative Home Secretary Michael Howard, want prison sentences to be both longer and more 'austere'. (Incidentally, in October 1998 Michael Howard spent one night in a relatively salubrious single cell in Brixton prison, to raise money for charity, with other 'top people' as neighbours, but this did not change his view, although he admitted that it was not like the real experience of imprisonment: *Guardian, Independent*, 3 October 1998). The reality is that the longer the sentences, the less harsh they have to be, both for humanitarian reasons and because of the need to keep order in prisons. If you have very little to lose, you can afford to be quite bolshie. People coming out of prison need extra help and after-care to get back on their feet, and this uses statutory and voluntary resources that could have been used for preventive work. Prisoners' families also suffer: in England it has been found necessary to establish a special charity, Aftermath, 'for the other victim, the families of serious offenders', as well as several groups for prisoners' wives. These efforts are chronically starved of resources. Politicians are in the habit of extolling the importance of the family; but imprisonment forcibly breaks up thousands of families, often permanently. The more often people are imprisoned, and the younger they are when locked up, the more likely they are to re-offend, but imprisonment continues to be official policy. Plainly something else is needed.

Rehabilitation or treatment?

At one time if you said 'rehabilitation' you meant some kind of treatment or therapy, as if delinquents were 'maladjusted', 'sociopathic', or in some other way pathological. If their behaviour was not their fault, it followed that it was wrong to punish them: they should be helped or 'treated'. I have two books with the title *The Crime of Punishment*. They are both critical of the theory and practice of punishment, and they both believe that offenders generally need help to enable them to survive without breaking the law. The first one was published in 1931, and it was written by Margaret Wilson, the wife of an English prison governor. She was impelled to write it by her forceful realisation of the unfairness and sheer inconsistency of punishment. She is one of the few writers to recognise the basically anti-moral lesson that punishment teaches:

> But the saddest thing about punishment is that undoubtedly it does sometimes deter adults from crime—and each time it does . . . , it to some extent perverts them. After infancy it can deter only by destroying moral standards. To say to a normal child after [the age of] ten, 'If you steal, you will be put into prison', is to destroy the very basis of morality. Because he will say at once, 'But I may not be caught' . . . . If you let a child think of all the pain which will be inflicted upon him, *instead of the pain which he will inflict*, you start him on the road towards crime (italics in original) (Wilson, 1931: 261-262).

The message given by punishment is: 'You'll get hurt if you're caught'. But think about it: surely that is not the message we want to send. In a society where people are encouraged to care for each other, the message should be: 'Someone else will be hurt whether you are caught or not'. The example set by those who punish is an anti-social one: it tells people that you can use superior force to stop other people doing what you don't want them to do.

After an extensively researched account of the brutalities of physical punishments, transportation and prisons, Mrs Wilson challenges:

> Ask them [lawyers] if for Christian courts a crucifix, an innocent man on a cross, would not be a better symbol of the workings of . . . justice than a blindfolded goddess with scales. Or would Pilate washing his hands in an attempt to shift responsibility be a still more fit emblem? (p.271).

The figure of justice flourishing a sword signifies, if it signifies anything, 'that though England has disarmed her citizens, she has not disarmed her law' (p.152 of that work). Mrs Wilson might have added that it is only through an accident of penological history that the symbol of Christianity is a cross rather than, say, a noose. She goes on to describe vividly the pain and poverty caused by financial speculators to many working people who 'are going to be nearer starvation because London gentlemen take risks with their money', and ridicules the idea that the reason for not committing such offences should be the prospect of 'silly penalties by discomfort for a few years in prison', rather than emphasis on the enormity of their crimes and the effects on other people. We should recognise, however, that less privileged malefactors simply do not have the same power to choose between right and wrong as those more fortunately placed.

Her plea for reform, in addition to social preventive measures and reducing prisons to a minimum, is to abandon the 'heathen conception of justice on which our primal law is based'. If she were writing today she would probably question the morality of introducing a market economy into countries which formerly had full employment, without planning to avoid the increased unemployment which has followed in country after country, opening the way to drug trafficking, prostitution and Mafia activity. If economic principles dictate that the economy should be based on market forces, social principles (and respect for fellow human beings) dictate that a way must be found, no less urgently, to prevent these foreseeable consequences.

As for attempts to deter other people, Margaret Wilson sums up the injustice of this approach in the words of a judge who is said to have told the man he was sentencing to death, 'You are not to be hung because you have stolen a horse. You are to be hung so that horses may not be stolen' (p. 260). But deterrence is not even effective. Mrs Wilson does not cite a source for her example, but I cannot resist quoting it:

> When the Bank of England first issued banknotes, the punishment for counterfeiting them was death . . . At one time a man was hung in London for making paper money, and soon after his body was taken to his house, the police entering, found his wife and family busily carrying on their counterfeiting, so busily, indeed, that when they were warned of the approach of the police, they stuffed their newly-made banknotes to hide them, into the mouth of the corpse (p.280).

The second book with the same title is by the American psychiatrist Karl Menninger, and appeared in 1968. He also gives many examples of 'the injustice of justice', especially towards those criminals who are misfits, wanting to be 'somebody': '*I suspect that all the crimes committed by all the jailed criminals do not equal in total social damage that of the crimes committed against them*' (p.28, his italics). He is far from uncritical of psychiatrists, but believes that in a majority of cases, if undertaken in time, education, medication, counselling, training can succeed in 'motivating or stimulating or arousing in a cornered individual the wish and hope and intention to change his methods of dealing with the realities of life' (p.257 of his work). Rather than have psychiatrists in the courtroom arguing about whether an accused is culpable or insane, and should therefore be punished or treated, he would have them meet outside the courtroom to decide on the best way to rehabilitate him. Dr Menninger calls for a 'therapeutic attitude' (p.260), which, combined with his proposals for crime prevention (p.268-274), could be called a problem-solving approach, although a treatment-oriented one. People who behave provocatively, even dangerously, have to be cared for and prevented from harming themselves or others; 'this requires love, not hate' (p. 260). He also recommends restitution, almost in passing (p.251).

A purely rehabilitative approach, if there were such a thing, would say that a young person with particular needs should be 'treated' (in both the everyday and the therapeutic senses of the word) in the same way whether he had stolen from a shop or beaten someone up. This is the position for children under ten in England and Wales (under eight in Scotland and Northern Ireland). The age is higher in most European countries: 13 in France, 14 in Austria, Germany, Italy, and several Eastern European countries, 15 throughout Scandinavia, 16 in Spain, Portugal and Poland, and 18 in Belgium and Luxembourg. The assumption is that children, and in other countries adolescents too, are learning, and should be dealt with informally if possible; this has been called the 'family model' (Griffiths, 1970), and its first priority is to try to educate the young person and keep him or her within the community.

What's wrong with rehabilitation?
There were three reactions against this approach. The first said that it was unfair to offenders, the second that it was too indulgent towards them, and the third that it ignored the victim.

Rehabilitation as unfair
The first, in the 1970s, in turn had several strands. It was recognised that many offenders were not suffering from a disorder, but were reacting rationally, though illegally, to their circumstances. It was unjust to sentence people to indefinite periods of treatment, regardless of the seriousness (or otherwise) of their offence. And doubts were raised as to whether treatment was effective. By the 1970s the despondent catch-phrase was 'Nothing works'.

If offenders were not 'sick', it would be more appropriate to try to rehabilitate them by 'persuading and enabling'; if we believe that society should use as little force as possible, we must rely on persuading people to obey the law, by building their self-esteem and making a law-abiding life-style accessible to them. It is right to allow people as much freedom as possible, and it is in any case impossible to coerce them beyond a certain point. This means of course that we need to try to build a society where everyone *has* opportunities and law-abiding behaviour *is* rewarded. Meanwhile we have to cope in the unreconstructed present; I'm not saying that 'it's all society's fault', but the methods we use should be of a kind that bring us towards that ideal, not further from it.

When the 'crime control model' is combined with rehabilitative methods, it is potentially unjust not only in the abstract, but in two very concrete ways. Firstly, since rehabilitative measures are based on the offender's needs rather than his actions or criminal intent, they may lead to too much or too little state intervention in his life out of all proportion to what he has done: too much, because his needs are great but his offence was minor, or too little because he has few needs but has inflicted serious harm. 'Treatment in the community' for juveniles, for example, is a pliable term: it could include reform schools which are as restrictive as some prisons but, because they are supposed to be caring institutions, are subject to fewer controls, so that low educational standards and even physical and sexual abuse of young people can go undetected for many years.

Secondly, in the 1960s people began to question whether this compulsion even worked. The medical, therapeutic policy was immensely well-meaning, but (the word 'well-meaning' always has to be followed by 'but'!) it suffered from some fatal flaws. It assumed that treatment could be carried out in penal institutions, and ignored the harmful effects and abuses which are endemic to prisons. The censorship of prisoners' letters, the absence of independent inspection and grievance procedures, and the resistance of most prison authorities to research effectively concealed the actuality of prisons, except when prisoners occasionally rioted or, after release when they couldn't be prevented, wrote books. Its logic required that the offender be kept in until 'cured', which is clearly unfair if the treatment doesn't work and arguably even if it does. The effects were most severe in some states of America, where sentences could be almost completely indeterminate (from one to 99 years in some cases); but they were felt in this country after the introduction of parole in 1968, and earlier than that for juveniles, who could be sent to approved schools or community homes until their eighteenth birthdays.

The unfairness of some rehabilitative programmes was made worse because officialdom tended to regard the 'model prisoner' as rehabilitated, and anyone who still had enough spirit to resist the regime as incorrigible. (The film *One Flew Over the Cuckoo's Nest* was about mental hospitals not prisons, but the point is the same.) Some of the objectors to rehabilitation went so far as to say that it should have no part in sentencing: the only criterion should be punishment, which should be proportionate to each offender's 'just deserts'. Those who based their ideas on the offender's rights assumed that such punishments would be largely symbolic, and they thought that prison sentences could therefore be kept fairly short.

Rehabilitation as 'soft'
This played into the hands of those at the 'tough' end of the spectrum, who thought that probation was altogether too lenient. According to them it encouraged offenders to put the blame everywhere except where it belonged: on themselves. Since they stressed the offender's wickedness rather than his deprived upbringing, it made sense to impose sentences that were proportionate to this wickedness – the trouble was that the sentence lengths that the liberals had in mind could be doubled or tripled and still be proportionate.

The second reaction against the therapeutic approach came in the 1990s. In this climate of opinion explanations were seen as 'excuses', even to the extent of removing (in October 1995) the requirement for probation officers to hold university-based social work qualifications; these were to be replaced by on-the-job training and a diploma in probation studies. The government thought that the service should recruit more former soldiers and fewer women (Schofield, 1997; *Howard Journal*, 1996: 176-7). The then British prime minister, John Major, called for 'a little less understanding and a little more condemnation', and in 1997 the Labour Home Secretary Jack Straw chose to call his White Paper about youth crime *No More Excuses*; the Crime and Disorder Bill which followed the White Paper is full of powers for the courts to *order* offenders and their parents to do various things (through parenting orders, child safety – i.e. control and supervision – orders, local child curfews, reparation orders, action plan orders, and detention and training orders) although, to be fair, it does envisage some assistance for them as well. If probation were to survive it would have to be 'tough' or even 'punitive'.

The media went to town over the case of a boy who was sent on a £7,000, 88-day safari trip to Africa in 1993, which the Politician referred to; this was intended to take him away from his surroundings so that he could think things out. Gloucestershire Social Services defended the decision, although he continued to offend afterwards, and they later sent another disturbed boy, aged 13, on a month-long canal trip with three others to prevent him from absconding before his trial (*Evening Standard*, 3 October; *Guardian*, 4 October 1996). This idea is not confined to Britain: in Darmstadt, Germany, a 13-year-old from a disrupted family background had committed over 150 offences (including criminal damage, theft, armed robbery, assault and sexual harassment). He broke out of institutions, and did not respond to group methods. Although he was only two months below the German age of criminal responsibility (14), after which he could have been locked up next time he offended, it was decided to send him on 'intensive social-educational individual care abroad', in the shape of a journey to Argentina with a social worker. The cost was 70,000 DM (currently about £24,000), but if he had been placed in care for more than 150 days at 470 DM (£160) per day it would have cost even more (*Badische Zeitung*, 30 June 1998; I am grateful to Michael Kilchling for drawing this to my attention).

Treating offenders, ignoring victims
The third criticism of rehabilitation is that, like punishment, it focuses on the offender and ignores the victim, who has seldom done anything to deserve the effects of the crime. More specifically, both 'do things to' the offender rather than make *him* do something positive to make up for the harm he has caused. This is true of the process of law as well as the outcome. Too often the defendant is a passive spectator at his own trial. In British courtrooms he cannot communicate with his lawyer, and often the dock is at the back of the court so that he has difficulty even in hearing what is going on (as the Howard League showed in its report *No Brief for the Dock* (1976)). Meanwhile the victim, if not called as a witness, may not even be told that the trial is taking place, although there are improvements, as the Victim Assistance Worker will be telling us.

So I think we have to accept that there is not so much a flaw as a large gap in the rehabilitative approach. It is not that it doesn't 'work'; there are plenty of ways of encouraging people to behave better, especially young people, and I think we have to proceed on the assumption that we can get better at it. I will say more about that in a moment. The serious gap is that it is based on the offender's *needs*, and ignores his actions and their effects on victims and the community.

We have to show that we recognise the distinction (which the Politician mentioned) between explaining conduct and condoning it: being deprived does not justify depriving or injuring someone else. We have to confront offending behaviour, by making the offender aware of the other person, the victim. If the victim wants to do this him or herself, a victim/offender mediation service can arrange it.

Showing concern for victims will help to meet the long-standing criticism from the victim's point of view, that the system in general and probation officers in particular focus on the offender and ignore the victim. Indeed one side-effect of punishment is, as I have said, that some spectators feel sympathy with the 'victim' of the punishment. We as probation officers are now required to take account of the victim—I mean the victim of the crime. The National Standards require us in pre-sentence reports to assess 'the consequences of the offence, including the impact on the victim' and 'the offender's attitude to the victim and offence and awareness of its consequences, . . . acceptance or minimisation of responsibility, remorse or guilt and any expressed desire to make amends' (Home Office *et al*, 1995: 9-10). This gives some acknowledgement of the victims' point of view, but they do not necessarily feel that they have been heard, since we do not interview them (it would almost double our pre-sentence workload if we did) but extract information from the prosecutor's files. What it does not do is to enable any dialogue to take place between the victim and the offender, so that they have the possibility of seeing each other as human beings and not as stereotypes, although this last point has been addressed to some extent by adding victim awareness to the range of methods of working with offenders. So long as the basic philosophy is a retributive one, there is a danger that the sentencer's thought processes will go something like this:

- decide appropriate punishment according to the conventional 'tariff'
- read report of effects on victim
- decide that heavier punishment is called for.

If the increased sentence had any value, there would be no objection to this; but it does not benefit the victim (except to a limited extent if the extra takes the form of a compensation order), it makes things worse for the offender and, in the case of imprisonment, for all other offenders by adding to prison overcrowding. It does nothing towards promoting any understanding of what the offender has done to the victim in human terms, and hence changing his future behaviour.

It seems to me that this will lead to four major developments for the probation service; in a number of places they are already happening. The first two I have already mentioned: referring to victims in pre-sentence reports, and including the victim's perspective when working with offenders. Thirdly, some members of the probation service will continue to be involved with Victim Support at a managerial level. Fourthly, there will be an extension of the work with both victims and offenders, which I expect the Victim Assistance Worker will mention, before the release of offenders from prison. The probation service will need to recognise, and get others to recognise, that being concerned for the needs of victims does not necessarily mean that one is harsh towards offenders, and *vice versa*. For all of these, especially the last, the probation service will need to shed its 'pro-offender' image. Probation officers are well placed to help establish and manage victim/offender mediation services.

We usually speak of the effects on the victim, but we have to remember that for many crimes the victim is a shop or institution, or the community. But then again, shops are run by individuals: the victim of an armed robbery is not the bank but the cashier.

PUBLIC OPINION

At this point I should like to say something about public opinion, because some politicians and sections of the media have used it as an excuse for encouraging the greater use of imprisonment. The courts appear to have believed their claims that they reflect public opinion, and that courts should do what public opinion appears to demand — two very questionable propositions. When even the politicians accept that imprisonment would be excessive, they have demanded that probation be made 'tougher' and more punitive. But this is a move away from the ideal of encouraging and inspiring offenders to develop internal self-control, towards external, authoritarian control; and it brings no benefit to victims, except those who want retribution, although statements of this kind often purport to be 'standing up for victims'.

We all know that public opinion is volatile, and the picture of it that is presented in surveys depends largely on the questions posed: what you ask is what you get. At one end of the spectrum, magazines and tabloid newspapers ask their readers to send their views to questions which point in a particular (usually punitive) direction such as 'Do you support tougher sentences for criminals?' The readers of any one publication are not a cross-section of the public, and those of them who respond to questionnaires are not representative either. At the respectable end are the polling organizations who use large balanced samples — but even their questions are not innocent of bias; they ask loaded questions, or ask questions about prison without referring to other options; but they should know that 'the more knowledge people are given, the more varied and thoughtful become their responses', and 'When people are asked what actually works in dealing with crime they tend to propose social measures' (Stern, 1998: 315, 316). A recent *British Crime Survey* (Hough and Roberts, 1998) found that many people greatly overestimated the proportion of violent crime and underestimated the proportion of people sent to prison for it. So far, so good: it has done a good job in showing that many people's attitudes are based on inaccurate impressions. But then it asks (p.18) 'In general, would you say that sentences handed down by the courts are too tough, about right or too lenient?' to which four out of five said 'Too lenient'. This question is firmly locked into a mind-set which assumes that 'toughness' and 'leniency' are the only dimensions on which sentencing can be based. It is a further example of the macho language of the 'war against crime', and disregards entirely the need for a 'peacemaking' approach: a rehabilitative philosophy which upholds the guiding principle that sentences (or at least some of them) should aim to enable the individual offender to avoid re-offending, and the restorative one which would base sanctions on holding offenders accountable by requiring them to make amends for the harm they have done.

The survey then asked people whether they thought that tough or lenient sentencing (about which many of them were misinformed) affected what they believed to be the increase or decrease in the crime (which many of them also got wrong); so many of them gave answers based on a single or double inaccuracy. (It does give a breakdown of the answers of those who got it right and wrong, but the total figure is the one likely to be quoted.) In addition, although admittedly the question allows people to say that sentencing has little or no effect, it clearly implies that sentencing can have a major influence on the crime rate, which criminologists know to be at best a very questionable proposition. As the report says, in a footnote in tiny type, 'There is general agreement among sentencing scholars that changes in sentencing severity will have little impact on the overall crime rate' (Hough and Roberts, 1998: 32); at least some of the public seem to recognize this, because only one in five thought that tougher sentences were effective in preventing crime. The Civil Servant will give some figures.

But the idea that sentencing should be aimed at something quite different, such as rehabilitating offenders or requiring them to make amends to victims or the community, is not explored; most respondents were offered a range of options including compensation and community service, but they are subsumed in the 'tough/lenient' mind-set of the rest of the questionnaire. The report mentions research showing that people with knowledge of the background of a case are less likely to think that the sentence is too lenient, but makes no attempt to provide such background in its specimen case of burglary; even so, 44 per cent wanted compensation and 26 per cent community service for such a case, and the survey confirmed that victims are no more punitive than others. The Civil Servant will give some more information, to supplement what he already provided after the Politician's talk.

Admittedly these surveys were carried out some time ago; it may be a sign of the political climate that there seems to be a dearth of recent surveys asking questions of this kind. (Here is a new hypothesis for social scientists to consider: that statements by politicians influence not only public attitudes but the questions asked by social scientists.)

THE FUTURE OF PROBATION

How does all this affect the Probation Service? Fundamental changes have been mooted, such as re-naming it as a national 'Public Protection Service' or 'Community Justice Enforcement Agency' which would 'deal more toughly with offenders serving their sentences in the community and to protect the public' (*Times*, 22 June; *Guardian*, 7 August 1998). Is this a move in the right direction? We have recognised that as probation officers we need to take account of victims, for several good reasons. This complements our work with offenders, in the ways I have just mentioned. Using information about the effect of crime on victims to make offenders face the consequences of what they have done is a step forward, but does not generally make as much impact on the offender as direct communication with the victim. Nor does it give the victim the chance to convey his or her feelings personally.

Work with victims
So I support the statement made by the Association of Chief Officers of Probation (ACOP) in 1996, *Probation Services and the Victims of Crime*, which accepts several of the principles which Victim Support has proposed about the rights of victims to be kept informed and supported; it also says that victims

> should be able to communicate with the offender, subject to the offender's informed consent and proper supervision and safeguards.

From the offender's point of view it says that

> the rehabilitation of offenders can be enhanced by increased awareness of the effects of their crime on victims, leading to a greater sense of responsibility for their actions, as well as by work that is also reparative and restorative,

and that

> the validity and authority of Probation Services will be strengthened if they take the needs of victims seriously and work to the principles of restorative justice.

It encourages Probation Services to develop mediation between victims and offenders, and reparation if practicable, subject of course to the needs and wishes of victims, and it has been backed up by a joint position statement between ACOP and Mediation UK in May 1998.

The *Victim's Charter* has given the English Probation Service the responsibility for working with victims of serious violent and sexual offences, and the families of murder victims, who are contacted after the sentence has been passed; they are given information and invited to express any anxieties. They are told for example about ways in which prisoners are prepared for release, sometimes by being moved to an open prison or temporarily released; the victim's concerns may affect the conditions imposed on the offender (but not the date of release). In some areas, such as West Yorkshire, this work is undertaken by workers from the Victim/Offender Unit, because victims see them as neutral and not mainly concerned for the offender; the unit's workers do not propose mediation, but when victims and offenders say they would like to meet (or communicate indirectly) before the offender's release, the workers are able to handle this. The Victim Assistance Worker will have more to say about this (see p.94).

Rehabilitation does work
With this new perspective of awareness of victims' needs, I should like to return to the question of rehabilitation. As a probation officer I know that many people drift into trouble because of the pressures they face: at best they have been deprived of physical and emotional necessities such as decent housing, education, work, food and love, and at worst they have been actively abused. This is not a deterministic statement. As I have said, I don't believe in 'causes' of crime, but in pressures towards it, including both the situation and the make-up of the individual. Poverty, inadequate parents and a low serotonin level do not make a person criminal, but combined with other factors they constitute the pressures upon him or her and the strength of his or her ability to resist them. Both the pressures and the resistance are different for everyone. One unemployed man will steal to feed his family, one business executive will commit fraud to 'keep up with the Joneses', and others will not; their circumstances and characters are different.

The fact remains that most of those who come the way of the Probation Service have considerable needs, and we are committed to do what we can to meet them. So we need a way of demonstrating that needs are understood and will be addressed, but that harming others is not condoned.

During the 1970s and 1980s the idea that 'nothing works' demoralised social workers and encouraged the advocates of 'just deserts'. But it has been challenged. I need not re-tell the well-known story of how the much publicised work of the American Robert Martinson was found to overstate the case for pessimism, and he himself partly recanted; for present purposes it is enough to quote some more recent work by the English researchers James McGuire and Philip Priestley (1995). They found little evidence that psychotherapeutic methods and counselling are effective, nor medical ones unless accompanied by a comprehensive programme of work. They also found, after reviewing findings similar to those described by the Psychologist earlier, that 'the failure of punishment to have a demonstrable effect on offence behaviour can be seen to be not only explicable but patently obvious' (p.14 of that work); indeed one review of research findings (what is called in the jargon a 'meta-analysis') found that 'deterrence-based programmes, interventions containing strong punitive elements, had a significant negative effect on recidivism and served to increase it by the order of 25 per cent' (p.16).

Meta-analysis has shown that there are types of programmes that stand a better chance of being effective. A Home Office review, *Reducing Offending*, has indicated the principles of 'what works' (Goldblatt and Lewis, 1998; see also PAPPAG, 1999). They should for example be based on those needs of offenders that are related to their offending, and should match their learning style, which for most offenders tends to require active and participatory methods of working; there should be adequate staff training and programme evaluation. Community-based programmes tend to be more effective than institutional ones, although programmes which take into account the other principles can be successful in any treatment setting; for example a recent Home Office study found that for highly deviant child molesters a long-term residential programme with a far greater amount of time undergoing treatment did more to change offenders' attitudes (Beckett *et al*, cited by Hedderman and Sugg, 1996). The same study found, however, that the community-based STEP programme — Sex Offender Treatment Evaluation Project — led to lower reconviction rates after two years compared to other groups of sex offenders). The more effective programmes were designed to teach problem-solving and other coping skills. Two Scottish programmes, using structured, 'challenging' group work weekly over six or seven months, have shown that men's violence towards partners can be changed; after 12 months the proportion of men committing five or more violent acts had fallen from 26 to seven per cent, whereas among those dealt with by other criminal justice methods it increased from 31 to 37 per cent (Dobash *et al*, 1996) — and the evaluations were made not on the basis of reconvictions but by their partners, who should know.

These findings are not exactly surprising; one which did stand out was that the most promising outcomes are based on combining two approaches:

- the cognitive, which means exploring how individuals interpret, understand and think about certain behaviour or situations, and then training them to find other ways of handling those which show signs of possibly leading to violence or other criminality; and
- the behavioural, which means using a combination of incentives and disincentives (carrots and sticks, if you insist) to promote the learning of new behaviour. Several of the techniques involve developing skills in interacting with other people; one study reported a 50 per cent reduction in recidivism rates after negotiation training to help resolve parent/child conflicts within families of delinquents.

Self-instructional training for the control of anger and other behaviour has been used, and training in moral reasoning can secure changes in juvenile offenders. Intensive probation supervision on its own did not have much impact, especially when the emphasis was on punishment and surveillance; some projects which did reduce recidivism were found to contain an element of treatment. Similarly, early research on American 'boot camps' found that the most punitive ones produced an increase in recidivism, but there was some reduction in three programmes where there were more purposeful, non-punitive and problem-focused activities such as alcohol-abuse and drug-abuse sessions, and where there was follow-up community supervision after release. Supervision that is not based on surveillance but on increased contact between clients and probation staff therefore seems likely to increase effectiveness (McGuire and Priestley, 1995; Vennard *et al*, 1997).

An assessment of research evidence by the Home Office has concluded, also not surprisingly, that no one method is likely to be effective on its own; an integrated strategy is needed, focusing mainly on prevention, and with 'interventions with offenders' quite low on the list (Goldblatt and Lewis, 1998).

A service for victims and offenders in the community
Finally we come to the way ahead. Let me say first what I do *not* want. I cannot accept the quasi-humane argument which says 'Prisons are expensive and damaging, but the public is punitive, therefore the only way to gain acceptance for reduced use of prisons is to promote punishment in the community'. This would concentrate on fines, curfews and electronic tagging; compensation and community service orders might be called restorative, but would be imposed primarily as punishment; victims and offenders would have no opportunity to communicate, and community service work would be chosen for its unpleasantness, not as the best way for the individual offender to make

amends. Probation officers would be enforcement agents, 'screws on wheels'. Of course supervision is necessary, but it should be a means to an end, not an end in itself.

But despite what I have said about the potential for rehabilitation, I do not see the future as a return to the idea of probation primarily as social work; that would lead back to the problems I described earlier, with probation officers – and offenders themselves – giving explanations which to many people sound like excuses.

My overriding duty as a probation officer has to be to the community, and I can start by taking an active role in passing information to the crime prevention policy agency. I am not talking about the kind of information that helps to detect crimes but information related to prevention. For example, if a high proportion of young offenders came from a particular school, or from an area of the city without adequate outlets for youthful energy, remedial action could be taken. I also have a special responsibility to those members of the community who are disadvantaged either by circumstances or by the actions of their fellow-citizens. This means that I must work to help offenders to be reintegrated, and must also be aware of the victims' needs, as the ACOP statement says. The British organization Victim Support recognises the need for offenders to receive fair treatment and has avoided calling for the weakening of 'due process' safeguards for the accused or heavier sentences for offenders.

People who were brought up on the rehabilitative ideal might see reparation as an extension of punishment, especially if it were in the form of cash payments by an offender who had little or no money. I agree that compensation and community service are seen as punishment by some, and the way they are presented in current political rhetoric encourages this; so I would, for a start, emphasise that both of them are a way of making good the harm caused, and are not imposed in order to cause unpleasantness to the offender through deprivation of time or money. An example shows what I mean.

Cleaning up the River Wandle in South London involves removing submerged car tyres, bicycles and other rubbish from the river bed, lifting them into a punt, then dragging it against the current to the collection point; a seven-hour day of that is certainly hard work. But one young offender asked to be transferred to what he called 'the punishment project on the river' so that the fish and wild life would return, and was proud to have worked there (Anon, 1997), and there are many reports of offenders who continued their community service voluntarily after completing their hours – it was therefore not punishment, but something better than punishment.

The point is not that the work was hard but that it was useful. Once again, politicians got it diametrically wrong. Just as sewing mailbags gave the message that work is unpleasant and ill-paid, Michael Howard's rehetoric on community service gave the message that working for others is unpleasant and unrewarding – exactly the opposite of pro-social, compassionate values.

Community service orders may also be used to educate the offender by probation officers whose training inclines them to a social-work approach, which misses the restorative dimension in a different way (Buonatesta, 1997). This tendency may be countered by a sentence such as the 'combination order' introduced in England by the Criminal Justice Act 1991 (section 11): a community service order is combined with a probation order, and the latter addresses rehabilitative needs.

However, while recognition of (and reparation for) the harm are appropriate, probation officers remain conscious of the needs which their clients face if they are to behave in the law-abiding way that is expected of them. What victim/offender mediation services have found is that many victims also recognise this, especially when they have met the offender. They do not always want any reparation for themselves – they may have claimed back the insurance, or the items stolen may have had sentimental rather than monetary value; but they want the offender to do *something* to show that he is sorry (to 'feel the pinch', as one victim put it), and many of them are actually concerned, particularly for young offenders, and want to encourage them to make better use of their lives. We do meet offenders who very much wish to offer apologies and make things up to the victim. So if the offender agrees to take part in a rehabilitative programme to meet his needs, for example to gain skills or overcome addiction, victims are often willing to regard that as reparation. The objections to rehabilitation in a punitive context do not apply, because the victim is involved, the offender agrees, the duration depends on the offender's needs and is not intended to be related to the degree of criminality. The offender is not having things 'done to him'; and at the end of the process, just as with other forms of reparation, he will not have the stigma of punishment which could make people turn him away from jobs or accommodation, but the credit for having completed the programme. This will make it easier for him to be re-accepted into the community.

FACTS AND STATISTICS

The Civil Servant
The Probation Officer has asked me to give further examples of deprived backgrounds of young offenders. To take just one recent study, Professor

David Smith and John Stewart of Lancaster University found that 80 per cent of young probationers had left school with no qualifications, compared with eight per cent of the general population (Smith and Stewart, 1997: 101). Twenty-two per cent of these 17 to 23-year-olds were chronically incapacitated through some form of disability, illness or addiction (p.102 of that work).

Among prisoners, 26 per cent had been taken into care as a child, as against two per cent of the general population (p.101). Only 17 per cent of young probationers had lived with one or both parents all their lives (p.102), and 38 per cent of under-21s in prison have been through the care system. There are very many studies which confirm these findings.

A study of 200 violent young offenders — a category of whom the public is especially fearful — found that 72 per cent had experienced emotional, sexual, physical or (rarely) organized/ritual abuse, and 27 per cent combinations thereof; 57 per cent had experienced bereavement, loss of contact with someone important, or both; only nine per cent had experienced neither abuse nor loss (Boswell, 1996, 1998).

The ultimate social exclusion is imprisonment, and this rose throughout the 1990s; from 40,606 at the end of 1992 to 56,440 in September 1996; it continued to rise after the change of government, and reached 62,481 by September 1997, an increase of 54 per cent in less than five years (Penal Affairs Consortium, 1997).

The Chief Inspector of Prisons found that 'Most young offenders had been *failed by the education system*' with over half being excluded (or excluding themselves) and many truanting on a regular basis. Almost a quarter had been under the influence of *alcohol* at the time of the offence, and almost two thirds admitted to *misusing drugs* at some time in their lives with cannabis being prevalent; although the Chief Inspector points out that 'This reflects the behaviour of young people as a whole'. He found that '*The main reason given for the young people's criminal behaviour was involvement with drink and/or drugs*' (Home Office, 1997, italics in original). This is confirmed by a Howard League study of 66 young men in Feltham Young Offenders Institution: 89 per cent had taken drugs, including alcohol, regularly, and over a third had taken Class A drugs (Howard League, 1998b).

Reconviction rates

On release from prison, 45 per cent of males are reconvicted within two years, but for 17 to 20-year olds the figure is 69 per cent and for those aged 14 to 16, 89 per cent. These figures are taken from *Prison Statistics 1994* (Home Office, 1996a), since when they have not been published in this form (perhaps because penal reformers quoted them too often!).

Probation reconvictions

Numerous studies have been made of what works and what doesn't work, and a picture is emerging of where the difference lies. Unstructured talk therapy is not successful, nor single-treatment methods: it is best to combine more than one. Punitive measures can actually make results worse: surveys of programmes such as shock incarceration and intensive surveillance showed re-offence rates 25 per cent higher than in control groups (Meta-analyses by M W Lipsey, quoted by McGuire and Priestley, 1995).

Programmes work best when they are structured and consistently applied, and use methods that are matched to the offenders' characteristics and learning styles. Those which include 'cognitive' methods, that is, encouraging offenders to think through the consequences of their actions for themselves and others, have a good record (McGuire and Priestley, 1995). These findings are supported by a Home Office review, which found that programmes teaching offenders the importance of reasoning and problem-solving were more successful; so is social learning, in which behavioural techniques are modified by cognitive ones, that is, observation of the outcomes of the behaviour of others. Thus after a 'STOP' programme (Straight Thinking On Probation), eight per cent were reconvicted of a violent or sexual offence or burglary within 12 months, compared with 21 per cent of those imprisoned (Vennard *et al*, 1997).

Public opinion

To add to the information I gave after the politician's talk: a recent *British Crime Survey* in 1996 interviewed 16,348 people aged 16 or over. In its report, *Attitudes to Punishment*, it found that many people based their views on a mistaken impression of the facts. About three quarters thought that recorded crime was rising when in fact it was falling; four out of five thought that more than 30 per cent of crime is violent, whereas the actual figure, excluding minor assaults, is six per cent. Over half the estimates of the proportion of convicted offenders sent to prison were substantially too low; for example over half thought that fewer than 60 per cent of rapists were sent to prison, whereas the actual figure is 97 per cent (Hough and Roberts, 1998).

When aware of other options, such as reparation, many people choose it. When the *British Crime Survey* asked people about sentencing, giving them a 'menu' of alternatives, considerably more chose compensation and community service, and fewer chose prison, than when no menu was provided (Hough and Roberts, 1998: 29). Previous surveys in Britain have found that:

- 85 per cent thought it was a good idea to make some offenders do community service instead of going to prison,
- 66 per cent wanted them to pay compensation to their victims
- 93 per cent thought that offenders should have to make good the consequences of their crime wherever possible
- 63 per cent thought that the money from fines should go to victims
- three-quarters thought that more adult offenders should be made to take part in community service instead of being sent to prison (Wright, 1989).

Despite this, community service orders in England have been moved away from the ideal of enabling offenders to show that they can make a contribution to other people's welfare: National Standards issued in 1995 required that placements 'should include at least one option providing hard manual work' (Home Office *et al*, 1995).

Similar results have been found in other countries; in Germany, for example, 90 per cent of those questioned had a 'restitutive' or 'very restitutive' attitude towards petty offences such as minor frauds, theft from a market stall or fare dodging; even for offences such as purse snatching, burglary and rape 25 per cent felt that way (Sessar, 1995). In one American state, four out of five people favoured spending on education, job training and community programmes rather than prisons in order to reduce crime, and about the same proportion indicated an interest in a face-to-face meeting with the offender in the presence of a trained mediator, if they were the victim of a non-violent property crime committed by a juvenile or a young adult. Nearly three out of four chose restitution by the offender as more important than jail. Similar findings are reported from six other national and local surveys in the United States (Pranis and Umbreit, 1992).

It has consistently been found that victims are not more punitive than the general population. In the study just quoted, 46 per cent of victims of violence were willing to disregard the punishment of their offender completely, and 30 per cent partly, if he were ready to make restitution (for burglary victims the figures were 32 per cent and 44 per cent respectively) (Sessar, 1995). The more directly affected people are, the less punitive: another study found that 54 per cent of victims of burglary thought that burglars aged 18 with previous convictions should go to prison, and 75 per cent thought that persistent burglars aged 30 should be imprisoned. But when asked how they would like the burglar *in their case* dealt with, only 29 per cent wanted custody. Remarks like 'Prison does no good to anyone' were common, and many of those who chose it did so only because they knew of no effective alternative. Although there was a minority of ten per cent who wanted personal revenge, corporal punishment or the stocks, the general message was that 'their' offender should repay his 'debt' in a useful way, by restitution or working for the community, and that if he could be reformed, other householders would be spared the experience (Maguire, 1982: 139-141).

DISCUSSION

Q. You have said that many offenders come from a deprived background, and the Civil Servant has backed this up with research findings. I don't question these, but couldn't they be interpreted in a different way? Many young people are unemployed because they can easily live off social security; they have low earnings because they bunked off school and acquired no skills (except street skills). Sometimes the schools have done little to contain them. This has happened partly because their parents (who are also often living on social security) either didn't make the effort to control them, or don't work at their marriages to keep them together, and when things get rough they are quick to put their children into care. When they do try to discipline the children, some social worker will be ready to prosecute them for assault, or even take them to the European Court of Human Rights. We should show them firmly where the boundaries are.

A. I couldn't agree more with your last point; the question is how we do it. You should not believe everything you read in the *Daily Mail*! Remember that it's only news because it's the exception; and even if the facts are accurate you can be sure they are incomplete. Firstly, I don't believe that there are children who are innately wicked; this is unprovable, of course, but I am sure it is the best working assumption. Some of them are certainly extremely disturbed, which is not surprising when you know the backgrounds many of them come from. Secondly, whether or not such 'bad' children exist, all the signs are that constructive treatment is more likely to be effective. If responsibility does lie with the parents, it is not fair to blame the children for that. It is vital that the way 'we' (or people on society's behalf) treat them models the way we want them to behave, and does not for example use violence to teach them not to be violent. Some truancy is because the children can see that the school is failing them; and it is accepted that many schools have been far too quick to exclude (that is, suspend or expel) children rather than attend to their needs—yes, including the need for *educative* discipline. Discipline should not be one-sided: adults should make specific undertakings, as well as expect them from children.

And finally, even if there are parents who fit the stereotype you have drawn, there are many more who genuinely want to do the best for their children but don't know how; we should be looking for ways of enabling them to do what they, and we, would want, for example through projects such as Home Start, which offers support, friendship and guidance to families with children under five, and I was pleased to hear the Politician endorse the High/Scope project which is similar. But I don't like the tendency of the last British government and the present one to threaten parents with fines, and certainly not with imprisonment, which is the surest way of making the family more dysfunctional.

Q. You haven't replied to the point about unemployment.

A. It's not a subject one can deal with in two minutes! Just two points. Firstly, I don't believe that there are so many people who prefer to be unemployed (although I confess that I'm looking forward to my own retirement!), and many of them, although not in paid work, are an asset to their communities in all sorts of ways. Secondly, if we (that unspecified 'we' again!) want people to have jobs, we must make sure that the jobs are available. We must look at overtime. The average industrial overtime is about eight hours a week, so five people's overtime could be one person's job, and a cut in the total working week would be even better. Of course this would not be easy, but the French have taken a step towards it. We should have to persuade people that more leisure is worth more than a pay rise; then they would have more time with their families and communities, there would be fewer crimes and other social problems, and therefore social workers could have a shorter working week too. With less unemployment, crime, and other social malaise, government expenditure, and therefore taxes, could be reduced, which would offset people's loss of income. Of course I am glossing over a load of difficulties, but I am convinced that this is the direction in which we must look if we are to have a stable, inclusive community.

Q. Among all the factors which you and the Civil Servant have mentioned, you have said nothing about the possible influence of nutrition on behaviour. Do you think it has any effects?

A. There are two main groups of factors here: individuals who are impaired because their brain is not properly nourished and those who have been exposed to poisons like lead from petrol which can damage the brain. These are frequently related. Numerous studies have found statistically significant correlations of raised levels of lead, cadmium and other heavy metals in the blood with poor academic performance, or anti-social or violent behaviour. Equally, deficiencies in the nutrients which nourish the brain—vitamins, minerals and essential fatty acids have been correlated with such behaviour. This is often due to eating snack foods that are high in refined foods and fat, with little nutritional value. A number of very precisely designed experiments in America have shown that improving nutrition can significantly reduce offending behaviour. A full-scale research project is taking place at a young offenders institution in Buckinghamshire, which should provide convincing evidence (Gesch, 1998).

Q. May I move the discussion to the Probation Service? Should it continue to be offender-oriented?

Q. If I may follow on from that question, Philip Priestley, who has written and spoken a lot about these matters, has proposed a 'Probation and Reparation Service', and I see that in the Czech Republic a Probation and Mediation Service is planned. What do you think of those ideas?

A. I would answer 'Yes' to the first question, but increased victim-awareness should help to promote victim/offender mediation. There should be safeguards for both victims and offenders.

With regard to the second, I don't think that a combined 'Victim and Offender Service' would be in the best interests of everyone, even if we were starting from scratch. There would be a danger that one type of user of the service would feel that they were not being treated as well as the other, and individual officers might experience a conflict of interest. So there are advantages in the separation which exists in England and Wales, with a statutory probation service (or an independent, government-funded one as in Austria), and a voluntary (non-profit) victim assistance organization, also receiving substantial public funding.

Mediation won't develop if it is only a secondary task for the people who do it. You need to have people whose job depends on making a success of it. So I would like to see an offenders' agency, one for victims, and a neutral one to promote communication (neutral as regards the individuals, but not of course as regards their offences). If this mediation service has to be organized on a statutory basis, it can be set up as an inter-agency joint effort by probation, social services, police, education, and of course Victim Support. The Probation Service may however play an active role in setting up independent mediation services, just as in the 1970s it helped to establish Victim Support in Britain.

So on balance it is probably preferable to operate the mediation services within an independent voluntary organization, under the auspices of a national umbrella body such as Mediation UK; they would have members of statutory services and Victim Support on their management committee. It might take them a little longer to win the confidence (and the funding) of people within the 'system', but it would also give them closer links with the local community, which is a great asset. Mediation services would offer other types of mediation as well; some of them, dealing with neighbour disputes, would contribute to crime prevention.

Q. A related question: as a probation officer will I have to learn to be a mediator?

A. No, we don't think that people should combine these two very different roles. If we as probation officers introduce ourselves to victims, they naturally think that we are asking for something on behalf of the offender, whereas mediators should be seen to be neutral. But an understanding of the concept of restorative justice should be part of every probation officer's training.

Q. For all the talk of offenders' accountability, many of them do come from very disadvantaged backgrounds, as you said, and need help and support. Does this mean that they won't get it, because they are expected to make reparation regardless?

A. No, experience with victim/offender mediation has shown that victims are realistic and do not generally ask for more than offenders can pay; often they do not ask for anything for themselves, but want the offender to do community service as a constructive way of recognising the harm that the offence caused to them. As regards the disadvantaged offender, it is often part of the reparation agreement that the offender will co-operate with programmes that address his needs.

In this way the help he needs is not imposed, but is undertaken voluntarily; and the community has an obligation to ensure that the necessary programmes are available, so that he can do what is required of him.

Q. You still don't seem to have overcome the basic difficulty which you mentioned at the beginning: rehabilitation is focused on offenders' needs, and not on the harm they have caused; it doesn't put right the harm, and isn't proportionate to it. Even if victims aren't vengeful, they often want the offender 'to sweat a bit', as one victim put it to me; they want it to 'cost' him, not necessarily money or pain for its own sake, but some sort of effort, acknowledging what he has done, apologising, and doing something tangible to show he means it.

A. We can get over the difficulty by looking at it in another way: the rehabilitative measures are part of the reparation. The effort which, as you say, many victims want to see, can take the form of co-operating in measures which not only help the offender, but encourage him to resist committing more crimes; and we find that this is another thing which victims often want.

SESSION 4

The Victim Assistance Worker

The contributors so far have spoken mainly about offenders; I should like to redress the balance by talking about victims, and particularly their position in the criminal justice process. I should begin by stressing that, like other contributors to this discussion, I speak as an individual and my views are not necessarily those of Victim Support or any other organization.

First I would like to say something about what it's like to be a victim. It's not only violence that causes pain, and men are as likely – indeed more likely – to be victims than women. Here is an account of one person's experience:

> He was deeply hurt by the fact that his house had been burgled while he was away. His state of mind "magnified this misfortune into a disaster much greater than the reality. The place was in confusion; cupboards had been ransacked and all his belongings scattered"; although apparently little had been stolen, "an outrage had been committed . . . which he, the mildest of men, had done nothing to deserve, and which he could never forget nor forgive. For many years it rankled".

The victim is well known to most English people: Edward Lear, the nineteenth-century artist and creator of immortal nonsense poetry, and the quotation is from his biography (Davidson, [1938] 1950).

The system is more aware of victims

My main concern to-day, though, is about the way victims are treated by what is loosely called 'the system'. I have to say that this is not the picture of thoughtless disregard of victims' needs that I would have described to you only two or three decades ago, when victims felt treated as 'non-persons' (Shapland, 1983). We have come a long way since it could be said that the victim is ignored, kept in the dark, and treated like just another witness, rather than as the person who was on the receiving end of the crime. The list of what has been achieved on behalf of victims in the United Kingdom is impressive; so much has happened in the last few decades that there is almost a danger of sounding complacent. I certainly want to acknowledge the progress. Some of the rough edges of the system have been made smoother; but not everything that exists on paper has been translated into practice, and I believe that there are built-in problems with the adversarial system which are bound to create difficulties and even dangers for victims. I will try to explain these, and suggest what needs to be done to avoid them.

Compensation by the state

Some of the developments have been outside the criminal justice system proper and independent of the power of the courts to order the offender to pay a sum (often inadequate due to his means) to the victim which I will deal with later in this session. The first in recent times was the compensation scheme for victims of violent crimes, introduced in New Zealand in 1963 and the United Kingdom a year later (and known in Britain as the Criminal Injuries Compensation Scheme). It is now available in a number of countries; the amount of benefit to victims varies widely. In Britain, changes in 1996 had the effect of reducing some of the larger awards to the most seriously injured victims, and compensation awards under the new scheme have been criticised, for example £18,500 to an 11-year-old girl whose mother and sister were murdered (*Guardian*, 2 and 3 April 1998), £7,950 to a six-year-old girl with a large facial scar (*Guardian, The Sun*, 26 August 1998) and £10,000 for a gang rape (*Daily Mirror*, 2 September 1998). These sums contrast with awards of £50,000 and £73,776 to women who were raped by their employers and sued in the civil courts for damages (*Guardian*, 5 November 1997). Even so, the sums payable are higher than in other countries, and their value is enhanced by the existence of the National Health Service, which provides much of the medical care free of charge. The Civil Servant will give details. Certain victims of violence are, however, excluded or receive reduced awards – those who have a criminal record, for example; and those who are dependent on social security payments may have these cut when they receive compensation because the Department of Social Security regards it as 'capital'. Affluent people, however, suffer no such deductions (Mawby and Walklate, 1994: 152). The Home Secretary has announced a review of the system, but without making more money available (*Guardian*, 17 September 1998).

In other countries maximum payments are lower, and they may have to be used to pay medical expenses. In the United States, the President's Task Force on Victims of Crime (1982: 36) found that rape victims were even required to pay for their own medical examination, which could cost nearly $200; one young man, permanently disabled, had medical bills of $30,000, but in his state the maximum award was $10,000 (p.40). Some countries compensate victims of only certain categories of violence, such as terrorism. In American states, and Belgium, it is common for compensation to be funded by levies on people convicted of other offences, but as Dame Helen Reeves of Victim Support has pointed out, this does not show a readiness on the part of the whole community to look after victims. In New Zealand compensation to victims of crime is treated in much the same way as to victims of industrial and other accidents; this has the advantage that it puts violent crime in perspective as a tiny proportion of the amount of injury to which people are exposed, and also that it compensates victims of offences against industrial safety legislation even if these are not processed through the criminal justice system. (Victims of corporate financial crimes, however, have to seek redress through the civil courts, as they do elsewhere.) Assistance to victims is not seen in purely financial terms, but counselling is provided to victims who need it (although it is not always available). The law was amended by the Accident Rehabilitation and Compensation Act 1992 which replaced lump sum payments by an independence allowance, payable where personal injury has resulted in disability of ten per cent or more (for 100 per cent disability the allowance was then up to NZ$40 per week). A survey of victim assistance agencies soon after this Act found that the scheme was felt to give recognition to victims, but the abolition of the lump sums was criticised (Lee and Searle, 1993).

Victim assistance
The second major development for victims was created by a voluntary group of concerned people, and most of its work is done by volunteers. Victim Support started in 1974 in Bristol, England, and spread rapidly through the country. Police give the names of victims to local Victim Support co-ordinators, who arrange for trained volunteers to contact them by letter or visit to see whether they need help. From 1989 a service was introduced in the Crown Court to support witnesses, and especially victims; this achieved nationwide coverage by 1995, and in 1999 Victim Support obtained government funding to extend it to magistrates' courts. Victims can ask to visit a courtroom before the case starts so that they know what to expect; on the day, they can ask to wait separately from the defendant and his or her family and supporters.

Victim Support also serves as a focal point for information from victims about their experiences in the criminal justice process, and the organization has campaigned to obtain improvements, some of which I will mention later. Comparable organizations now exist in other countries, such as the National Organization for Victim Assistance (NOVA) in the United States, the Institut National d'Aide aux Victimes et de Médiation (INAVEM) in France, and the Weisse Ring (White Ring) in Germany; and in 1988 a European Forum for Victims' Services was established, with member organizations in 14 countries currently (UN Commission, 1998). There are other organizations offering help to victims of specific types of crime, such as rape crisis centres, refuges for victims of domestic violence, and the National Society for the Prevention of Cruelty to Children.

Procedures which recognise victims
Governments have also begun to improve the system from victims' point of view. In 1990 the British government, for example, published a *Victim's Charter*, with a second edition in 1996. This gives a number of undertakings about how victims will be treated, and there is also a *Courts Charter* which relates specifically to court procedures. Neither document has much to say about what redress is available if the targets are not reached, however. In 1993 the Crown Prosecution Service issued statements on prosecution policy in cases of domestic violence, and on the treatment of victims and witnesses, and in the same year the Royal Commission on Criminal Justice (1993) recommended several reforms. As a result of these initiatives, victims may now expect, for example, that:

- they will be given a leaflet and the name and telephone number of a police officer, and another leaflet if they are called to give evidence
- the prosecutor will introduce himself or herself, and keep them informed if there is a delay. The family of someone killed as a result of crime can ask the CPS to explain its decision on prosecution
- there will be a separate waiting area for them in the court building
- court staff will try to arrange seats for them in the courtroom
- their addresses need no longer be read out in court
- their identity will not be published where the charges include rape or certain other sexual offences
- pre-sentence reports (PSRs) on offenders by probation officers will include information about the financial loss and other suffering experienced by the victim, although at present probation officers rely on the files of the CPS for this information
- they will be informed if a suspect is caught, reprimanded or charged.

Not all of these policies are followed throughout the country yet, however. With regard to the provision of information to the victim, a 'One-Stop Shop' pilot project has been conducted in seven areas, in which victims of domestic burglary, assaults (including domestic violence and sexual assaults), robbery, racially motivated offences, and criminal damage over £5,000, were also asked if they wanted to be told the date of the first court hearing in a magistrates' or youth court, the date of the plea and directions (preliminary) hearing, the date of a Crown

Court trial, and the verdict and sentence of the court. The project appears to have made victims 'marginally more satisfied', but it raised their expectations without always meeting them (Hoyle *et al*, 1998: 23). The Home Office is considering whether to implement it nationwide. Nearly all Crown Court centres, and most magistrates' courts, offer familiarisation visits to victims before the trial; most have separate waiting rooms, or can make them available, but there are still problems of intimidation (Shapland and Bell, 1998).

For the families of homicide victims, arrangements for giving them an information pack and keeping them informed already exist in most areas; for sexual offences and homicide, information is also given about appeals against conviction or sentence. Plans to notify victims about bail have yet to be implemented in Britain.

In England the legal profession has accepted the need to recognise victims' needs. The *Code of Professional Conduct* of the General Council of the Bar has been amended to say that barristers 'must not suggest that a victim . . . is guilty of crime, fraud or misconduct or make any defamatory aspersion on the conduct of any other person' unless this is material to the defendant's case and supported by reasonable grounds. The rule which prevented barristers from having any contact with witnesses, and used to make victims feel they were being ignored, has been removed; prosecuting barristers can now introduce themselves, answer questions about procedure, and have a responsibility to put nervous witnesses as much at ease as possible (Bar Council, 1997).

There are restrictions on questioning a victim of rape about her previous sexual history, in an attempt by the defence to discredit her, but there are still complaints that this rule is not enforced rigorously by judges (Interdepartmental Working Group, 1998: 67-9), and plans to change it. The evidence of child witnesses can be pre-recorded on video tape; they may still be cross-examined about it, although this can be done by a live video link or, for adult vulnerable witnesses where there is a danger that they could be intimidated, from behind a screen to spare them from facing the accused in court. This, too, however, requires the consent of the judge, which is not always given.

Compensation by the offender
European criminal courts outside Britain have the possibility of hearing from the victim regarding compensation: a civil action is joined to the criminal one. In Britain, criminal courts were given the power in 1972 to order offenders to pay compensation to victims; the Criminal Justice Act 1982 said that this should take precedence over fines and court costs. Victims' enthusiasm for the measure has, however, been muted. Some were not consulted about whether they wanted compensation at all, and

if they did, how much; when payments are made they are often small and irregular; and in 12 per cent of cases compensation was written off. Courts make limited use of the orders, and when they do, they often order some of what the offender can afford to pay to be treated as a fine instead of going to the victim, despite the 1982 Act; magistrates appear to feel that punishment is necessary in addition to compensation (Newburn, 1988: 12, 40). Since the Criminal Justice Act 1988 they have a duty to make a compensation order or explain why not, but they continue to find reasons for not doing so, one of which can be that the court has imposed a prison sentence (Moxon *et al*, 1992: 14). Compensation has to be paid to the court, so it feels more like paying a fine than compensating the person you have harmed, and courts have been uneven in the efficiency with which they chase slow payers.

The solution proposed by Victim Support is that the court should pay the compensation in full, and collect it from the offender later. This idea has been criticised: people have asked 'Why should the court, in effect, lend the offender money?' But this is, as so often, an offender-centred way of looking at things; I would rather ask, 'If the offender can't pay the full amount at once, and may not pay it at all, why should the victim be the loser? Shouldn't the whole community support the victim by sharing the burden?' A different approach is used in some parts of Germany. A 'resocialisation fund' is set up, for example by private benefactors or from prosecutorial fines, from which the compensation is paid; in addition, where the offender was in financial difficulties, negotiations take place with creditors such as gas, electricity and hire purchase companies, on the basis that they can accept a percentage of the amount due, or risk that the offender will be sent to prison and be unable to pay at all. The offender then repays the fund, under the moral pressure that if he fails to do so, it will not be available for some other person in the future—and the perhaps more potent prospect of a suspended prison sentence being implemented. Very high repayment rates are claimed, although it has to be said that there is some selection of 'good risks', so that victims and creditors of 'poor risks' may not benefit; and there are obviously greater problems in areas of high unemployment. In Quincy, Massachusetts, the 'Earn-It' scheme encouraged local employers to provide short-term jobs so that offenders could pay compensation, but when it was suggested in England (Wright, 1983) the reaction was 'Why should offenders jump the queue for jobs?'

Victims and the release of prisoners
One way in which the *Victim's Charter* recognised concerns of victims relates to the release of prisoners, as the Probation Officer mentioned (p.76). Many victims of violence do not know when the offender will

come out of prison, and are anxious about what will happen when he does, especially if he knows them or is a relative; some of them have told Victim Support of their fear or anger at seeing their attacker at large when they thought he was still in prison. In some cases the offender will have changed while in prison and be able to reassure the victim; in others, the offender himself may be apprehensive and be reassured about the reception he will get when he returns. The *Victim's Charter* accordingly provides that where a prisoner has been sentenced to life imprisonment (that is, for an indefinite period followed by release on licence for life), or to a fixed prison sentence for serious violent or sexual offences, the probation service will contact the victim or victim's family within two months of the sentence being passed, to ask if they want to be told about any plans for releasing the prisoner, and take their concerns into account when planning the offender's supervision after release. Victims do not have any say in the actual length of time the prisoner serves, and in the UK it is generally accepted that they should not do so, but conditions may be attached, such as a restriction on where the ex-prisoner will live.

Probation officers, however, have found that contacting victims is unfamiliar work, and some victims and families have been unwilling to be visited by an officer whom they see as working in the interests of the offender. In at least one probation area, West Yorkshire, these enquiries have been made by trained mediators from the victim/offender mediation service, who are used to meeting both victims and offenders impartially. When they make these visits they do not promote the idea of mediation, but if a victim spontaneously suggests that contact with the offender would be helpful or they have questions they would like answering, the enquirer/mediator will be sensitive to this and can suggest mediation, face-to-face or indirect (Johnston, 1994: 38-39; Leeds Victim/Offender Unit, 1996). In many cases the victim and the offender will of course remain hostile; but at least the system should allow the victim to tell the offender how he or she feels as a result of the crime and what effects it had; and if the offender feels regret, he or she should have the chance to say so and possibly to express it in a tangible form. This is best done outside the court setting. Few probation areas, however, have pursued this possibility, and so far, in my opinion, it has been a missed opportunity.

In some parts of the United States victims of the most serious crimes, including causing death by drunken driving or by armed robbery, are being given the opportunity to meet offenders in prison. After long and careful preparation, both victims and offenders have found that communicating or meeting gave them deeper understanding. In some cases the offenders were on death row – hardly a restorative outcome, but even in such circumstances there is evidence that dialogue between the victim and the offender can be helpful to both (Umbreit, 1995).

Two more developments are that a helpline for victims who have received unwelcome contact from a prisoner was established by the government in 1994, and that Victim Support has obtained government funding for a national helpline for all victims, launched in February 1998.

Information from victims to courts: a problematic reform

These and other reforms could be said to make the system less hurtful, although all of them could of course be improved as I have indicated, especially as regards giving information to victims and the way they are treated in court. But what information should be conveyed *from* the victim *to* the court? This is relevant to the victim's experience of the criminal justice process, but it can also be hijacked by those who claim that victims are helped by 'tough' policies on the sentencing of offenders. Victim Support in Britain has always had a firm policy of not commenting on sentencing, except with regard to compensation (restitution) which directly affects victims, and in matters of courtroom procedure it has maintained awareness of the rights of defendants. It has pointed out, for example, that, as the Politician mentioned, from the victim's point of view a wrongful conviction is as serious as a wrongful acquittal, because in both cases the true perpetrator is not brought to justice.

There have been comparable initiatives elsewhere; in the United States, for example the Victim and Witness Protection Act of 1982. In New Zealand the Victims of Offences Act 1987 laid down similar principles for the treatment of victims; a survey of victim agencies a few years later gave mixed views as to how well its intentions were being put into practice (Lee and Searle, 1993).

Statements by victims

One of the concerns expressed by victims, when organizations had come into being to give them a voice, was that their hurt should be recognised in the criminal justice process. One way is through the 'victim impact statement' (VIS), a much publicised example of which was the eloquent statement made by Mrs Deborah Eappen after the conviction of Louise Woodward for the second degree murder (later reduced by Judge Hiller Zobel to involuntary manslaughter) of her eight-month-old son Matthew (*Guardian* etc., 1, 11 November 1997). But when and how should this statement be presented, should it influence the sentence imposed by the court on the offender, and should the victim be allowed to express specific views about the sentence? It seems to me that within the existing system there is no right answer to some of these questions, and I will try to explain why. But first I will try to outline the arguments and the present position.

At first sight it seems no more than an unfortunate omission that can now be put right. If A reports that he has been robbed or assaulted, and B is charged, it is an offence against the state and under English and American law A is not a principal party in the case. He or she may be called as a witness, or not even that if B pleads guilty. So A gets no chance to say publicly what effect the crime had on him or her. If the attack led to the victim's death, the court process allows no opportunity for relatives to acknowledge the person they loved and the loss they have suffered (although in the coroner's court, whose function is only to ascertain the cause of death, some coroners permit a statement of this kind). So isn't it fair and humane to give the victim the right, as proposed by the US President's Task Force on Victims of Crime in 1982, 'to be present and to be heard at all critical stages of judicial proceedings'? The United Nations (despite reservations by the United Kingdom) adopted in 1985 a *Declaration of Basic Principles of Justice for Victims of Crime and Abuse of Power*, which recommended *inter alia* 'Allowing the views and concerns of victims to be presented and considered at appropriate stages of the proceedings where their personal interests are affected, without prejudice to the accused' (quoted by Wright, 1995).

Before answering, we need to pause and ask, firstly, what is meant by 'being heard' and 'presenting views and concerns'? In nearly all states of America (all but two, according to Elias, 1993: 93), and other countries such as Canada, New Zealand and Australia, victims are now allowed to give written 'victim impact statements' (VISs) to the court. Some go further and allow the 'right of allocution', that is, the victim may make an oral statement in court. The US Department of Justice (ca. 1997) regards this as a 'restorative justice practice'. Others go further still, and invite the victim to express a view on what the sentence should be (35 states: Elias, *ibid.*). Secondly, what will be the effect of that? It may have a cathartic value for the victim, letting him or her feel that the pain caused by the offence has been publicly recognised, and this would fill one of the gaps in the criminal justice process. But is the courtroom the right place for it, and could it and should it also influence the sentence?

Here the question becomes more complicated. Sentencing is traditionally based on the harm that the offender intended to inflict. This is qualified by other factors, as the Judge will explain. If a statement by the victim about the degree of pain suffered were considered as a further factor in determining sentence, it would introduce a new principle into justice. The late Lord Chief Justice of England, Lord Taylor, suggested that an assessment of the impact of the crime could be included in the prosecution file, and 'If appropriate, it could then be included in the prosecution case put before the judge at the sentencing stage' (Taylor, 1996: 8; *Guardian*, 13 April 1996). But with respect (as lawyers say), one wonders whether his lordship had thought through the implications; when, for example, would this be 'appropriate'? Lord Taylor himself recognised, as Victim Support had pointed out, that victims might then be exposed to hostile cross-examination, to make sure they had not exaggerated. Victim agencies in New Zealand felt that victims might fear retaliation because the offender may see the statement; there were also practical problems about who should help the victim prepare it, and whether statements are made as often as they should be (Lee and Searle, 1993: 12, 42). Participation in the process may be a necessary ingredient in healing, and its benefits may outweigh its costs, but some victims are disillusioned if they expect it to influence the outcome, and it doesn't (Erez, 1991: 694; 1994: 24). Change is not necessarily a bad thing in itself, and there is a case for using harm rather than criminal intent as the criterion; but to use it *in addition to* all the other criteria would be an extra complication in the already convoluted calculus by which sentences are arrived at. This would make it harder for sentences to be fair, and to be seen to be fair. The offender did what he did; should the sentence be heavier or lighter because the particular victim was more, or less, affected? The Justice Committee on Victims has pointed out, however, that if sentencing were to move to a restorative model, this information would be essential, because restoration of the victim's sense of emotional well-being and financial status would become a core priority (Justice, 1998: 89). This is the Judge's territory, of course, but I want to show that victim assistance workers, in Britain at least, are aware of the difficulty.

Part of the case for VISs is that they are helpful to victims by allowing their feelings to be recognised; but are they likely to influence sentences, even if they do not intend to? One small-scale study suggests that they are (it used reports as compiled by probation officers, but these contained information about the experience of victims, so the effect would probably be similar). Two groups of magistrates were presented with ten simulated cases, based on actual facts, and accompanied by traditional social inquiry reports or by pre-sentence reports (PSRs) which recognised both offenders' responsibility and the effects of their social situation, and contained information on the experience of victims. The latter type of PSR led to sentences more than double those imposed after the social inquiry reports, but there was a tendency to use reparative sentences such as community service orders (Cooper and Cooper, 1995). It sometimes looks as if victims are being used by politicians as a pretext for introducing policies that are assumed to be vote-catching; for example, laws which institute harsher punishments, but do nothing to protect victims, are given names like 'Child Sexual Abuse Prevention Act' and 'California Child Protection Act' (McShane and Williams, 1992).

The right of allocution is even more problematic: should the sentence be influenced by the victim's grief, anger, eloquence, sincerity, histrionics, or for that matter forgiveness? In those jurisdictions where the victim actually proposes a sentence, the dilemma is greater. If the courts accept the recommendations of victims, sentences will inevitably be even more inconsistent than, despite the best efforts of the courts, they already are; but if they do not, victims' expectations will be disappointed. Victim Support has suggested that the burden of conveying this to the court should not be placed on the individual victim; instead, judges and other lawyers should, as part of their training, be made more aware of the effects particular types of crime have on victims, and should act on that basis.

Not all victims would welcome the opportunity to make statements: in California, only three per cent did so (Elias, 1993: 95); but this might be simply because they are not told that they can. The possibility should be available even if only a minority want it – unless the benefit to them was bought at the cost of making things worse for other victims or causing unfairness to offenders. It might not be cathartic but delay the victim's psychological healing (Elias, 1993: 64, 93), and Victim Support (1995: 15) says that many victims would find it a cause of anxiety, especially if it were linked to the sentencing decision. They might feel guilty if their intervention led to a heavier sentence than they thought the offender deserved, and they might even be subject to intimidation by the offender or his associates. If their statements were likely to lead to a heavier sentence, the offender would have a right to challenge them, so that the victim would be forced to undergo another ordeal in the witness box; in New Zealand, victims, especially of domestic violence, were inhibited or feared retaliation because the offender would see the statement (Lee and Searle, 1993: 12). Lawyers (in Britain) and many victims appear to agree that victims should not have a say in sentencing; Professor Andrew Ashworth (1993), for example, has pointed out that the victim's statement might be inaccurate or irrelevant. From an American perspective, however, Professor Edna Erez (1999) maintains that VISs do not affect the harshness of sentencing, but should be encouraged because they have therapeutic advantages for victims.

In England Victim Support, as the main organization representing victims, has opposed the use of VISs for the reasons I have given (Reeves, 1993); but it has recognised that if courts are to have a complete picture they should receive information from the victim. There are three stages, apart from sentencing, at which this can be important. Firstly, when the court is deciding whether to remand the accused in custody, or impose bail conditions, it should know whether the victim has reason to fear that the offence will be repeated; this applies particularly in cases such as domestic violence. Secondly, when the accused has been found guilty, the CPS has issued guidelines saying that in accordance with the *Victim's Charter*, it will challenge statements made by the defence to try to obtain mitigation of sentence if these contain unjust criticism of the character of the victim or witness (CPS, 1993); in order to do this the prosecutor needs information about the victim, so as to know whether the criticisms *are* unjust. Thirdly, and independently of the sentence, the court needs to know about the victim's losses and injuries when making a compensation order. To meet these needs, Victim Support has suggested that at the beginning of the process (when a suspect is charged) a 'Victim Statement' should be made. (This is sometimes called a 'Victim Effect Statement', to distinguish it from the PSR VIS; but 'Pre-trial Victim Statement' would be a clearer term.) A Victim Statement Project is being piloted in six areas (five of which are also running the One-Stop Shop which I mentioned as one of the procedures which recognise victims); in three of them victims were asked to complete a questionnaire, and in the other three the police compiled the statement from information given to them by the victim relevant to compensation, emotional effects of the crime, and any threats or continuing fears about safety. Only 30 per cent of victims took up the opportunity. Of those who did, three out of five wanted to express their feelings, and some specifically wanted the offender to hear them. A somewhat smaller percentage wanted to influence the court in regard to conviction, sentence or compensation. The researchers found that 'There is little doubt that many victims have much to say that cannot be contained in evidential statements. For the more traumatic cases, full disclosure will rarely be made other than to someone else in person' (Hoyle *et al*, 1998:29). Most were glad to have made the statement. Some were pleased that it was read out in court, a few were angry because it was not, and some did not want it to be, because they feared the offender's reaction. The researchers conclude that the *purpose* of the statements needs to be clarified (p.46).

A washed leopard still has spots

If all these improvements are being made, you may ask, isn't the system at least on the way to doing almost everything necessary to treat victims with respect? The answer is 'No', and the reason lies in the nature of the system itself.

It is common to criticise the very fact that it is adversarial; but we need to consider why it is adversarial, and the problems that would not be resolved even if the system were changed to an inquisitorial one. The state accuses an individual of a crime, for which he is likely to be punished if convicted. Because the consequences of conviction are serious, numerous safeguards are built in. The accused is generally represented by an advocate — an immediate barrier to any personal communication or resolution between offender and victim. The standard of proof is higher than in civil matters, and the advocate does all he can to get his client acquitted, on a technicality if necessary, or to mitigate the sentence. There is protection against self-incrimination, although in England this has recently been weakened in the Criminal Justice and Public Order Act 1994.

A judge from New Zealand has identified some of the problems. To start with, the defendant is made to feel at a disadvantage by the use of unfamiliar legal language, and (in New Zealand and Britain at least) by being placed in the dock. He is asked 'How do you plead?' (a word which Judge McElrea proposes should be abolished, because it 'suggests the prostrate suppliant offering up a prayer for relief from a kingly presence'); and if the defendant pleads not guilty it does not necessarily mean that he denies guilt — it may only mean that he hopes that the prosecution cannot prove its case 'beyond reasonable doubt'. This, Judge McElrea says, encourages offenders to try to deny responsibility that they or their lawyers think cannot be proved, 'and of course the more punitive the sentencing regime the greater is the incentive for a guilty person to rely on the presumption of innocence and put the State to the proof, i.e. not to plead guilty', especially if the consequences of conviction are rejection, isolation, and destruction of self-respect (McElrea, 1998). None of this is in the victim's interest. In New Zealand, Judge McElrea reports, instead of the language of guilt the family group conferencing process for juveniles encourages an admission of responsibility and finds offences 'proved'. There are current efforts to simplify English legal terminology; perhaps they will take account of these points.

The lawyer's approach to a criminal offence is somewhat like a grammarian's approach to language. Lawyers look at legal categories, and at contradictions in the details of testimony, rather than at the web of events and relationships which are relevant in human terms — but not in law (especially when victim and offender knew each other). Two criminologists have summed up the reasons for victims' frustration like this:

> Their role in the courtroom is simply as evidentiary fodder for the legal digestive system. They must stick to the facts and suppress their opinions. Consequently, they often emerge from the experience deeply dissatisfied with their day in court. For victims and their supporters, this often means they scream ineffectively for more blood. But it makes no difference when

the system responds to such people by giving them more and more blood, because the blood-lust is not the source of the problem; it is an unfocused cry from disempowered citizens who have been denied a voice (Braithwaite and Mugford, 1994: 148).

The legal system pares down 'the facts at issue', stripping away the emotional background which is 'irrelevant' in legal terms, so that in turn the trial seems irrelevant to the victim. This point is made by two researchers in Bristol, Antonia Cretney and Gwynn Davis, who studied the way offences of violence were dealt with by the courts, and produced a devastating chronicle of the way the system serves its own ends, not the victims' needs. The aim is not to discover 'what happened' as a lay person might understand it, but to test the defendant's guilt in relation to a specific charge. It also limits any therapeutic potential the court process might have. Thus a man who lost the sight of one eye in an attack, having previously lost his girlfriend of 15 years to his assailant, was given no recognition of these wrongs and saw the case bogged down in legal technicalities about 'intent' and 'recklessness' as a result of which the jury felt unable to convict of the *crime*, although there was no doubt about the *harm* (Cretney and Davis, 1993: 147-149). As a rape victim put it, 'I felt as if he wouldn't let me say my piece' (Victim Support, 1996b: 33).

The difficulty of making marginal improvements to an unreconstructed system is shown by the experiment with victim statements, as I have just described. Although they have a wider use than sentencing, they still may be taken into account for that purpose; defendants may therefore see them, if found guilty, and victims may be cross-examined on them, so that's one of the difficulties raised by VISs that pre-trial VSs fail to overcome. Both the VIS and the VS are addressed to the court, and therefore do not achieve what some victims want, which is to let the offender know what his action did to them; nor do they allow any dialogue with him, so that the victim may understand him and his actions better, and obtain answers to some of the things they want to know.

The defence and the victim
There are other reasons why an adversarial system has a built-in tendency to give victims a hard time. The defending advocate proceeds in logical stages. Firstly, can he create doubt in the mind or minds of the court or jury whether the accused committed the act at all or whether it was a crime; for example, in the case of alleged sexual assault or rape, did the victim consent to it? This may entail techniques, not to say tricks, to make witnesses, including victims, appear unreliable or even untruthful. The defending lawyer may for example pick on discrepancies

between what a witness said in a written statement and the evidence they have given in court; these may be trivial, and of little or no significance for the alleged crime itself, but they are intended to sow doubt in the minds of the magistrates or the jury about the major issues. This can be a distressing experience, especially for the victim of a serious offence who knows that he or she is telling the truth, but does not remember every detail or is confused by the way defence lawyers frame questions, which does not allow the victims to describe things in their own words; sometimes the defence may use these tactics to goad the victim into a display of petulance which may undermine his or her credibility with the jury (Cretney and Davis, 1995: 143, 153). Two young boys, giving evidence against two teenagers accused of sexually abusing them, broke down in hysterics under cross-examination, and a third boy, aged 12, was told by the defending barrister that he was a bad boy who had done bad things and was trying to blame it on someone else; when he heard that the teenagers were appealing against conviction and he would be put through it again, he was suicidal. His mother felt that the choice lay between irrevocably damaging the three boys and not getting justice (*Guardian*, 30 January 1998).

Secondly, the defender asks, if the accused performed the act, can this be excused in any way? The state gives him the opportunity to ask for a lesser punishment, which he, or usually his lawyer, often does by making excuses, minimising the seriousness of the crime, or trying to put some of the blame on to the victim — for example by persuading the court or jury that the victim was promiscuous, willing, or a troublemaker. 'Tanya', a rape victim, said 'It was awful. They made you feel that it's all your fault. They twist and turn your words . . . They don't understand' (Victim Support, 1996b: 45). It is all very well to argue that defence lawyers should be more aware of the victim's feelings; but as long as their success is measured by winning acquittals or lower-than-expected sentences, they will continue to regard making mincemeat of victim-witnesses as part of the game, or at best an unfortunate necessity.

These problems have been seen in a stark form in a case in 1996 where a man accused of rape was conducting his own defence, and took the opportunity to distress his victim as much as possible while questioning her over several days. The Home Secretary, Jack Straw, has announced that he will put a stop to this, and a government working group has recommended that in cases of rape and serious sexual assault it should not be allowed; in other cases the court should have discretion to prohibit it, subject to safeguards (Interdepartmental Working Group, 1998: 64-67). The Youth Justice and Criminal Evidence Act 1999 addresses this issue. It may be that these were sadistic men who would have behaved similarly in any system; but the present system makes it more likely that defendants will see the victim as an adversary to be defeated. If they do have the capacity to realise the effect of their actions on another human being, the adversarial procedure does nothing to encourage it. It has been suggested that such painful episodes should be prevented, for example by compelling the defendant to have his case conducted by a lawyer; but that would do nothing to reduce the gap in understanding between the two people, and defence lawyers can also, in a different way, cause pain and frustration to victim-witnesses.

The prosecution and the victim
Criminal justice agencies such as prosecutors have their own agendas, which are not necessarily those of the victim: they measure their success by, for example, the number of convictions, whereas victims want vindication and recognition of what they have suffered. Because getting a conviction is difficult (and time-consuming), the practice of negotiating pleas has grown up. The offender can escape the most serious punishment by pleading guilty to a lesser charge, for which the maximum sentence is lower; although victims may be relieved at being spared the ordeal of giving evidence, they are also disappointed because the offence is hardly described in court at all, which prevents the victim's feelings or the full seriousness of the offence from being recognised (Cretney and Davis, 1995). Prosecutors and courts, however, welcome guilty pleas because without them they could never get through all the cases. The Crown Prosecution Service is beginning to explain the reasons for such decisions, but that gives only limited comfort to the victim.

What is the process for?
All these traditional processes are based on the premise that the purpose of the court is to determine whether the accused committed the offence, and if so to punish him. There is a 'right' outcome, the accused is guilty or not guilty. If the process is an ordeal for the offender, no one protests much; it may even be felt to be a degradation ceremony, part of the punishment. (If the accused is acquitted, it is merely unfortunate that he had to go through the ritual anyway.) Until the 1980s few people except victims and other witnesses noticed that it was an ordeal for them too. Not only that, but it did not give them what they wanted or needed.

The common assumption was that they wanted the offender to be punished; but the *British Crime Survey* and other research found that victims were not more punitive than other people (Hough, Moxon and Lewis, 1987: 128; Hough and Roberts, 1998: 42); if they recommend imprisonment it is often because they are not aware of any other options such as community service, treatment, or restitution (Erez, 1994: 21). Objections on grounds of leniency often come from victims, or relatives of victims, of offences such as causing death by careless driving, where the sentence is based on the criminal intent or negligence of the offender, but the consequences of the act are out of all proportion to it.

Dissatisfaction with the process goes wider than this. It stems from a feeling that victims want the seriousness of the crime and its impact to be recognised, especially by the offender. If the offender pleads guilty, or the victim did not witness the crime (for example a burglary), the victim has no part in court proceedings. (There is a guilty plea in eight out of ten cases in magistrates' courts, and more than half in the Crown Court — Home Office, 1995.) If the victim is called as a witness, his or her evidence is constrained by the questions put by counsel, which are designed to make legal points about guilt or innocence rather than to convey the victim's feelings. Lawyers do not acknowledge how important the event was to the victim by inviting him or her to describe what happened in their own words and asking how they felt; instead they ask closed questions, which are not even well-suited to getting a full and accurate account of the crime, according to psychologists Mark Kebbell and Steven Deprez (*Guardian*, 10 September 1998). In courts (and coroner's courts) the death of their loved one may not be material as evidence when a motorist is charged with, for example, 'driving without due care and attention'; they feel aggrieved that no importance seems to be attached to their loss (Victim Support, 1994: 22).

But however much it is improved, there are certain things the conventional process is not suited for. Victims talk in terms of wanting their assailant to understand what it is that he has done to them; they need re-affirmation of their right to personal security (Cretney and Davis, 1995: 157, 166). But the process does not enable the victim to communicate with the offender, either to find out more about the crime or to consider appropriate reparation. It gives neither victim nor offender the chance to tell the story in their own words, but only in a form which fits the picture the lawyers want to paint, and relevant to the points of law on which they hang their case. If they were friends who have become estranged, they remain estranged; if they were strangers, they come no closer to understanding one another. We know that victims often have a strong need to resolve questions like these, and a system that prevents them ought to be changed.

The other main reason why, despite reforms, criminal justice systems make difficulties for victims is that, whether adversarial or inquisitorial, they are essentially based on punishment (although for juveniles some European countries have held on to the rehabilitative/educative philosophy). Certainly victims want action taken towards the offender; but the more punitive that action is, the harder the offender (and his lawyer) will try to avoid it. Hence the devices of the defence advocate, which I have described. The dilemma is at its most intense for abused women and children who want the abuse to stop but do not want the abuser to be sent to prison, for example because they are fond of him in spite of all, or because they are afraid of what he will do when he comes out, or simply because the family depends on him as breadwinner. But other potential solutions are disallowed from the start by the presumption that the offender must be punished and that the punishment must take the form of imprisonment. All the improvements in child witness information packs, facilities for giving evidence from behind screens or by closed circuit television, and other support, do not alter this basic problem. I am not saying that abusers should never be locked up, and of course some would continue to deny their offences even if the system were less threatening. But there are other possible ways of protecting children and families, as the Probation Officer mentioned. If they were used some children would find it less difficult to report the abuse and to take part in the process, and some families would be healed instead of being torn apart.

Behind all this some writers, like the American Robert Elias, discern a political dimension, which is not necessarily in victims' best interests. 'Get tough' policies do not work, and are therefore not in the interests of victims, and a 'war on crime' is a kind of civil war; but politicians find that these ideas are easily expressed as sound-bites, so they promise them in the name of victims, who are thus re-victimised once again. It is easiest to crack down on the least powerful criminals, who are usually the most disadvantaged. It is simplest to give the impression that victims are mostly female, elderly or blameless, despite the fact that many of them are young, male and have themselves been in trouble with the law. Victim assistance and state compensation, and even prisons, cost less than comprehensive social policies which would have some chance of being 'tough on the causes of crime', to use a sound-bite of the New Labour party in Britain. Other measures, such as victim impact statements and the undertakings in the *Victim's Charter*, cost little, especially if the agencies charged with implementing them are given no extra funds and there is no mechanism for redress if the standards are not complied with; some of them are aimed as much at getting victims to co-operate in the criminal justice process as at helping them (McShane and Williams, 1992; Elias, 1993). The manipulation may not be quite so blatant in other countries as in the United States; nevertheless, beware of politicians promising gifts for victims.

One further factor remains unchanged despite the reforms in the way victims are treated in the criminal justice process: the media. They are, of course, on the side of victims—aren't we all?—but that didn't stop them harassing victims or their relatives, naming victims of rape until legislation prohibited them, exploiting loopholes in this legislation until further legislation was introduced, and reviving painful memories by re-telling, as entertainment, the stories of terrible crimes. They also publish statements about victims made by defendants who are pleading for a mitigated sentence, without checking on their accuracy or considering the effect of such reporting on victims and their families (Victim Support, 1996a). I am speaking of the United Kingdom; in some European countries, notably Sweden, the journalistic code protects victims (and offenders) from being named, and there is no evidence that this harms either the public interest or the circulation of newspapers. A change in the system would not necessarily change the way it is reported; but if the official system replaced the 'script' of the drama, which at present gives messages such as 'Judge cages evil monster', and substituted something like, say, 'Abuser says sorry, accepts treatment', explaining that he was himself a victim of child abuse and has agreed to treatment to prevent him repeating abuse on his own children, there would be some hope that eventually this would influence the way the information was passed on by the media. It suits the media, politicians, and even some victim assistance organizations to exaggerate crime, and especially violent crime; in Britain, however, Victim Support has set the reduction of fear as one of its aims and has therefore avoided this type of publicity.

Hearing the victim—Out-of-court

How do we get out of this dilemma? We have a system which was not designed with the victim's needs in mind—nor the offender's, come to that, except on some occasions when rehabilitative intentions have taken precedence—and now it is trying to become more victim-friendly. It has succeeded to some extent, as we have seen, but in some ways the nature of the beast makes it difficult or impossible. The system is based on a 'battle model' of winning or losing, and on punishment, which many offenders try to avoid by any means from procedural devices to extreme violence. Instead we could use a 'family model': when a member of a family harms another, the normal reaction is to work out how he or she can make things right so that the family can go on living together. This analysis does not mean that the system should, or even could, be abolished overnight, nor that if it were, offenders would immediately change their behaviour.

But it does suggest that we might try a different approach, and see where it could lead, starting not with the system and attempts to modify it, but with victims and what they want. I accept that they cannot automatically get everything they want, because there are other considerations; but the victim is the person who has suffered, or at least been inconvenienced by the crime, and it is appropriate to take his or her needs as a point of departure. What I shall argue is that some of them can best be provided *outside* the formal system, so that, although reforms are very necessary, we should be putting our effort and imagination into developing a parallel process free of the built-in problems of conventional justice. Later in this discussion the Mediator will be making the case for mediation; I will consider it from the point of view of the victim's experience of criminal justice.

Victims' needs

One Victim Support representative, Teresa Reynolds, has listed things that victims want (Reynolds, 1997). The first group are those which both the conventional system and mediation claim to provide: to be treated sensitively and with respect, to know and understand what's happening in the case, to receive public acknowledgement that wrong has been done, and to feel it is worth pursuing the case. Some also want compensation. These are mostly points which have been addressed in the *Victim's Charter* and the other recent initiatives that I have described; as I said, things are getting better, but there is still some way to go. The criminal justice system is beginning to take them on board, but some people claim that restorative justice meets these concerns better, and I look forward to hearing from the Mediator how she believes this happens.

Victims also want quick resolution of the case, Reynolds says; they want to be heard and taken seriously, to know 'Why me?' Some also want an apology from the offender. On current form, diverting a case from the system means that it is dealt with more quickly than bringing it to court, and the more cases are diverted, the more the courts' backlog is reduced. As for the other points, victims are often not heard in court at all, or, as we have seen, are limited to answering specific questions. If they were allowed to make a statement in court this would cause complications in relation to the punishment of the offender; and in any case it allows for no dialogue with the offender, no opportunity for those human questions to be asked and answered, such as the very common one 'Why did you pick me as your victim?' or even for apologies or offers of reparation. The court's layout and procedures just do not make it the right place for this.

The other needs of victims include help with the practical/emotional effects of crime, and reassurance to know that the offence will not be repeated. Victim Support in Britain offers practical and emotional help, but not financial assistance, for which people have to turn to social security or charity (compensation, whether from the offender or the state, is very slow). Its German counterpart *Der Weisse Ring* (The White Ring) does provide cash help in many cases. For some people the opportunity to communicate will help the process of recovery, by closing the incident, and some people maintain that victims have the *right* to an active part in the process (Mawby and Walklate, 1994: 191); Victim Support, however, maintains that most want to be free of decisions about the offender. Research in the United States showed that the percentage of victims afraid of being re-victimised by the offender fell from 23 per cent before a mediation meeting to ten per cent afterwards (Umbreit and Coates, 1992: 12; Umbreit, 1994: 71). Victims are naturally concerned for their own safety, but also many of them feel that, although what was done to them cannot be undone, they would like an opportunity to try to persuade the offender to do better. As Teresa Reynolds says, there are those who want retribution; but often what they really want is vindication, and retribution is the only form in which the system offers it. Researchers have found that 'the denunciatory function' is what they are seeking, and that 'they also talk in terms of wanting their assailant to understand what it is that he has done to them'; while some victims may have a generalised preference for tough sentences, their views as to what should happen to the offender in their own case often shows more understanding (Maguire, 1982; Cretney and Davis, 1995: 157, 215).

One of the concerns I come across as a victim assistance worker is that victims will be targeted again, and I was impressed to see that research in Australia found that the proportion of victims who expect the offender to repeat the offence is half as much after victim/offender conferencing as it is after a court case (31 per cent and 67 per cent, respectively). Victims offered a conference were also far more likely to receive an apology, restitution or both, to be informed of the proceedings, and to attend. Of those who took part in conferences, 60 per cent felt angry with offenders beforehand but only 30 per cent afterwards; conversely, 23 per cent felt sympathy for the offender before the conference but nearly twice as many, 43 per cent, after it (Sherman and Strang, 1997).

Obviously not all victims would want to communicate with the offender in this way, but a substantial number would. Cretney and Davis, although they were researching violence, found some who wanted some form of mediated encounter. One, who had been 'mugged' outside his home and as a result was fearful of venturing out, was firm in his wish to meet his assailants and confront them with the harm they had done. Two student nurses, assaulted by a stranger wielding a stick as they walked home, both expressed a wish to meet their attacker, provided of course that they felt protected. The incident was totally unprovoked and they wanted to know what lay behind it. A young man who had been 'mugged' said 'I would rather speak to him and ask him why he did it . . . I would like to explain to him that it's not a nice thing to do . . . I'd like him to try to understand that from my point of view' (Cretney and Davis, 1995: 175-6).

In New Zealand only six per cent of victims said they did not want to meet their offender (Maxwell and Morris, 1996: 99). Victims did not necessarily want anything for themselves; although some attended from a sense of curiosity, many came from a willingness to attempt to help or support the young person and as a social duty (Maxwell and Morris, 1993: 81). They also commented on two other specific benefits for them: providing them with a voice in determining appropriate outcomes, and meeting the offender and the offender's family face-to-face so that they could assess their attitude, understand more why the offence had occurred and assess the likelihood of it recurring (Maxwell and Morris, 1996: 100). If such substantial numbers of people would like this opportunity, it seems to me that it should be made available, provided they aren't pushed into it by someone who thinks it will be good for them.

Victims and new laws in England and Wales
The danger in recent legislation in England and Wales is the opposite: that victims may be pushed into it by someone who thinks it will be good for offenders. Under the Crime and Disorder Act 1998, reparation may take place in the context of a police reprimand or final warning, or a court sentence such as a reparation order or an action plan order. It is true that Home Office guidance expresses the hope that victim/offender mediation will provide benefits to the victim, but the emphasis is on the effect it may have on the offender. In pilot schemes introduced in 1998, there has been such pressure to process cases quickly that there is often no time for victims to consider their response, nor to take part in the process of discussing with offenders how they can best make amends. These sections of the Act apply only to children and young persons, so the development offers nothing to victims of adult offenders.

There are also concerns about the Youth Justice and Criminal Evidence Act 1999, which changes the whole English juvenile justice system. Courts will have to refer most first-time young offenders to youth offender panels; it has been suggested that these should be conducted on the lines of family group conferences, but there is no provision for asking the offender's extended family to attend – a basic feature of the conferencing idea – and the Act says only that the panel 'may' allow the victim to attend. As with reparation orders, the emphasis is on the nature of the reparation which the offender will have to make, and not on the value which victim/offender mediation can have for both of them. The primary aim is said to be the prevention of re-offending, so there are fears that there will be more emphasis on 'confronting' the offender than on the interests of the victim, or for that matter the welfare of the child. Training of the facilitators of the panel meetings will be crucial. Evaluations and consultations are, however, in progress, so there is still hope that these issues will be addressed and Victim Support is recommending its members to take part (Victim Support, 1999).

FACTS AND STATISTICS

The Civil Servant

Both the second edition of the *Victim's Charter* and the *National Standards for Witness Care* were issued in 1996, but research published early in 1998 found that in magistrates' courts they were not being adequately met. Only 54 per cent of witnesses were called to give evidence on the day they were required to attend court. Over a third of prosecution witnesses were not told how to get to court, and half were not told what to do on arrival; even more defence witnesses had these problems. Over a quarter of prosecution witnesses, and 96 per cent of defence witnesses, were *not* given a 'Witness in Court' leaflet. Many of them simply wanted more information; four in ten of both prosecution and defence witnesses were worried about not understanding what was going on in court (Plotnikoff and Woolfson, 1998; see also Shapland and Bell, 1998).

There have been similar problems in Scotland. Of a sample of 139 victims, 55 per cent were not told formally whether their case would go to court. Waiting time at court was over three hours for 32 per cent; two thirds of those called to court were not asked to give evidence (MacLeod *et al*, 1996).

Children suffer especially; a survey by the NSPCC found that 75 per cent of children who had given evidence in cases of alleged child sex abuse found the experience so traumatic that they would not report abuse again, and a quarter of them said that the ordeal of giving evidence was as bad as the original abuse they had suffered. They are often bewildered by legal language and procedures (Brown, 1998). A report by the Crown Prosecution Service Inspectorate found that some Crown prosecutors wrongly thought that the CPS could stop children having counselling therapy to ease the trauma of abuse, in case this might 'contaminate' their evidence (*Guardian*, 30 January 1998)

Compensation

The maximum compensation in most of the United States is $15,000 to 25,000. In Norway it is 200,000 kronor (about £15,000); in Sweden 704,000 kronor (about £50,000); in The Netherlands fl.50,000 (about £15,000); in some countries there is no maximum (Austria, Denmark, France, Germany). In the United Kingdom the maximum tariff award is

£250,000; in certain very serious cases there may be additional payments, for example for loss of earnings or nursing care, to a maximum of £500,000 (CICA, 1999).

Annual figures of Victim Support

In 1996-97 Victim Support offered help to over 1.1 million victims of crime; its witness service supported nearly 100,000 victims, witnesses and their families. This work is done by 15,000 volunteers and nearly 900 staff in England, Wales and Northern Ireland (Victim Support, 1997).

Helplines

The Prison Service helpline is for victims or their families to contact if they are concerned about a prisoner being released on a temporary licence or home leave; their views will then be considered, with other relevant information, when the decision is made. People receiving unwanted letters or phone calls from a prisoner can ask for this to be stopped. The telephone number is 0345 585112.

The Victim Supportline, staffed by 30 volunteers working four-hour shifts, is open from 9 a.m. to 9 p.m. on weekdays, 9 a.m. to 7 p.m. at weekends and holidays. The number is 0845 30 30 900.

Research on victims' attitudes to mediation

The first major research on Victim Support, by Mike Maguire and Claire Corbett, reported a finding from the 1984 *British Crime Survey*—at a time when this idea had not received much publicity. This showed that about half of the victims interviewed said they would have accepted the chance of a meeting to agree a way in which the offender could make a repayment for what he had done. This number was higher (56 to 67 per cent) for thefts and burglary, and lower (29 to 44 per cent) for robbery and assault. A further 20 per cent would have liked an out-of-court agreement without a meeting; so almost seven out of ten would have liked some form of reparation agreement. Of these, 30 per cent would then not want the offender prosecuted and punished as well.

There is some evidence that when victims feel supported they feel less punitive. One study of two groups of individually matched victims, all of whom had been substantially affected by the offence, found that fewer of those who were visited by Victim Support workers felt more punitive towards offenders generally than those who were not visited (eight per cent and 46 per cent, respectively), and they were much more likely to be willing to accept mediation (42 and 12 per cent respectively). The first reasons people thought of were to ask why the offender did it and to see what he was like; it was only when prompted by the interviewer that they added further reasons, such as to give the offender 'a good piece of your mind', to arrange for the offender to pay compensation, and 'so he could see the effect the crime had on you' (Maguire and Corbett, 1987: 170, 227-231).

Mike Maguire's early research (1982) on burglars and burglary victims found that people who were punitive towards offenders in general were less so when asked about 'their' burglar. The *British Crime Survey* of 1992, however, found that more victims wanted imprisonment for their burglar than for the hypothetical one in a 'vignette', and still more so for victims of car theft; the authors suggest that in both cases this was probably because on average their actual loss was more serious than the one in the vignette (Hough and Roberts, 1998: 40-41).

DISCUSSION

Q. You have described powers given to courts to order compensation to victims, and schemes to help offenders to make reparation. Couldn't these be described as 'restorative'?

A. Yes, but only to a limited extent. They make things better instead of making them worse, but these measures are for victims *or* offenders, not both: they lack that additional element of allowing victims and offenders to communicate, which is the hallmark of restorative justice. No doubt the Mediator will tell us more about this, and I believe the Philosopher has some ideas about it.

Q. What do you think about Victim Support's argument that victims shouldn't be burdened with any decisions about the offender? Surely some decisions, such as whether to report the crime at all, are unavoidable?

A. Yes, they are. I think Victim Support has a point if it is referring primarily to decisions about the *punishment* of the offender, for reasons I discussed earlier; but to me it seems entirely appropriate for victims to discuss *reparation*, which affects them directly, provided there are safeguards to make sure that they are not under any pressure to take part (and safeguards for offenders too, of course). On the other hand, they should have the right to do so if they wish. I know that good mediation services have given much thought to this, and no doubt the Mediator will have something to say about it.

Q. Isn't there a risk that offenders might threaten a victim who does not wish to take part in mediation because they might get heavier sentences?

A. In a punitive system there is always a risk that the accused will try to intimidate the victim—that is part of the price paid for relying on punishment. The Home Secretary's Interdepartmental Working Group (1998) has made proposals for witness protection, including relocation and change of identity in the most serious cases. If mediation is offered after sentence (or diversion), the question does not arise. If it is offered at an earlier stage, good mediation services have taken account of this in several ways. One is to offer the offender the chance to do community service, or to take part in a victim/offender group, if the victim does not wish to be involved. Some services offer indirect mediation instead of face-to-face, or someone else can speak on behalf of the victim, which many victims find acceptable. It can be done in the same way as a caution: the victim's views are sought, but it is made clear to the offender that the mediation service decides whether to go ahead, so that the service takes responsibility for the decision, but of course they don't proceed against the wishes of the victim.

Q. You have mentioned 'good' services; what about the others?

A. Of course it is important that all services should meet proper standards. There is a Restorative Justice Consortium in Britain which has drawn up standards (RJC, 1999); and Mediation UK has also published practice standards (Mediation UK, 1998); it has a system for accreditation of mediation services, and a National Vocational Qualification for individual mediators is on the way.

SESSION 5

The Judge

One of the tasks of English judges is that they sum up, so I will begin by summing up the main points made by other contributors to this Symposium, in relation to the main conventional aims of sentencing, and I will comment on them from a judicial point of view. Of the five generally listed, three have already been covered: containment, individual deterrence and rehabilitation; I will begin by looking briefly at these, and at the different perspective of the Victim Assistance Worker. The others are general deterrence and retribution, which will form my main contribution.

The Psychologist has spoken about punishment as individual deterrence, and I will say a little about two specific forms of punishment currently in use in this country and elsewhere. (I speak, of course, as a lawyer, but I have endeavoured to inform myself about criminology, and shall bring in some findings of that discipline.) I shall try to explain how judges balance conflicting requirements such as consistency, proportionality, the effect of the crime on the victim and the exercise of compassion towards the offender. More recently the question of compensation has been added to the list, although it is in a different category from the others because it is intended to affect the victim and not only the offender. Other points affecting the victim have to do with procedure rather than sentencing; they were validly raised by the Victim Assistance Worker, but my concern here will be about sentencing. Finally I will offer some thoughts on how we can assess judges' performance.

Restraint/containment

The Politician's primary concern is with the maintenance of public order. She wants to keep crime levels as low as possible, and everyone will surely welcome the part of the Crime and Disorder Act 1998 which puts more emphasis on preventive strategies which I believe are the only effective ways to reduce crime. Politicians are also responsible for deciding the principles on which law breakers are to be dealt with (individual cases of course being dealt with by judges and magistrates); she concentrated mainly on one aspect of this, the use of containment to prevent offenders from re-offending. There was a time when politicians rather irritatingly reduced this to the one-dimensional claim, to which she referred, that 'prison works' because it keeps offenders out of circulation. Anyone who has given serious thought to the question knows that it is more complicated than that, as I shall show; on the other hand, even liberal reformers accept that on occasion 'reasonable force', including restriction of liberty, has to be used to restrain physically those who are very likely to commit further very serious offences. The problem here is how long to detain them and how to decide when to let them out, and I will return to that later.

As the Politician rightly pointed out, there are other means of protecting the public against individuals which do not involve locking them up, but politicians should therefore provide the necessary legal measures for the courts to use, and the resources for the relevant agencies to carry them out. That still leaves judges with the question of the duration of these measures; but when a person is under supervision in the community it is easier to assess whether the restrictions are still necessary. Judges are also conscious that even if the reason for a sanction is purely preventive, its impact will be different on different people; for example, if their crime was committed in the workplace, the restriction might preclude them from continuing to earn their living in the same way.

I think, though, that where the offender is not violent, selective restrictions make more sense than the total incapacitation of imprisonment; and by the way, is it not ironic that the word 'incapacitation' is doubly apt, because despite the best efforts of prison governors and staff prisons notoriously 'lead to incapacity for effective life' when they come out, if I may borrow a phrase from the Psychologist, and extra effort is needed by probation officers and others, including ordinary citizens of good will, to help them to recover? (I am interested in the significance of words, as you may notice!) Surely this is yet another reason why custody should be used as sparingly as possible.

Individual deterrence

Next the Psychologist considered, in the light of scientific research, the use of punishment to deter individual offenders from repeating their offence, in other words, individual deterrence. The main points from his talk which struck me were that punishment only teaches people what not to do, not what to do; and that it only works under certain conditions, which are seldom present in the criminal justice process. There seems to be unanimity that if behaviour is to be changed, another form of behaviour must be available, and that reward is more effective than punishment in shaping behaviour. He also spoke about some specific issues, such as the effects of shame, from a psychological point of view, and I should like to add a few criminological comments.

This should make us all re-think our intuitive belief that punishment 'works'. In the meantime, however, judges have no option but to use the existing system. This leaves us with some dilemmas. One is, 'How long a sentence is needed to deter a particular offender?' I may be out of touch (which judges are often accused of being), but I have never heard of a psychological test which says 'This offender is likely to be deterred by a sentence of at least x months or years, and results cannot be guaranteed with anything less', or 'A court appearance on its own will be quite enough to deter this person in future'. Judges sometimes speak of the 'clang of the gates theory', by which we mean that for many people the sound of the prison gates closing behind them for the first time is enough to deter them for ever, so that it is unnecessary to sentence them to more than 24 hours' imprisonment; this is the explanation of some unexpectedly short sentences. (It has also led some courts – quite wrongly – to refuse bail without justification to accused people while they were still unconvicted, to give them 'a taste of prison'.) In practice we simply have to assume that if the previous sentence was not long enough to deter, this one will have to be longer; but this is of course overridden by other considerations such as the 'going rate' for the offence, within limits laid down by Parliament, and by considerations of general deterrence, to which I shall return later.

If I am frank, as the circumstances of this Symposium fortunately allow me to be, the giveaway for both the Court of Appeal's decisions and Professor David Thomas's analysis of them is that they only ask 'What sentences were imposed in other comparable circumstances?' and never 'What effect did those sentences have?' We do not know whether Burglar Bill lived blamelessly ever after, or emerged from prison with plans for bigger and better burglaries, or spent his time picking up tips on how to switch to credit card fraud, or resolved to go straight and was dragged down after release from prison by his inability to find a home, work or non-criminal friends. So our current legislation, the Criminal Justice Act 1991 (as amended), retreats into the retributive principle: everything is based on seriousness, except that section 2(2)(b) allows longer sentences for violent or sexual offences if there is evidence that the accused is likely to commit further serious offences of the same kind. The sentencing 'tariff', despite its inconsistencies, does have some logic.

There is further unfairness because punishment inflicts 'collateral' pain, for example because the offender loses his job, or his family suffers as a result of his punishment. Should a big businessman or politician get a lesser sentence because they have lost more in other ways? Should they go to an open prison because imprisonment of any kind hits them harder than others?

Rehabilitation

Rehabilitation has been among the official aims of sentencing for a century, since the Gladstone Report of 1895, and the Probation Officer spoke about this—and about how it is incompatible with the other aims. Firstly, he said, the aim of punishment is to hurt, while rehabilitation tries to help; secondly, the amount of punishment is based on the seriousness of the offence, while the amount of rehabilitation is based on the offender's need. This can work either way: it can lead to a major intervention in someone's life because of a small offence, or a person who has caused great harm to a victim may receive treatment which seems to an onlooker almost like a reward. It may well be in the public interest, if it results in the offender's refraining from committing more crimes against more victims, but if it is not accompanied by some recognition of the harm caused by his offence, the man or woman in the street feels that something is lacking. In some cases we have to make a choice between what is optimistically called a 'deterrent' sentence and a rehabilitative one; this is a complex balancing act in itself, and more so when we have to consider fairness towards others who have committed similar offences, especially if they were co-accused in the same crime. The Court of Appeal spends a lot of time wrestling with these puzzles, as Professor Thomas's *Current Sentencing Practice* (1984-) bears witness.

There are arguments about whether rehabilitation 'works', that is to say, whether it persuades and enables offenders to live law-abidingly; and there is further controversy about whether it has been given a fair chance or starved of funds, and whether the research was properly conducted. That is a matter for probation officers, criminologists and others to assess; the difficulty that concerns me as a judge is that sentences are generally based on the seriousness of the offence, but rehabilitation is based on the needs of the offender. What we do as judges is to balance these criteria in the light of the circumstances of individual cases; often a similar case has been decided by the Court of Appeal, which we can apply.

Victims and criminal justice

Fourthly, we heard a different perspective from the Victim Assistance Worker. His concerns were firstly with the criminal process, and secondly with reparation to victims. He emphasised that the criminal justice system has until recently been focused either on its own priorities or on the protection of the offender's rights, with little regard for the effect on the victim. There have been considerable improvements in recent years (although some of these, such as victim impact statements, are themselves problematic), but he said that some of the difficulties are built-in to a legalistic system, especially if it is adversarial—although an inquisitorial system would still be bound by much the same legal logic.

He pointed out that there are repercussions for victims in the fact that the accused, if convicted, is likely to be punished. There is likely to be plea bargaining, which is unsatisfactory for victims because it leads to inadequate recognition of the seriousness of the offence; but if plea bargaining does not take place, the accused is more likely to try his luck with a plea of not guilty, which often means that the victim is subjected to cross-examination in the witness box. Victims feel responsible for initiating the process which ends in the offender's punishment, and as a result in some cases they do not report the crime or they refuse to give evidence, either because they feel guilty or because they fear reprisals as the offender intensifies his efforts to escape punishment, by means which may range from hostile cross-examination to intimidation and the threat of revenge when he is released from custody.

The Victim Assistance Worker's other main concern was with reparation, which judges have to consider because it affects sentencing; we also heard that there are different views on how best to convey relevant information to the judge. (What the judge does with it is another question, to which I will return.) For the victim not merely to describe the effects, but to express a view about sentence, as is done in some of the United States, opens up another whole range of problems.

Community service orders also have a reparative element; many victims do not require compensation, perhaps because their loss is covered by insurance, perhaps because nothing can make up for it—or even because they do not want to burden the offender with payments he cannot afford. They feel, however, that the offender should 'put something back', and working for a charity or for people in need is a practical way of doing so. Community service orders require the offender's consent, and when first introduced in 1972 were based on the offender's abilities rather than on the nature of the offence or the unpleasantness of the task. Recent regulations, however, have stipulated that the work should include 'hard manual work', as the Probation Officer mentioned; they are supposed to be 'demanding in the sense of being physically, emotionally or intellectually demanding', which few would quarrel with, but they are also supposed to combine punishment with reparation and reintegration into the community (Home Office *et al*, 1995: 34), so that the reparative element is diminished.

I understand that the ethics of sentencing will be dealt with by the Philosopher. So I will turn to the aspects I mentioned at the beginning: general deterrence and retribution.

GENERAL DETERRENCE

This is the first of my specific concerns. General Deterrence still has many supporters, despite the dishonourable discharge of his side-kick Corporal Punishment. But if there is such a thing as a just war against crime, he has no place in it. The concept of general deterrence is based on the simple principle that we cannot detect all lawbreakers, but we will make an example of those we do catch, doing such fearsome things to them that although the risk is very small, the consequences are so serious that it is not worth taking. Using the threat of unpleasant consequences to deter potential offenders is presented as a basic justification for punishment. The doubtful effectiveness of this has been recognised at least since the 1660s when John Bunyan wrote in *Pilgrim's Progress* of 'them that pick pockets in the presence of the judge, or that will cut purses under the gallows'; and a long prison sentence did not deter Bunyan himself from the 'crime' of preaching non-conformity.

The word 'deterrence' comes from *terrere*, the same Latin root as 'terror'; it is incorrect to use it as if it were merely a synonym for 'prevention'. The idea is that the penalties imposed on the offenders who are convicted will frighten other people into obeying the law. At first sight this appears self-evident, but on closer scrutiny turns out to be at best a half-truth.

I think we should constantly remind ourselves—both judges in chambers writing judgments and academics in libraries writing textbooks—that punishment is not abstract, but does drastic things to people's lives; as Sir Walter Moberly put it:

> The original wrongful act has caused pain and therein lies its wrongness; but you do not necessarily mend matters by punishing. On the contrary, the one thing you do, immediately and certainly, is to cause more pain. Unless you can expect some further useful consequence of punishment, you are only making matters worse. You are adding a second evil to the first; and one and one make two and not zero. The executioner pays the murderer the compliment of imitation (Moberly 1968: 45).

We have to be clear what we are trying to frighten potential offenders with. It could be the prospect of *being caught* at all, or the *shame* that results, or the *pain* of the actual punishment. If it is the prospect of being caught, this is substantially undermined by the fact that only a small number of crimes are even reported, let alone cleared up. The *British Crime Survey* has shown that under 50 per cent of all crimes are reported to the police. The proportion cleared up is 4.9 per cent, and only 2 per cent result in a conviction (and a further 0.7 per cent in a caution (Home Office 1995: 25). Moreover, it is of course precisely those who offend most often who are most aware of their chances of getting away with it; the less experienced often *over*-estimate the likely sentence but commit the offence anyway. Many more do not stop to think whether they are likely to be caught, either because they have little to lose, or their crime was committed in the heat of the moment.

It is true that the most serious crimes are more likely to be reported; they are also more likely to be cleared up, both because the police allocate more resources to them and because the victim and the assailant are often known to each other. The clear-up rate for homicide is 88 per cent, and for violence against the person and sexual offences about three-quarters; but for violent crimes by strangers, such as robbery, the clear-up rate is only 22 per cent (Home Office, 1995: 26).

Thus many people know that they are unlikely to be punished, or do not care too much if they are, or do not stop to think about it. This is probably compounded by misleading newspaper reports suggesting that the courts are more lenient than in fact they are. As the Home Office said in its handbook for sentencers, *The Sentence of the Court* (1990):

> The inference most commonly drawn from research studies is that the probability of arrest and conviction is likely to deter potential offenders, whereas the perceived severity of the ensuing penalties has little effect.

The second way in which general deterrence tries to influence people's behaviour is through shame. Although fear is a powerful emotion, and its effects should not be underestimated, before we conclude that punishment is therefore effective, we should ask what potential offenders are afraid of: not necessarily the punishment itself, but other consequences. The shame of having to face family and friends, for example, arises from the conviction; the punishment often does not add all that much to it. There are people who want to use humiliating punishments — the trial process itself has been described as a 'degradation ceremony' and one still sees reports of people, apparently in earnest, calling for the return of the pillory — but I will say no more about that aspect of shame because the Psychologist has already done so and I understand that the Mediator also intends to speak about it.

Thirdly, general deterrence tries to control people by the threat of pain (which I will use as a general term to cover everything from 'hitting people in the pocket' to physical pain and partial or total restriction of liberty). The Psychologist told us about the effects of pain on individuals; I should like to look at the effects of the threat of pain on the behaviour of people in general, and the effects of two particular forms of pain, fines and physical punishment. The Psychologist and the Probation Officer have already given their indictment of imprisonment.

A policy based on deterrence can have paradoxical effects. In some cases the victim would like the offender brought to justice, but fears that the law's reaction will be excessively harsh; for example, when someone catches a neighbour's son stealing, or a woman wants her husband to stop abusing her but does not want him to be sent to prison. Many women refuse to give evidence in such a situation, and it has been pointed out that the position would be worse if the law obliged the court to pass a lengthy sentence on the accused because of his previous record; as Baroness Mallalieu put it in the debate on the Crime (Sentences) Bill – and she is an experienced barrister, and no 'softie'!:

> More victims of sexual assault, who are often required to give evidence against close relatives – and that applies particularly to children – often in situations where affection continues to exist or where there is heavy family pressure, will refuse to testify in cases where the consequence of conviction will be a life sentence, with the result that more guilty people will escape justice (House of Lords, 23 May 1996, quoted by Penal Affairs Consortium (1996: 2)).

One form of deterrence which some politicians find attractive is to threaten certain repeat offenders with a specified minimum sentence, but this also has side-effects. Juries may refuse to convict: the nineteenth-century abolitionist Sir Samuel Romilly cited cases in which, for example, a woman was convicted of stealing a ten-pound note, but because stealing more than forty shillings (£2) from a private house was a capital offence, the jury brought in a verdict of stealing thirty-nine shillings, and Lord Suffield said in the House of Lords in 1833 that he had a list of 555 such cases over 15 years, and that over 11,000 jurors must have perjured themselves in this way. In the past seven years, he said, only 18 per cent of non-capital charges led to an acquittal, but on capital charges the figure was 28 per cent, so that 'ten persons out of every 100 escaped with impunity, because the nominal penalty was death' (*Hansard* [HL], 2 August 1833, col. 279-80). Even without the death penalty, minimum sentences distort the system: the accused has no incentive to plead guilty in order to get a lesser sentence, so that the victim is likely to suffer the trauma of giving evidence in court, and the court's costs and delays will be increased.

The alternative is for the accused to plead guilty to a lesser charge that does not require the minimum sentence; this is unsatisfactory for the community, and especially for the victim, who knows that what actually took place was more serious. Once the offence has been committed, the threat of punishment can lead offenders to try to conceal what they have done, as the Psychologist has shown. Police know all about this: whether they are investigating gangland violence, or misconduct within their own ranks, they all too often come up against a wall of silence, and the reason is clear—the potential witnesses know that their evidence may lead someone else (or perhaps themselves) to be punished.

We know that offenders often do not calculate the possible results of their actions, and this is one of the factors which undermines the supposed effects of deterrence. But neither do those who impose punishments, and this is not so commonly recognised. Nor, I believe, is the fact that there are occasions when sanctions produce not deterrence but defiance, and this is likely when offenders do not accept the legitimacy of the sanction and do not have bonds of respect to the authority that inflicts it (Braithwaite, 1998b).

The effect of general deterrence on the whole of society also needs to be considered. Many people, perhaps most, would prefer to live in a society which was held together by trust, self-control and incentives to good behaviour rather than by fear, authoritarian control and the threat of punishment. This ideal state of affairs is of course never likely to be completely realised; but insofar as we have a choice, would it not make for a pleasanter and more stable society if we tried to work towards this ideal rather than in the direction of control through fear and repression?

I have been talking about general deterrence in general, so to speak, but there are special considerations in relation to specific forms of punishment. Besides imprisonment, which the Psychologist spoke about, two of the commonest types are fines and physical punishment (which of course is no longer part of the penal system in most Western countries, but still widely used informally).

Fines

Fines tell people that their conduct is illegal, but do nothing to make them think about *why* it is illegal—for example, that it causes inconvenience or harm to others. If fines are imposed for property offences, or those related to, for example, begging or prostitution, there is a well recognised risk that the offender will simply re-offend in order to pay the fine. It might make more sense to help someone extricate himself from financial difficulties, rather than add to them. (There is a system for doing this, which the Victim Assistance Worker described.) This argument must however be used with care by advocates of restorative justice, because reparation often takes the form of cash payment, whose effect on the offender's pocket is no different.) But when the offence was not committed out of need, the difference lies in the purpose to which the mulcted money is put. If a company has damaged the environment, every pound paid to the state is a pound less that it can spend on restoring—or improving—the air, land, water or lives that it has harmed.

It makes more sense to require railway companies or airlines to spend money on safety instead of dividends, rather than to fine them.

Physical punishment

The case against physical punishment may be made in terms of human rights: that people, including children, have the right not to be physically assaulted, whether by each other or by agents of the state. The Psychologist has pointed to some of the reasons why punishment in general, and physical punishment in the home in particular, can be counterproductive. I will look at it in the context of criminal justice, where although there are some who support corporal punishment on purely retributive grounds ('Give them a taste of their own medicine'), the argument most often used is the pragmatic one: that birching or whipping will deter crime. But the facts are not on the side of the floggers. Although Acts permitting the use of judicial corporal punishment for specific offences were passed after various scares (for example, for garotting in 1863 and for procuring for prostitution in 1912), the courts, whose outlook was not markedly radical, did not feel that birching was effective, and progressively reduced its use almost to nothing, until it was abolished in 1948; the Civil Servant will give the figures.

It is almost folklore in Britain that good policing includes giving young offenders a 'clip round the ear' – the phrase used to describe what PC Christopher Hirst did to a 16-year-old youth at Chesterfield police station. Judges cannot condone this: Mr Hirst was fined £200 and later dismissed. A chief constable, however, was quoted as saying that 'hooliganism would not be such a problem if parents took a stronger line and administered the occasional "clip round the earhole"', but a spokesman for Hampshire police attempted some damage limitation by emphasising that the chief constable was 'certainly not' advocating that policemen hit youngsters (*Daily Telegraph,* 2 August 1988). A few years later the same phrase was back in the news: PC Steve Guscott did it to a youth who had been abusing a pensioner by knocking on her door and running away. In fact the 14-year-old boy was hit on the nose and taken to hospital, and his nose was still bleeding when the police brought him home (*The Times,* 14, 15 June; *Guardian,* 15, 16 June 1994); but when magistrates fined Mr Guscott £100 and ordered him to pay £50 compensation many members of the public offered to pay on his behalf, and at least one tabloid newspaper ran a campaign of support for the officer and abused both the youth, as a 'foul-mouthed lout', and the 'snooty' chairman of the magistrates, Lady Sarah Wright, as an 'upper-class twit'. The father of the youth asked for police protection after receiving threatening phone calls (*Daily Star,* 15 June 1994); apparently the supporters of law and order were planning to follow PC Guscott's example, by using violence against a man they considered guilty of inadequate parenting.

The Psychologist has told us more about how 'discipline' can become abuse, and as he reminded us, in September 1998 the European Court of Human Rights awarded an eight-year-old boy £10,000 in damages, plus £20,000 costs, because being repeatedly caned by his stepfather was not 'reasonable chastisement' but 'inhuman or degrading punishment' (*A v. United Kingdom, ECHR Human Rights News*, 23 September 1998). The then British Health Minister, Paul Boateng, accepted the need to change the 1860 legislation, but despite a call by 140 children's organizations for an outright ban on corporal punishment, he said that the government affirmed a parent's 'right' to smack a child 'within a caring and loving environment' (*Daily Mail, Daily Telegraph, Guardian, The Times*, etc., 24 September 1998). He said nothing about a child's right not to be assaulted in the name of discipline, perhaps because parents have votes and children don't; nor did he refer to the government's duty to try to reduce, by legislation and public education, the amount of violence in society, including within the family.

Competing demands on the sentencer
Returning to judicial penalties that are still in use, let us pause for a moment to take stock. There are two primary decisions that judges have to make when sentencing: what type of sentence to impose, and how much of whatever it is. The current baseline for sentencing in Britain is the Criminal Justice Act 1991 (as amended in 1993); but as the authoritative *Current Law Statutes Annotated* (1991) says, 'There exists no concise declaration of philosophy, objectives or principles in this Act' (p.53-5). In effect, although the Act does not spell it out clearly (Criminal Justice Acts seldom do!), it says that there are three grades of punishment: financial penalties, community sentences, and imprisonment. Financial penalties are at the 'bottom of the range' (apart from discharges and binding over). Next, courts are not supposed to think of community sentences (probation, community service orders, and so on) as a 'soft option': the Act says that the offence must be 'serious enough' to justify such a sentence. The top category is imprisonment, which I cannot impose unless I consider that the offence is 'so serious' that only a custodial sentence can be justified or (in the case of a violent or sexual offence) is adequate to protect the public from serious harm *from that offender* (in other words, it is only for containment, not for general deterrence).

Another way of deciding which principle to employ is that the sentencer should choose the objective that is most likely to be achieved.

The Supreme Court of Victoria, Australia, put it like this: 'where it is not possible to have much or any confidence that the sentence imposed will do anything by way of deterrence or rehabilitation, substantial retribution must be exacted' (Victorian Sentencing Committee, 1988, quoted by Walker, 1991: 126). On this basis offenders who were considered capable of being rehabilitated would be fortunate, unless the court thought that their rehabilitation would take a long time and therefore imposed a long sentence; the others might not notice much difference between sentences intended to deter and those which were exacting retribution, except when a judge decided that, although their crime was serious, it wouldn't take much to deter them. (It is not clear from this quotation whether the writers had general or individual deterrence in mind.)

How long or how much?
The German word for sentencing, *Strafzumessung*, reflects the common assumption that punishment is accurately 'measured out', but this implies a precision which does not exist, and the English word 'sentencing' recognises this: it comes from the Latin *sententia*, which means nothing more than 'opinion': *quot judices, tot sententiae*. And it is salutary to remember that the word 'arbitrary' is derived from the word for 'a judge'. After deciding the type of sanction, judges have to consider another question (I nearly said they have to answer it, but if truth be told I think it is unanswerable). It is this: supposing that despite all these reasons a judge decides to base a sentence on general deterrence, how long should that sentence be, or how large the fine? As I said, we have no research evidence to guide us. Here again we have a conflict of principles. Suppose for a moment that potential offenders are deterred by sentences passed on others, the amount necessary for some is likely to be much more than the amount deemed to be proportionate to the individual offender and his or her offence—and for others it will probably be much less. Faced with all these contradictions, we as judges have to try to find some rational basis.

Thus since nobody has the faintest idea what is the 'right' amount of deterrence for a particular offender, and since the amount of rehabilitation, if any, needed by any individual bears no relation to the seriousness of the crime (from, say, the intelligent, calculating murderer to the schizophrenic who steals a cabbage) we turn to another principle. This is variously called retribution or denunciation. They are not quite the same (one focuses on making the offender actually suffer, and the other on showing the rest of society how much he is made to suffer, so that it may be only ceremonial, like a suspended sentence—Walker, 1978: 396), but both attempt to be proportionate to the seriousness of the offence. This sounds reasonable at first sight, but here we have another unanswerable question: how much of any particular sanction is enough to express denunciation? What is the correct sentence for a serious offence which fortunately did not affect the victim very badly, or *vice versa*?

If on the other hand restriction of liberty is used as 'containment', to prevent re-offending, a decision has to be made as to how long it should last. We ought to be clear on which principle this decision is based, but I'm afraid we aren't consistent about this. In theory the duration should then be based on the probability of re-offending, whatever the seriousness of the offence; but in practice it comes back to seriousness: if the offence is not very serious, the public is not protected from it for very long. Under the Criminal Justice Act 1993, however, a person with several previous convictions can be given a longer sentence; this might be justified on the grounds that the more often a person has offended the more likely he or she is to do it again, but as lawyers we are uncomfortable with this, because it feels as if the offender is being punished for the current offence and then re-punished for the offences that are over and done with.

There are two basic options: either the judge decides, at the time of sentence, for how long the offender is to be kept under restraint; or the decision is left to a later assessment. There are two compromise methods, which are often combined: one is that the judge can impose a sentence which in effect sets the maximum and minimum period, within which a parole board may assess when to release the prisoner, and the other is that the sentence may include a period under supervision after release. If the judge sets the length, it is likely to be based on retributive criteria, and is almost certain to be longer or shorter than required for protection of the public or for rehabilitation. If there is an element of assessment, this means predicting future behaviour, which can obviously not be done with any great accuracy, and there is a danger that parole boards 'play safe', keeping too many people locked up for too long, which is unjust and expensive (or perhaps to 'play soft', if they are of a liberal-minded disposition). Preventive custody places an added moral responsibility on the authorities to provide suitable programmes before and after release, to give the offender the greatest possible chance of becoming an ex-offender – for his sake and everyone else's. But they often fail to do this. I am also unhappy about predicting future behaviour for the reason given by the Probation Officer when he talked about risk assessment: we do not know how a person's behaviour in an institution will translate into the world outside, nor do we know what conditions he will face: will he get a job, does he have family and friends who will support him?

Mercy

In many ways consistency is a virtue; but so, on occasion, is flexibility, which is why judges so strongly defend their power to exercise discretion. One thing we hold to strongly is the power to exercise mercy. Some thinkers have argued that in a perfectly just system mercy would be not only unnecessary but wrong; but perfection is unlikely, and Dostoevsky expressed the other view: 'You have no mercy, only justice, therefore you are unjust'. The Court of Appeal has reduced custodial sentences to community service orders where a young man with an appalling record had formed a relationship with a 'sensible, level-headed girl' with whom he had had a baby; where a man had amended his ways between the offences and the sentence, so that 'the man who committed the offences was not the man who was appearing before the judge'; and where 'there is any indication that he is beginning to realise the extent of his past criminality', so that one might achieve 'at any rate some change of heart' (all cases from *Current Sentencing Practice*, all between 1980 and 1983). Other offenders have earned mitigation by attempting to rescue three children from a burning house while on bail, apprehending men carrying out a robbery, and raising the alarm when prisoners escaped from a van. I do not know how these examples will appeal to the Philosopher's logical mind, but to me, as a pragmatic lawyer, it seems both reasonable and humane to temper justice with mercy.

Victims' requests for mercy get a mixed response from the courts. The Court of Appeal refused to reduce a four-year sentence for the rape of a relative, although she wrote to say that she 'begged for mercy and intimated that if she had known that a sentence like this might have resulted she might not have complained'. The Court said that 'the complainant's subsequent attitude relating to the degree of sentence is a completely irrelevant consideration'. So much for the victim's right to be heard. But the three-year sentence on the secretary of a social club was reduced when 440 of the 500 members petitioned; the court said that 'when the only part of the local community affected by the offence asks for leniency in these terms the Court can properly give some effect to their request' (Walker, 1980: 135-6). In another case (*Attorney-General's Reference No. 18 of 1993, R. v. Kavanagh*) a man who used severe violence on his three-year-old step-grandchild during a family row was given a two-year probation order, subject to treatment for alcohol dependency, to which he had responded well. The Attorney-General asked the Court of Appeal to review the sentence on grounds of undue leniency; but the man had spent four months in custody before sentence, and in the light of letters from members of the family, the Court did not increase his sentence (*Criminal Law Review*, 1994: 467-8).

RETRIBUTION

It comes down to this: usually I end up saying in effect (like the Victorian Sentencing Commission which I quoted earlier) that if none of the other objectives provides a coherent reason for a particular length of sentence, I must impose a punishment anyway, whether it is effective or not, and base it on retribution. A tariff has been constructed, a kind of 'exchange rate', using the seriousness of the offence as a yardstick. This has been done with great care; each time a new set of circumstances arises, a judge will try to interpret it in the light of previous sentences, and if the offender appeals (or it is referred to the Attorney-General on grounds of excessive leniency) the Court of Appeal reconsiders it likewise, and it gets added to the law reports and textbooks for future judges.

The length of the sentence has to be 'commensurate' with the seriousness of the offence. The implication is that seriousness is the only criterion (except in the small number of cases where physical protection of the public is an issue). The old problems of balancing it against deterrence and rehabilitation are no longer supposed to be part of the equation; if they occur, they are by-products, which depend on the regime provided by the prison or the community supervision, although the White Paper which preceded the Criminal Justice Act 1991 Act said:

> The lifestyle of many offenders, especially young adults, is often disorganized and impulsive, particularly if they drink too much or are addicted to drugs . . . Each order should be tailored both to the seriousness of the offence and the characteristics of the offender. A comparatively short order may make more severe demands on some offenders than more severe orders would on others (Home Office, 1990, para. 4.9).

The context makes this sound a rehabilitative consideration, and so does the word 'tailoring', with its connotations of individually designed garments which enhance the wearer, but the word 'severe' sounds punitive, and the idea that sensitive souls should receive milder punishments is unworkable because neither the sensitivity nor the impact of the punishment is measurable. If in addition the effect on the victim is taken into consideration, it can in this 'just deserts' context only be to increase (or possibly decrease) the level of seriousness. Assisting the victim's recovery is by implication also secondary. Some may get compensation, but it is seldom available from people who are imprisoned, except in the few cases where the prison pays realistic wages or the offender has realisable assets.

All this gives us little guidance as to what sentence is 'commensurate' to what offence; the only basis seems to be what is customary. Even that can change markedly in a few years: in England

and Wales, the proportion of those sentenced to imprisonment for indictable offences in magistrates' courts doubled between 1992 and 1996, from five to ten per cent, and in the Crown Court it rose from 46 to 63 per cent. The average length of sentences has also gone up for most categories of offence; for adult males for indictable offences it increased by 29 per cent from 18.3 months in 1986 to 23.6 months in 1996 (Penal Affairs Consortium, 1997: 8; Home Office, 1997 Table 7.16). The Lord Chief Justice himself, Lord Bingham, has more than once admitted that the reason for the 'exponential increase' in the prison population in recent years is 'the vocal expression of opinion by influential public figures that custody is an effective penalty'; he regards this as a source of concern, as being potentially both excessive and ineffective (NACRO, 1997: 1; 1998: 20). Although we are independent, we judges do not like being told that we have got it wrong, whether by politicians and the media or by judges in higher courts, so we often err on the side of sentences which we think will avoid criticism.

The picture is further clouded by the Crime (Sentences) Act 1997, which compels judges to impose life sentences on second-time serious sexual and violent offenders. My senior colleagues have objected strongly to this. It is not a matter of judges wanting to hang on to their powers, as has been claimed: the point is that this is completely contrary to the principle of 'just deserts'. As regards protection of the public, this should be used only when it is strictly necessary, on grounds of justice (to say nothing of economy). There might be strong mitigating circumstances, or good reason to believe that the offender would be no danger in future, and yet judges are forced to impose a life sentence (save in very exceptional circumstances – a small concession which the judiciary managed to wring from the then Home Secretary, Michael Howard). As Lord Bingham has also said, there is a strong case for allowing judges to use their experience and discretion not only in these cases but also for murder, to enable us to reflect the wide differences in the circumstances of different cases (*Guardian*, 8 October 1998); or if life sentences are used, it should be judges, not politicians, who decide when an offender can be released on licence.

In short, as one law professor has put it, 'everywhere, criminal justice is strangely uncertain in its goals . . . A commercial enterprise similarly unenlightened could not long survive and certainly could not prosper' (Gross, 1979: 5).

And so if I'm honest (which is one thing everyone expects judges to be) I have to admit that this exchange rate has no gold standard; the going rate varies in different parts of the country and still more between countries (the Civil Servant will give examples), and the 'hard currency' is imprisonment. In a sense, therefore, this intricate edifice of precedents is quite arbitrary.

I am reminded of the fable of the wolf and the lamb.

> A lamb was drinking in a mountain stream, when a hungry wolf came up; but as the lamb was so helpless, even the wolf felt a little guilty about harming it. So he looked for an excuse. 'You are fouling my water', he said. 'But your majesty', said the lamb, 'please don't be angry with me, because I am 20 paces downstream from you, so I cannot be harming your water'. 'Yes you are', said the wolf, 'and what's more, last year you called me names'. But the lamb replied, 'Last year I was not born'. The wolf tried again: 'If it wasn't you, it was your brother'. 'I have no brothers'. 'Well, it was one of your family; and your shepherds and their dogs are always chasing me. So I am entitled to my revenge'. And with no further pretence at a trial, the wolf carried off the lamb and devoured it.

In other words, if we don't have a basis for choosing which type of sanction to use, we tend to fall back on retribution; and if we don't know how much of any sanction to impose, again we turn to retribution, under the guise of proportionality. Thus we have resorted to a symbolic function, a way of measuring the seriousness of the crime and letting the public, and the victim, know the assessment. As we have seen this was the solution adopted by the authors of the Criminal Justice Act 1991, with its emphasis on the word 'serious', except where it specifically provided for departures from this principle in the interests of protection of the public.

COMPENSATION

Despite the criticisms I think we judges do a pretty conscientious job of balancing the different factors against each other to arrive at tolerably consistent sentences. I know there are variations between judges, but in a field which is based on the assessment of individual circumstances I think that is inevitable, and there is an elaborate procedure for correcting any that are too far out of line, through the Court of Appeal (Criminal Division). But the purpose of this Symposium is to look for possible improvements, and I am not so complacent that I can't think of any. I do have one major suggestion, apart from the obvious question of trying to improve consistency. As Professor Walker has pointed out, the philosopher Kant considered that dealing with offenders was a 'categorical imperative', but he did not explain why this must be done in a *punitive* way (Walker, 1991: 77). I myself do not see why, in principle, the denunciation could not take the form of reparation rather than punishment. This could also be proportionate to the offence, although some would say that it is a move towards applying the civil law, so that it should instead be proportionate to the harm done. If I may confuse you with a little more etymology, the original meaning of the word 'retribution' is 'to pay back', from the Latin *retribuere*, to restore or repay. We have got into the habit of using it to mean 'repayment' of harm *to* the offender; but it could make better sense (and better Latin!) to regard it as repayment, making amends, *by* the offender.

I can see two problems which would have to be overcome. One is that if the reparation took the form of monetary compensation, there would often (perhaps usually) be a disparity between what the victim ought to receive, and what the offender is able to pay. The other is a practical one: if a very serious offence required an amount of reparation, or community service, which would take many years to complete, would this be unduly onerous, especially to a young offender (some would have little sympathy with this), or would it be impractical to enforce over a long period? These are some of the issues which I hope the Mediator will address.

At present, I have to say that most of my colleagues in the judiciary and magistracy do not appear to think of compensation in this way. They see it either as a form of punishment, which is meted out in proportion to its unpleasantness for the offender rather than its benefit to the victim; or as something less than punishment, which has to be supplemented or even replaced by 'real' punishment. Thus, as the Victim Assistance Worker pointed out, Home Office research has found that magistrates have often imposed fines in addition to compensation, even when this has meant that the offender will be able to pay less to the victim; and of course we commonly send people to prison although we know that this will generally make it impossible for them to pay any substantial compensation, or to make reparation in any other way. Similarly, the proportion of cases resolved by a compensation order alone has always been very small, especially in the Crown Court.

It is true that at present the court (or in some countries the prosecutor) can order the offender to pay compensation. But because it is an order, and (in England at least) the arrangements for paying are no different from those for paying fines, offenders are given little chance to feel that they are making amends. Victims, similarly, receive an impersonal cheque from the court, usually for small amounts at irregular intervals; these are of little practical help – one large sum would be much more useful – and many victims probably sense the reluctance with which they are paid. It has been proposed that courts should pay the compensation all at once, and collect it in instalments from the offender; after all, the victim has already endured the crime, why should he or she suffer further inconvenience, and lose out again if the offender fails to pay? But this distances the offender still more from the victim. Another method, which overcomes some of the difficulties, was described by the Victim Assistance Worker.

I should also like to make a point about 'denunciation'. This is a shorthand word for punitive action to show how strongly society condemns the crime. It seems to me that we could demonstrate this more imaginatively, and on occasion we have. After the discovery of the many murders committed by Fred and Rosemary West at 25 Cromwell Road, Gloucester, the house was demolished, after consultation with relatives of the victims, and replaced by a shrub-lined walkway, with no plaque, memorial garden or benches (*Times*, 5 and 18 October 1996). The Broad Arrow Café in Port Arthur, Tasmania, where a gunman killed 35 people in April 1996 was also dismantled (*The Times*, 2 December 1996). When the then Prime Minister, John Major, and Opposition Leader Tony Blair visited the school gym in which 16 children and their teacher were killed in March 1996 by Thomas Hamilton at Dunblane, Scotland, Mr Major said 'They must tear it down'; after consultation with the bereaved parents this was done while the school children were away for Easter, and the area planted with bulbs (*The Times*, 16 March, 5 April 1996). In this case further significant action was taken: the children's parents launched Gun Control Network, a powerful campaign to restrict the availability of hand guns, which led to the Firearms (Amendment) Act 1997 banning all handguns above 0.22 calibre. (There have been similar calls for gun control in the United States after repeated multiple killings, but there the anti-control lobby has been stronger.) The men guilty of such terrible crimes would inevitably have been imprisoned or sent to secure mental hospitals if they had not committed suicide, and in many American states they would have faced the death penalty; but it is possible to find other means of expressing concern. Denunciation could take the form of commemoration, and might include the planting of a tree, naming a park, or the institution of a charitable fund, according to the wishes of the bereaved family (United Nations, 1998: 53-54).

KEY PERFORMANCE INDICATORS FOR JUDGES?

All in all I have to admit, ruefully, that if some keen researcher wanted to assess how well I and my fellow sentencers had performed during the year, or — perish the thought — if performance-related pay were introduced for judges (or periodic assessments for magistrates, since in England they are with some exceptions unpaid), it is hard to see what criteria could be applied. If the basis were post-sentence reconviction rates, we should be tempted to put as many people as possible in prison — unless someone took notice of the possible increase in offending after the prisoners were released. But in that case would it be appropriate, or practicable, to assess us on the basis of decisions made years ago? In any case re-offending depends so much on factors over which courts have no control (housing, employment, family support . . .) that the judges would feel unjustly treated — or perhaps it would encourage us to take a greater interest in reducing the social and economic pressures to which offenders are exposed, if our own remuneration or promotion depended on the consequences. Should the criterion be the total crime statistics for the area, with all the well-known problems of statistics in general, and crime statistics in particular? In that case it would be impossible to distinguish the effects of the sentences of individual judges, and once again the results would depend on many factors which had nothing to do with judges' performance as sentencers.

If the basis for assessment were the denunciatory effect of the sentences, which is *de facto* the overriding criterion, who could possibly measure whether we had got that right? Would the researchers decide? —judges would not like that! Would it be on the basis of public opinion surveys? If so, would it depend on cases reported in the media, which almost by definition means the sensational or controversial ones, or on an elaborate survey in which the public were given a précis of the facts available to the judge? Would the respondents have to undergo a short course in the principles of sentencing as well? The remaining possibility would be to apply the yardstick often used when evaluating restorative justice programmes: whether the victim felt better as a result, and whether the offender felt justly treated. This would have the advantage that it would bring into the equation the whole of the process, not just the outcome, and at present it is aspects of the process which cause much of the dissatisfaction and hurt. But that would be an additional complication, because many other people, such as the police, prosecuting and defence counsel, court ushers, and since the early 1990s the Crown Court Witness Service, have an influence on the participants' feelings about the handling of the case.

So we judges have inherited a system which has in recent years been streamlined, and is governed by a vast amount of case law. If you start being analytical you can be a devil's advocate and find all sorts of contradictions, as I have done, and perhaps you will think that I have been hard on myself and my fellow judges; it is far from perfect, especially with regard to the mandatory minimum sentences which have been introduced, but I take comfort from the fact that not very many sentences are varied on appeal, either upwards or downwards, and I think this shows that, with care, we can balance the competing demands and find for each offender a place in the tariff which corresponds reasonably well to the seriousness of his offence and his individual circumstances, while not being too far out of line with other sentences for comparable cases.

FACTS AND STATISTICS

The Civil Servant

Unequal sentencing
One study of 30 courts in England found that the proportion of convicted offenders sent to prisons or juvenile institutions varied from three to 19 per cent; the proportion fined ranged from 46 to 76 per cent (Tarling, 1979: 9). In West Mercia (in the Midlands of England) the Crown Court imprisons 74 per cent of offenders, but in Gloucestershire, in the West, only 39 per cent; the average sentence in Kent was 27.9 months, compared with 16.7 months in Staffordshire (Penal Affairs Consortium, 1997: 9; Prison Reform Trust, 1997).

International comparisons are harder to make, but there are wide variations. Some of these are attributable to differences in crime rates and the efficiency of the police and courts, but some must be due to variations in sentencing, notably in England and Wales, where the prison population went up from 76 to 120 per 100,000 between 1993 and 1998; in Italy, from 58 to 85 between 1991 and 1996; and in The Netherlands, where the proportion of prisoners trebled to 75 per 100,000 between 1980 and 1995. At one end of this league table are

Belarus (1995)	505
Kazakhstan (1995)	560
United States of America (1996)	615
Russia (1996)	690

Figures in Central and Eastern Europe are also relatively high, but the trend is downwards: in Poland, for example, the proportion fell from 170 in 1995 to 149 in 1996, and further changes in legislation in September 1998 are expected to bring numbers down further. At the other end of the scale are countries like

India (1992)	23
Cyprus (1995)	30
Slovenia (1996)	31
Japan (1992)	36
Bangladesh (1992)	37
Croatia (1994)	50

(Penal Reform International, 1998; Stern, 1998: 31-2)

Corporal punishment

Its use by English courts fell from 2,079 cases in 1913 to 130 in 1930; after a temporary rise during the second world war, the number declined to 25 in 1945. Research had long supported the magistrates' growing reluctance to use it. Research published in 1920 showed that 76 per cent of 574 boys birched in two towns were charged with new offences within two years, 25 per cent of them within a month. A study of men flogged for robbery with violence in 1921-30 showed that the proportions reconvicted were as follows (with the proportion of men not flogged in brackets):

reconvicted of serious crime 55.0 per cent (43.9 per cent);
reconvicted of serious violent offences 10.6 per cent (5.4 per cent).

The Home Secretary reported that in nine months before abolition, there were 711 robberies with violence, and in the corresponding period after it 597, a fall of 16 per cent (Fry, 1951: 235). Corporal punishment was abolished in 1948; within penal establishments its use also declined, until it was formally ended in 1967.

Deterrence

Much has been written about the inconclusive results of deterrence (summarised for example by Wright, 1982: 172-182). Another example, of an unsuccessful attempt at deterrence through minimum sentences, comes from South Africa: the Dangerous Weapons Act 1968 prescribed a minimum sentence of two years for assaults with dangerous weapons (without mitigating circumstances). The number of such assaults in 1969 was 73,934; by 1972 it had risen steadily to 85,926 (quoted by MacKenna, 1978: 426). Of course there is no evidence that the increased sentences actually *caused* the increase, but they clearly did not prevent it.

The judge mentioned the ideal of attaining consistency of sentencing, but it has always proved difficult. The American criminologists Michael Tonry and Norval Morris report one test of 50 federal judges, in which the sentences they proposed for one case varied from three to 20 years, and for another from probation to 7 years and six months. They comment that 'the norm was the absence of a norm' (Tonry and Morris, 1978: 438).

DISCUSSION

Q. You said that knowledge of the undesirable side-effects of imprisonment had not entered the public consciousness; would it not be true to add that it has not percolated to the Court of Appeal either?

A. I think the diplomatic answer to that, in the words of the devious politician in the television series *House of Cards*, 'You may say that, I couldn't possibly comment!'.

Q. All the evidence suggests that most hardened criminals are hardened in prison. The reconviction rate is particularly high for juveniles: as much as 89 per cent for 14 and 15-year-olds. So in the absence of leadership from politicians, should not the courts simply cut down on their use of custodial sentences, and explain to the public why they have done so?

A. That's all very well, but unless the Politician is successful in pushing her idea for resourcing the Probation Service, I foresee that probation officers would not be able to give adequate supervision and support to their increased numbers, there would be much-publicised recidivism, and the hard-liners would claim that they were right. Before we can undertake anything like that, I think the Probation Service needs to do a much better job of 'selling' itself to the public, and telling everyone some of their success stories, of which there are many.

Q. You said that many people offend despite being aware of the penalties; do you have any evidence for that?

A. It depends on the crime, of course; with impulsive crimes, they simply do not stop to think. But a study of 15 to 22-year-olds found that most of them *over*-estimated their chances of being caught (Walker, 1969: 64-65), and a Home Office study of car offenders found that they consistently *over*-estimated their likely sentence (Light *et al*, 1993). And in a different context there have been several reports of young people in Northern Ireland, who are well aware of the violent self-appointed 'para-police' and in some cases have already been 'knee-capped' by them, yet they continue to take cars, as an act of defiance or to provide some excitement in their grim lives.

Q. Judges are supposed to guard their independence jealously against interference, especially from politicians, and simply to impose sentences within the limits laid down by Parliament; so how does it come about, as you admitted, that during the 1990s the level of sentences went up so sharply even for crimes where there was no change in those limits? It looks very much as if the judges allowed themselves to be bounced into increasing the tariff by right-wing politicians and headlines in the tabloid newspapers. You yourself admitted that sentences are arbitrary; surely the fact that the sentence for a given offence can be months or years longer now than it was a few years ago is clear evidence of that?

A. Firstly, I didn't say that individual sentences are arbitrary – they are worked out with great care by balancing the various factors, as I explained. What I said was that the general *level* of sentencing is arbitrary: the tariff has passable internal consistency, but there is no logical starting point. Secondly, judges should not take account of anything politicians say about individual cases; but insofar as we are acting on behalf of the public we are bound to take account of what we believe to be public opinion, otherwise we lose credibility. But we have resisted the pressure as much as we could, as evidenced by the fact that the government of the day had to resort to introducing the Attorney-General's power (in the Criminal Justice Act 1988) to refer a sentence of the Crown Court to the Court of Appeal for reconsideration on the grounds that it is excessively lenient, and (in the Crime (Sentences) Act 1997) it compelled judges to impose minimum sentences in certain cases. The latter Act in particular was strongly opposed by senior judges as it went through Parliament, and slightly modified as a result; and as I mentioned some judges such as the Lord Chief Justice, Lord Bingham, have spoken out against excessive reliance on prison (for example, in his lecture to the Police Foundation, *Daily Mail, Independent,* 11 July 1997). Judges have also objected to the British system, which amazes lawyers in European countries, by which a politician, the Home Secretary, has the final say in deciding when some life sentence prisoners are released.

Q. Won't community service be very difficult to control, and have persistent young offenders laughing up their sleeves?

A. It depends on the type of work, and I think the Probation Officer was right when he stressed the importance of the way it is presented to the offender and the community. Research has found that the more it resembles a 'chain-gang', the more reluctant the offenders will be (Vass, 1986). The ideal work is demanding and useful; the point is not whether it is hard or enjoyable (it can be both) but that it shows the offender what he or she can contribute, and hence there will be less slacking and absenteeism.

SESSION 6

The Philosopher

My contribution to this debate has two aspects: a critique of what we do now in the name of criminal justice, and a vision of a way of dealing with criminal activity, taking account of criticisms of the present methods and building on ethical principles.

To start with, I should like to make some general points. Firstly, as has often been pointed out, there is no such thing as 'crime' — that is to say, there is no list of qualities that are possessed by all criminal acts and not possessed by any non-criminal acts. All crimes are crimes because the law-giver says so; there are harmful acts that are not criminal, and criminal acts which are not very harmful. In some countries such as France a more precise distinction is attempted between *contraventions* which are socially undesirable but do not physically hurt a victim (such as irregular parking, speeding, riding a motor cycle without a helmet, driving without a licence), harmful or potentially harmful acts such as *délits* (fraud, receiving stolen goods, threats, sexual assaults other than rape, drunk driving, unarmed robbery), and the most serious *crimes* (armed robbery, drug trafficking, rape, murder).

Secondly, it is commonly assumed that crime and punishment belong together like lightning and thunder — indeed crime is usually *defined* as an act or omission punishable by law. It would be true to say that crime is an act *prohibited* by law; but as the Judge rightly said, the sanction need not be punitive. Historically reparation has been a common response; among the ancient Germans, for example, through a payment of cattle and sheep, or money, to the victim's family (Schafer, 1968: 15); and in some cultures, to this day, even homicide can be atoned for by the payment of substantial compensation, as in the case of the Australian nurse Yvonne Gilford, for whose murder in Saudi Arabia in 1996 two British colleagues were sentenced, respectively, to execution and to eight years' imprisonment and 500 lashes but were eventually reprieved.

The 'common sense' idea that the threat of pain discourages people from certain behaviour was elevated into a philosophical theory by Jeremy Bentham in the early nineteenth century. According to his 'utilitarian' principle, people choose what gives them most pleasure; so if they get pleasure from unacceptable behaviour, such as stealing, we must arrange for some pain to outweigh it. It was only on that basis that he advocated punishment, which he described as 'evil'. (In passing, I am always surprised that Christians do not seem to attach significance, in this context, to the precept 'Do not return evil for evil, but drive out evil with good', which is repeated several times in the New Testament, for example in *Romans* 12: 17, 21; *I Thessalonians* 5: 15) On the basis of this 'common sense', criminal law has become punishment law; in modern French and German this is the word used (*Code Pénal, Strafrecht*). In addition it has come to be assumed that to harm a fellow-citizen also harms the state, which therefore takes over the conflict. In medieval times kings benefited from the reparation which went to them rather than to the victim, but for modern states with their dependence on prisons punishment is a source of expense rather than revenue.

Another interpretation of this social contract is that the state prohibited private vengeance, and relieved the victim of the burden of private prosecution; in return, it also took over the imposition of sanctions. It is widely assumed that punishment is so old and universal that it must be accepted as normal. But blood feuds were also a very ancient tradition, and every country as it becomes civilised tries to stop them. The subordinate status of women is another custom of great antiquity, which many people are working hard to eradicate. In recent Western history the tendency has been towards the reduction of 'cruel, inhuman and degrading' punishments such as mutilation, torture, public degradation and the death penalty, although the last two have been reintroduced in parts of the United States in the late twentieth century. In many countries corporal punishment is forbidden in schools, as the Psychologist has pointed out.

I should make clear that I use the word 'punishment' to mean measures whose primary purpose is the infliction of pain or deprivation, and not as a general term for sentences imposed by courts, which, following the Psychologist's terminology, I will refer to as 'sanctions', rehabilitative, reparative or punitive as the case may be. Some sanctions can be seen in different ways according to how they are applied; community service orders, for example, should ideally be reparative but were made more punitive by the British government in 1995, as the Probation Officer mentioned (Home Office *et al*, 1995). This is inappropriate because they do not depend for their effect on being unpleasant; their main goal should be to show that offenders can do helpful work and be valued for it. They can however have beneficent side-effects; one research study found that community service orders 'beat probation at its own game', by helping offenders to increase their understanding of others, their self-respect, and their sense of integration with the community (Thorvaldson, 1980). When offenders on CSOs were given work that was not degrading and allowed them to have contact with other people, they often continued after the order had been completed. Those who found the work to be very worthwhile had on average fewer reconvictions within three years of sentence: 2.9 as compared with 4.6 (McIvor, 1992: 87, 169).

With that in mind, let us begin by examining current theory and practice, which will in turn be divided into two: sentencing policy in general and, since it looms so large in people's thinking, punishment in particular.

SENTENCING

The point about sentencing, as the Judge conceded, is that it is trying to achieve several different objectives. What she did not fully recognise, I suggest, is firstly, that several of those objectives are impossible, and secondly, that even if they weren't, they are incompatible with each other. Let me take her main points one by one. The aims of sentencing are broadly divided into the utilitarian and the symbolic. The first utilitarian aim is general deterrence, and there is a surprising unwillingness of the public in general, and judges and legal theorists in particular, to recognise that to inflict on one person more punishment than he deserves for his own offence, for the sake of what others might do, is ethically problematic to say the least, because if there were such a thing as a just punishment for a particular offence (which is questionable, as we shall see in a minute), it would not be just to inflict more than that on an offender who is caught, *pour encourager les autres*. Yet that is what general deterrence does. A slightly different but related point is that it is not permissible to punish a whole neighbourhood for a crime assumed to have been committed by one unidentified inhabitant. I would remind the Judge that it was an eminent Law Lord, Lord Justice Asquith, who said (in 1950): 'an exemplary sentence is unjust; and unjust to the precise extent that it is exemplary' (quoted by Wright, 1982: 191).

In this Symposium the Judge has admitted that the fate of the tiny proportion of offenders who get brought to justice is not likely to make a significant impact on the whole population, and reminded us that the Criminal Justice Act 1991 accepted this, choosing instead to make retribution the primary principle of sentencing. Both the Psychologist and the Judge have pointed out that punishment intended to be deterrent can have some paradoxical effects which make it counterproductive. It is supposed to deter individuals from offending again, but in many ways it makes it harder for them to keep out of trouble: fines aggravate their financial difficulties, imprisonment causes them to lose their job, if they had one, or even their home, or makes it harder for them to get one because of the stigma of being an ex-prisoner. When it comes to undesirable side-effects, prison is in a class of its own: in addition to the stigma, it breaks up families, encourages people to share criminal expertise, provides a setting in which the strong can bully (or even sexually assault) the weak, and these days often introduces them to the use of drugs. In 1998 a new feature of prisons came to light: it enables paedophiles to get in touch with each other, especially when they are segregated in special wings of prisons to protect them from other prisoners.

The second aim is individual deterrence, and we have already heard the Psychologist's contribution (which the Judge also summarised). I should just like to comment on the 'clang of the gates' theory which the Judge mentioned: that for some people just hearing the gates close behind them and spending a day in prison is enough to make them say 'Never again'. (As we heard earlier, it didn't have that effect on Michael Howard!) That may be so, but of course it makes nonsense of the idea that sentence lengths should be proportionate to the crime; and for such offenders the deterrence probably took place much earlier, when they were convicted, or even when they knew they had been found out. And *saying* 'Never again' is one thing; the reality of the stigma of a prison record with the substantial disadvantages that are inseparable from it is quite another. I'm afraid that the 'clang of the gates' is one of those euphemistic metaphors used by lawyers (and, to be fair, by many others) to conceal a harsh reality, which may mean the loss of a job and trauma to the offender's children — to say nothing of the fact that (like mandatory minimum sentences at the other extreme) it throws the idea of 'proportionate' punishment out of the window. Rather the same thinking lay behind imposition of 'a taste of prison' by refusing bail, which the judge rightly criticised. Another such phrase is the 'clip round the ear', which the Judge also mentioned. Judges refer to a 'deterrent sentence' either to mean one which they rather hope, without much evidence, will be deterrent, or as a euphemism for a retributive one. I won't labour the point, but I do urge people, and especially lawyers, to use the same precision of language when talking about sentencing as they do in other contexts.

A further conventional aim of sentencing is rehabilitation. The Judge spoke of balancing this against other factors such as retribution, but the problem here is that either there is an attempt to combine it with punishment, in which case the two aims are in conflict and undermine each other; or it replaces punishment, in which case there is a problem of fairness as between an offender who is punished and another who, after committing a similar offence, is given a rehabilitative sanction. Just to complicate matters, rehabilitation can also be unfair by being oppressive, as the Probation Officer explained. Some people have argued that this is a matter of rights—a person has a right to be treated as a responsible autonomous individual and not demeaned by being labelled as maladjusted or inadequate; but it is also important in a very tangible way, because states have shown an inclination to deprive people of their liberty for long periods in order to 'cure' them. In English approved schools, not so long ago, this meant that wayward young people, even if their offences were petty, could be sent to an institution until their eighteenth birthday, which might be the equivalent of a prison sentence of several years; and in some American states offenders were sentenced to long indeterminate periods of imprisonment, which could be quite disproportionate to the offence, especially if the prisoner stood up for his rights, or those of other inmates, and was therefore labelled a troublemaker. A famous example was the Black activist George Jackson, author of *Soledad Brother*, who was sentenced for an indeterminate period for a robbery of $70, and because he would not respond to 'treatment' was still in prison 11 years later when he was killed in a prison fight.

The rehabilitators have damaged their case by going up two blind alleys: the 'medical model', which regarded all offenders as suffering from a psychological defect which could be 'treated', and the social deterministic one, which went so far towards blaming social conditions for delinquency that it seemed to deny offenders' accountability for their own actions. Probation officers in their social inquiry (pre-sentence) reports and lawyers in their pleas in mitigation have seemed to encourage this attitude: they imply that 'with such a background, he couldn't help it'; and it is not surprising that some of the offenders used similar arguments to justify their behaviour. But the advocates of 'just deserts' (the new name for retribution) were themselves in a more unpleasant dead-end; at least the rehabilitators, despite some excesses, were in the main trying to help people, not to hurt them.

According to the often-quoted dictum of the liberal prison commissioner of the 1930s and 1940s Alexander Paterson, you cannot train people for freedom in conditions of captivity. I do not deny that it is possible for rehabilitative activity to take place in prisons: vocational training, the Alternatives to Violence Project, the Sex Offenders Treatment Programme, and many more; but as long as prisons are primarily places of punishment, any benefit will take place in spite of them rather than because of them: the punitive and the rehabilitative effects are in conflict, and the demands of security and a growing prison population make inroads into the funding available, so that few prisoners can benefit from these programmes.

From the offender's point of view, blaming 'maladjustment' or 'social conditions' tends to devalue the offender's own responsibility: from the point of view of human rights and dignity it seems to deny free will, and leads to C S Lewis's strictures. From the point of view of retributivists it looked like making excuses to escape punishment. Philosophers like Hegel wrote of the 'right to be punished', and Lewis claimed that 'to be punished, however severely, . . . is to be treated as a human person made in God's image' (quoted by Walker, 1991: 61). They were reacting against the idea of human beings being manipulated by 'men in white coats' and treated, in Lewis's words, like 'infants, imbeciles and domestic animals'. That was a reproach which could be made against some versions of the 'medical model', before it was understood that in many situations crime can be a rational choice, but for many people it is not exactly a free choice, because of the pressures they are under, and rehabilitation can take the form of helping people to make better informed choices. In any case punishment itself is a fairly crude way of trying to manipulate behaviour, and a demeaning one at that: an odd way of recognising that people are 'made in God's image'.

How much punishment or rehabilitation?

The Judge said enough to show that the problem of the length of sanctions is already daunting enough if we take the various aims of sentencing singly. Let us look at the example of deterrence. Suppose that a woman has committed a fraud and we want to deter her from doing it again. If she was previously regarded as a respectable citizen, the conviction alone will act as a severe sanction; but the more she was driven by necessity, for example to feed herself and her family, the more severe a punishment will have to be to deter her. In any case there is no means of knowing how much is necessary to have this effect on her, and almost any punishment will make her situation worse. If however we punish her differently or not at all, or use a rehabilitative sanction, this could be seen as unfair to someone else who has committed a similar crime in different circumstances. There is no right answer within a retributive framework.

If we consider the amount of time that will be needed for rehabilitation in isolation from the seriousness of the offence, there is still no way of predicting how long will be required; insofar as it can be assessed, it is a clinical judgment, not a judicial one. It is hard enough to assess after the individual has taken part in the programme, and almost impossible before.

If the court attempts to combine more than one principle in one sentence, the contradiction becomes even more intractable, because we are no longer comparing sentences for different offenders: for one and the same offender a short sentence for a minor offence may not be enough to rehabilitate him if he has been severely damaged by a disastrous upbringing, whereas a longer one, imposed with worthy rehabilitative intentions, would be disproportionate to the seriousness of the offence.

So although the Judge said that she and her colleagues try to balance the conflicting criteria, these are in totally different dimensions, and I don't see how the two can be reconciled. To say that they are weighed against each other (in the scales of justice, presumably) is a fudge; any resulting sentence will be too long for denunciation and too short for rehabilitation, or vice versa, except when the two may accidentally coincide. This should make us think about the primary purpose of the criminal justice system. The Crime and Disorder Act 1998 makes local authorities and the police responsible for crime prevention policy, but it does not acknowledge the corollary: that this should therefore no longer be regarded as a primary function of the courts.

Given the difficulty of determining the lengths of sentences on utilitarian grounds, practitioners, academics and politicians have turned to symbolic ones: the sentence should be proportionate to the seriousness of the offence. This seems self-evident until we look at it more closely. Should punishment be imposed even if there were reason to believe that it would make matters worse? (A thoroughgoing retributivist would presumably say 'Yes'.) Should it be proportionate to offences or to offenders? Should it take account of differences in the impact on different offenders (and if so how can we assess them?). The American Professor Michael Tonry has pointed out that 'just deserts' focuses on crimes and criminal records, to the exclusion of ethically important differences in their circumstances. Two years' imprisonment in a maximum security prison may be no more than a rite of passage for a Los Angeles gang member, but for an attractive, effeminate 20-year-old it brings the terror of repeated sexual victimisation. For the 40-year-old head of a household, it could mean the loss of his job, his home and his family; and for a 75-year-old in poor health it could mean death. Thus the 'just deserts' concept follows the first principle of equal treatment under the law, to treat like cases alike, but fails to observe the second, to treat different cases differently (Tonry, 1996: 13-19).

There is no basis for the claim that a certain punishment is equivalent to a certain offence. Professor Walker makes a distinction between absolute equivalence, or commensurability (a given offence is 'worth' a given amount of pain), which nobody nowadays regards as an achievable aim (Walker, 1991: 101), and relative equivalence, or proportionality. Offences can be graded in degrees of seriousness, and so can punishments, but there is no agreed base-line or scale: it is as if an offence were assessed at, say, 60 degrees, but there was no basis for deciding whether the scale of Fahrenheit, Centigrade or Réaumur was being applied. We measure guilt in months and years, or in money; but the symbol of justice is a pair of scales, which presumably measure it in kilograms. It is even more difficult to claim that there is a 'right' punishment if we look at different countries: in Sweden, 95 per cent of prison sentences are for two years or less, and none for over ten years, while in the United States 67 per cent are for over four years, including 43 per cent over ten years (Tonry, 1996: 187-8). The difference cannot be convincingly explained by differences in the crime rate, because no one can prove the 'direction of causality': in other words, a hard-liner might say 'We have to use prison a lot in America because we have so much serious crime', but it could just as well be argued that the high crime rate is the result, among many other factors, of the large numbers of people coming out of prison, harmed or embittered by the experience and with little support in the community.

The same amount of punishment can have very different effects on different people, as Professor Tonry pointed out; so should there be less harsh prisons for white-collar offenders because they are not used to roughing it, and/or because they have suffered more in other ways, such as loss of status and career prospects? (This is what often happens in practice at the moment: such offenders tend to be classified as good security risks, partly perhaps because their social standing makes a good impression on interviewing officials, and so they are quickly sent to low-security prisons.) It has been suggested, apparently in earnest, that electric shocks would be a suitable punishment. An American professor believed that they compared favourably with some of the revolting punishments used in the past, including Jeremy Bentham's whipping machine (which is not much of a recommendation); they leave no body scars or mutilations (hence their popularity with the world's torturers) and can be precisely graded in intensity. The professor notes that a medical examination would be necessary to establish the offender's fitness to receive punishment, but does not say what he would do instead with a person with a weak heart, or a pregnant woman (Newman, 1983). In fact electric shocks have been used, and not in the carefully graduated way Newman suggested: Ronnie Hawkins, convicted of theft in Los Angeles, was blasted with 50,000 volts for eight seconds, leaving him 'as stiff as a board', for the offence of repeatedly interrupting the judge. This 'stun belt' has been used 27 times since it came on the market, eight of them 'accidental' (*Guardian*, 10 July 1998).

Flexibility

Should the system be flexible or inflexible? Both have disadvantages. I will say something about inflexible guidelines in a moment. Flexibility brings its own problems, such as the confusion which the Probation Officer described when well-intentioned judges tried to mix mercy with retribution. The Judge also gave some examples of merciful sentences, which many people would applaud, but is there a coherent principle behind them? Professor Nigel Walker, to whose ideas I am much indebted in this section (Walker, 1995), distinguishes between leniency and mercy. The latter, he says, must be motivated by compassion, not expediency, and must not be whimsical, random or corrupt. Under these headings he includes personal favouritism, bribery, and sentimentality such as 'Christmas sentencing'. He counts as expediency the practice of relieving overcrowding in prisons by early release (now offered to some categories of prisoner in England if they submit to electronic tagging); but it could be argued that this is not expediency but justice, since in overcrowded prisons people experience a given amount of pain in a shorter time. Nor is it true mercy if an offender is given a shorter sentence in order to correct some injustice, for example when the full sentence would cause an offender to suffer unduly on account of youth, age or a serious medical condition, or because he has suffered 'natural punishment', as when his drunken driving led to the death of people he loved. Another reason could be some unusual hardship which the punishment would cause to the offender's innocent dependants; the 'usual' suffering of spouse and children is not considered enough reason for mercy, so how great must the additional suffering of innocent dependants be, in order to qualify? If that criterion were generally applied, it would rule out many fines and most imprisonment.

Walker distinguishes two main classes of mercy. The first is where justice requires leniency, but rules have not yet been formulated for its application, for example reducing the just sentence because an equally guilty accomplice has been sentenced more leniently. The second comprises cases where the 'tariff' sentence would be unfair, such as aged, ill or disabled offenders, but how old or ill do they have to be? Or those who have behaved well since an offence committed a long time ago, but how meritorious must their conduct have been, how long must have elapsed since the offence, and is this unfair to others who do not have such claims to sympathy? It is hardly possible to draw up rules. And then, of course, there would be the equally unanswerable question, How much of the sentence to remit?

Walker's candidates for 'mercy' include, for example, reducing the punishment because of the offender's subsequent remorse, but if remorse is a ground for mercy, how can it be measured? The Judge gave examples of how mercy may (or may not) be exercised in response to a plea from the victim or the victim's family, or because of meritorious conduct unrelated to the offence. The ground for mercy may be unrelated to the offence: a good army record, or saving a child from drowning, or the fact that the penalty would cause distress and harm to the offender's dependants. But these are also difficult to quantify, and the last-named applies to the majority of prison sentences. Should pregnant women be exempt from imprisonment, or mothers of small children (up to what age?), and if so why not fathers?

Harm by numbers

The difficulty in compiling a scale is illustrated by the efforts of two just-deserts theorists, Andrew von Hirsch and Nils Jareborg (1991), to devise yet another yardstick, in addition to blameworthiness and rehabilitation: they propose a method of gauging criminal harm as a scale of seriousness of offences, to be used for determining punishment. They say that seriousness should be based both on the offender's culpability and on the harm done to the victim's standard of living, which immediately creates difficulties, because it is not clear which should take precedence. Next they try to assess a measurement of the 'standard harm' caused by a typical crime of a particular type; but they admit that the impact of, say, a typical burglary will vary between cultures as well as between individuals. They base their assessment of harm on its effect on the victim's living standard. This does have the advantage of providing a single measure of the impact of different types of harm, such as assaults and burglaries; but it is still dependent upon subjective judgments such as the degree of importance to be accorded to privacy (and hence to its invasion by a burglar). Since it is aimed entirely at determining punishment, this theory is of limited use to victims unless they happen to be retributively inclined; the authors admit that it is not oriented to improving matters in future, and the same may be said of retributive punishment; in that case, one may ask, what use is it?

This is all in addition to the basic question which just-deserts theorists do not satisfactorily answer: why does an offender 'deserve' punishment at all; would it not be just as valid to say that he deserves to be required to make amends?

It is hard enough to agree an *order* of seriousness of offences. If we accepted a scale of seriousness based on, say, a public opinion survey, some quite different crimes would end up with the same rating. For example, most people would say that violent crimes are worse than non-violent ones, but it is hard to predict whether defrauding the Inland Revenue of £100,000 would be regarded as more or less serious than, say, hitting someone so that he loses half a day at work. It is just as hard to put punishments in order of severity: would ten years' probation be more serious than even one week or one month in prison? Some quite different punishments would be given the same rating. That would still not tell us what should be the *type* of punishment for a given crime, or what should be the increments by which it is increased, or, most fundamental of all, where the 'anchor' point should be. The Judge claimed that the tariff has internal consistency, but even if those problems were resolved there is no logical means of assigning appropriate *amounts* of punishment to particular offences. One defendant was sentenced to eight years' imprisonment for stealing a Rolls-Royce and driving it for several months (and for having a long criminal record). He pointed out that another man had just been given ten years (or rather, had ten years taken from him) for tormenting his little daughter to death, and said to the judge 'You have made me four fifths as bad as him'. Even if there were a logical basis for the quantum of punishment, the impact of a similar punishment on different people will be very different. For some, prison is a home from home (so where is the punishment? — and what sort of society offers some people a less unpleasant existence in prison than outside?); others become miserable or even suicidal: there were 436 suicides in English prisons between 1990 and 1997, including 88 young people aged from 15 to 21 (Howard League 1998).

If the actual (as opposed to the intended) effect on the victim is brought in to the calculation, logic and fairness become if possible even more unattainable. To take an actual case:

> Two young men have committed similar crimes, but one has no mitigating factors, while the other has gone straight while waiting for trial. The judge performs the necessary mental gymnastics to decide that the first should get a 12-month prison sentence, while the other gets a 200-hour community service order; the sentence on the first is then reduced to six months to reduce his sense of grievance at the disparity, although the Court of Appeal admitted that this 'might be slightly illogical' (*Current Sentencing Practice*, Case 506/1).

Now suppose that these two young men had had different victims, of whom the first pleaded for leniency, and the second told the court that the crime has had a drastic effect on her and her family: does the judge then have to re-calculate, so that perhaps both offenders get the same sentence after all? Or if the attitudes of the victims were reversed, would the gap between the two offenders' sentences be increased, regardless of a possible sense of grievance?

How can we judge that the criminality of a lawyer defrauding clients of £8 million (*Guardian*, 21 December 1995) is of the same order as that of an accomplice to a gang rape (*Guardian*, 19 April 1997)? Both offenders were sentenced to ten years' imprisonment. How can we compare a step-parent convicted of excessive discipline of his step-children (*Guardian*, 29 November; *Observer*, 1 December 1996), a social security fraudster (*Guardian*, 25 March 1983), and a teacher who sexually molested boys

(*Daily Telegraph*, 5 February 1992)? All were sentenced to 15 months, though in the teacher's case the sentence was suspended, prompting the newspaper headline that he was 'freed by judge'. Is attempting to steal £31.8 million (five years' imprisonment: *Guardian*, 1 March 1995) twice as bad as stealing £109,000 (two and a half years: *Guardian*, 5 April 1997)? These are cases culled at random from British newspapers; are the results more coherent if we take a more systematic approach? Judges say that many apparent discrepancies are accounted for by the background to the case, which newspapers often fail to report, and the study which the Civil Servant described after the Politician's talk supports this; but that doesn't help in putting a *figure* on these influences.

Even if we confine ourselves to one category of crime (for example violent, sexual or against property), and within an individual category we agree on the ranking of the offences, we have no rational means of deciding the position of the bottom rung of the ladder or the distance between the rungs. Professor Walker uses the metaphor of 'a ladder with rungs that are both sliding and elastic' (Walker, 1991: 138), which sounds odd, but perhaps no odder than the situation it describes.

Puzzles of this kind led to a return to the retributive philosophy of the 'just deserts' movement. It started in the United States, where the inconsistencies were the most glaring, and has spread to Europe, saying in effect that these anomalies give justice a bad name and are inevitable where different principles are being applied; so let us have a single standard: what does the offender deserve for the offence? This line of argument soon exposed the lack of any agreed standard. The original proponents of 'just deserts', such as von Hirsch, being of a liberal persuasion, thought that as the function of the punishment was to be a purely symbolic, public declaration of the relative seriousness of the various crimes, the sentences need not be very long; but influential people on the Right who still believed in retribution and deterrence wanted the sentences to be not only proportionate but severe, and the 'just deserts' theorists had no convincing answer.

In the United States attempts have been made to draw up inflexible grids, representing the seriousness of the offence and the offender's previous convictions (Minnesota Sentencing Guidelines. Commission, 1982; United States Sentencing Commission, 1987a, b; for a dissenting view, although from a conventional standpoint, see Robinson, 1987). The only discretion allowed to the judge is a small increase or decrease to reflect aggravating or mitigating circumstances; this reduces judges' ability to show mercy, and shifts discretion to the prosecutor, who may mitigate what he regards as excessive severity (or encourage the accused to plead guilty) by bringing a less serious charge. The US Sentencing Commission grades some 2,000 offences, from minor assault in category

3 (there seem to be no categories 1 or 2) to first degree murder in category 43, mostly with one or two additional offence characteristics. Taking for example (and simplifying somewhat) category 25, we find:

Attempt/conspiracy/solicitation to murder (planned, weapon brandished, for money);
Kidnapping/abduction (held over seven days, or under 24 hours if weapon used or serious injury);
Burglary of a residence (value over $5 million and planned or weapon possessed);
Robbery ($50,001-250,000 if weapon used, or $1,000,001-5,000,000 if bodily injury not serious or permanent); and
Certain categories of forcible extortion.

Several drugs offences are in categories 24 and 26. Different offence characteristics increase or decrease the categories. Lower down the scale, say at category 20, we find:

Attempt [etc.] to murder;
Aggravated assault (for money, weapon brandished);
Burglary of a residence $50,001-250,000 (or less if planned, weapon possessed, etc.);
Robbery $10,001-50,000 (or less, cf. burglary);
Bribe involving public official $2 to 5 million;
Certain levels of drugs offences;
Financing extortionate credit;
Arson: property damage by explosives (reckless disregard for safety);
Laundering monetary instruments;
Tax evasion over $5 million (sophisticated).

There is a certain logic in all this, but where does it get you? It is rather like trying to measure the precise attractiveness of a number of Miss World contestants to the nearest gram: wickedness, like beauty, cannot be quantified.

Opponents of 'just deserts' therefore claim: 'For all the rhetoric of just deserts, no retributivist can answer any question about what is the deserved punishment for any act', and 'The spuriousness of retributivist precision in calibrating commensurate deserts should be unmasked' (Braithwaite and Pettit, 1990: 178, 179). Seven years after the Criminal Justice Act 1991 the Court of Appeal was still grappling with the question, 'When is an offence "so serious that only a custodial sentence could be justified?"' (*R v. Howells, The Independent* (Thursday Review), 1 October 1998). Professor Walker (1991: 139) also cannot find a valid justification for retribution: 'If one is a retributivist the choice is between the unquantifiable and the indefensible'.

Therefore I think that the inescapable conclusion is that fair punishment is unattainable; harm is not quantifiable, nor is it possible to inflict an equivalent amount of pain on equivalent offenders, because there is no such thing as an equivalent offender.

Since the fashion in this Symposium is to tell stories, I will do the same; and this is the one I have chosen.

A Lord Chancellor was monstrously fond of fine clothes. One day two weavers came and said that they could make the loveliest material, and clothes made from it also had the property that they were invisible to anyone who was either unfit for his situation or was intolerably stupid. The Lord Chancellor gave them a large sum of money to make these marvellous clothes. Soon he thought he would like to know how they were progressing; so he sent his trusted minister to the weaving shed, where the fraudsters were working at a bare loom.

He couldn't see any material; but he didn't want to admit that he was unfit for his job, or stupid, so he said that the cloth was charming, and reported back to the Lord Chancellor. The weavers now demanded more money for silk and gold thread. A second official was sent, and was likewise unwilling to admit that he was stupid or incompetent, so he also praised the beauty of the material. At last the Lord Chancellor himself went to inspect it, and seeing nothing, wondered whether he was stupid, or unfit to be Lord Chancellor; to show that he was not, he too gave his highest approval to the weavers and their work. The swindlers asked him to take off his clothes, and acted as if they were handing him each piece of the new costume. He walked out in a procession through the streets, and everyone praised his finery, until a little child said 'But he hasn't got anything on!' People in the crowd started to say the same, and the Lord Chancellor began to suspect that they were right; but he said to himself that he must go on with the procession, and walked on, bearing himself more proudly than before.

By re-telling this familiar story, I am pointing out that legal theory has been dressed up in elaborate robes which are supposed to consist of the 'right' sentences for particular crimes with particular aggravating or mitigating circumstances, attempting to balance the factors I have mentioned. But in fact this is an impossible task: there is no such thing as the 'right' sentence, and this fact will not be altered by the Court of Appeal's sentencing guidelines, nor the sentencing panel to advise the Court of Appeal, both provided by the Crime and Disorder Act 1998. It is not merely that in an imperfect world no one will achieve perfection; the whole enterprise is unachievable, using elements which will not mix for purposes which conflict with each other, as if one were trying to paint a picture with a combination of sticking plaster and sulphuric acid. In a word, to mix the metaphors thoroughly, not only does the Lord

Chancellor have no clothes, but he lives in a labyrinthine castle built on sand, from bricks made without straw.

PUNISHMENT

Hence to the question of punishment itself. It sometimes seems as if people are determined to punish other people; if one justification won't stand up, they find another—and another (as the Judge admitted in her fable of the Wolf and the Lamb). We punish the offender because it will make him behave better. He doesn't? then we punish him to deter others. Is that unethical, or ineffective, or both? Then we do it because society needs to symbolise the fact that laws must be upheld. Some claim that people in general have a *Strafbedürfnis* ('need to punish'); as I mentioned at the beginning, a few philosophers, like Hegel, have even claimed that an offender has a right to be punished. But the state does a lot of things to citizens already; if it is going to inflict pain on them, possibly by locking them up or even killing them, it needs some very clearly thought-out reasons.

We have spent some time examining how to decide how much punishment can be justified; but in doing so we have left the fundamental question till last: is punishment justified at all? The public, the judiciary, politicians and the media do not appear to see the irony of responding to the harm committed by the offender by inflicting further harm on him. The Norwegian criminologist Nils Christie (1982) has reminded us of what should be obvious: that punishment is the deliberate infliction of pain by the state on its citizens. Unless there is some overriding justification, this is an abuse of power.

Ethics of punishment

We need to re-examine first principles. Is punishment, the deliberate infliction of pain, ever justified, and if so when and why? There are four positions for which a case can be made.

The first is that *punishment is justified for its own sake*, even a duty. For believers in retribution, this may appear self-evident; the philosopher Kant put it dramatically: 'Even if a civil society were to dissolve itself by common agreement . . . the last murderer remaining in prison must first be executed so that . . . the blood-guilt thereof will not be fixed on the people' (quoted by Walker, 1991: 77). But as Professor Walker asks, even if to deal with offenders is a 'categorical imperative', Kant does not explain why this must be done in a *punitive* way? (p.77 of that work). Kant also says that retribution can be defended on the grounds that an offender has gained an unfair advantage at someone else's expense, and punishment is necessary to restore equilibrium by depriving him of that advantage. As in other contexts, however, this does not explain why the scales could not be balanced through making reparation. Less often quoted is Kant's further point, that each individual has the right to be dealt with solely for what he has done: 'One man ought never to be dealt with *merely* as a means subservient to the purposes of another' (quoted by Walker, 1991: 53), so his punishment should not be determined by its possible effect on other miscreants.

The second position, on the contrary, is that *punishment can only be justified if it works*. As Bentham said, all punishment in itself is evil; more questionably, he maintained that this evil is acceptable as a means to a good end. Indeed since it involves the deliberate infliction of pain (deprivation of liberty), it can be justified only if it works not merely as well as but *better than other responses to wrongdoing*, which is questionable to say the least.

One common argument is that the state has to inflict punishment in order to persuade people not to resort to lynch law. It could be argued that there are more lynchings in the American states with more draconian punishments – apparently the state's punishments serve as a role model, a justification, rather than as a catharsis or lightning conductor. Populist newspapers and television programmes can find people who declare their intention of taking the law into their own hands if they are not satisfied with the official response, both reflecting and perpetuating a culture of exclusion and retribution. To some extent this may be a reflection of inadequate support for victims, as the Victim Assistance Worker pointed out, because it has been found that victims who have received support are less punitive: fewer of the people visited by Victim Support felt more punitive than before the offence, and more of them would accept victim/offender mediation, as compared with those who had no contact with Victim Support (Maguire and Corbett, 1987: 170). What victims and their relatives commonly say is that they want some good to come out of their painful experience.

Thirdly, there is the relatively humane principle implied by the European Convention on Human Rights (Article 3; the Convention has been incorporated into English Law by the Human Rights Act 1998) and the Universal Declaration of Human Rights: that *punishment is justified so long as it is not cruel, inhuman or degrading*. In my opinion, another condition should be added: punishment should not be *excessive* (though I question the implication that punishment is acceptable so long as it meets these criteria). In all of these (especially the last) there are problems of definition. The European Court of Human Rights has distinguished:

• Torture: deliberate inhuman treatment causing very serious and cruel suffering;

- Inhuman treatment: treatment that causes intense physical and mental suffering;
- Degrading treatment: treatment that arouses in the victim a feeling of fear, anguish and inferiority capable of humiliating and debasing the victim and possibly breaking his or her physical or moral resistance.

It has held that severe beating in police custody can be inhuman and degrading; complete sensory and social isolation can be inhuman, although in one case isolation for 17 months was not considered to be of such severity as to fall within Article 3 (Clements, 1994: 111-9). The Eighth Amendment to the United States Constitution states that 'Excessive bail shall not be required, nor excessive fines imposed, nor cruel and unusual punishments inflicted'. By this standard one American court has found that forcing people to live and sleep in a space of less than 50 square feet (about 4.6 square metres) contravened the Eighth Amendment; other courts set higher or lower limits (Powers, 1982: Part 3 Topic 12). But overcrowding is endemic in American prisons, and there is little comfort in the fact that it is less serious in Britain, and much worse in some other countries, as Vivien Stern of Penal Reform International has documented (Stern, 1998; Prison Reform Trust, 1997a). How can we define what forms of punishment are justified?

I will be provocative to make the point: what is punishment? – and where can we draw the borderline with torture? They have in common the deliberate infliction of pain, although the purpose of torture may not, strictly speaking, be punishment; the United Nations Convention against Torture defines it not as exceeding a threshold, but by its purpose: severe pain or suffering inflicted or allowed by an official, for purposes such as obtaining information or a confession; it does not include pain or suffering arising from lawful sanctions (the full text is quoted by Stern, 1998: 213). Most people would surely say that torture is never justified, even if for example it extracts information which helps to combat terrorism and possibly saves lives – mainly because it is simply wrong (the end does not justify the means), but also because it is likely to be counterproductive: the information or confession it extracts may be false, and it gives the terrorists an excuse to continue their fight for freedom from such a barbarous state. Many people consider that the torturer is the terrorists' best recruiting sergeant.

But is it torture, or 'merely' inhuman and degrading, to lock people up where they may live in fear of being assaulted or homosexually raped; or where they constantly agonise over the fate of their partners and children, or are subjected to months or years of grinding boredom;

or to subject them to gross overcrowding or, at the other extreme, to solitary confinement for an indefinite period? In what way is the argument different in the case of punishment? It may be argued that it inflicts a much smaller degree of pain. Western countries do not inflict physical punishment or mutilation, and do not (with the exception of the United States) judicially kill people. But in this country branding and flogging were considered by many to be acceptable, and so were humiliating punishments such as the stocks, and there are still apparently serious calls for them to be brought back, besides the lunatic fringe such as the clergyman who demanded that the thieves of twelve statues of the apostles should have their hands cut off (*Oxford Mail, Guardian*, 10 September 1997). In years to come we may consider it unacceptable to separate people, especially youngsters, from their families and friends in bleak institutions, or to force people who are already poor to pay fines to the state. (Young people who break the law are usually denied the sympathetic term 'youngster'.) When the death penalty was in force, there was revulsion against inflicting it on the young or on pregnant women; now there is unease about separating a young woman offender from her baby (for example *Guardian 2*, 19 May 1998).

So even if the principle of punishment is accepted, the boundary between acceptable and unacceptable forms is a flexible one, usually but by no means always moving in a more humane direction. We must hope (and work) to see the abandonment of measures which today are tolerated, or at least are ignored except by penal reform campaigners. Quite apart from the morality of subjecting people to such conditions, it is not likely to help them to be capable of leading 'a good and useful life' after release, or even to persuade them to want to; to adapt a remark of Talleyrand, ill-treatment of prisoners is worse than a crime, it is a mistake.

The fourth position is simply that *punishment is never justified*. It might be described as a 'pacifist' position: there should be 'disarmament' of the criminal justice system. This position is outlined in a pamphlet by a group of Quakers, always anti-war and anti-slavery, who now questioned criminal justice, on the basis of their respect for the value of every human being, even those who have committed terrible acts. Instead of 'the doubtful exercise of trying to determine the precise degree of pain we should inflict' they propose restorative action, 'a realistic and sometimes rigorous response', arrived at where possible with the offender's co-operation; this may at times be painful to the offender and others, but unlike punishment it causes pain as an incidental by-product, not a primary aim (Six Quakers, 1978: 28). There would be opportunities for the offender to make amends through restorative action, and to apologise to the victim. For the few who would not or could not control their violent impulses there would be small self-contained communities whose purpose would be compulsory segregation, with constructive employment and humane treatment, not punishment.

Thinking on similar lines a criminologist from The Netherlands, Herman Bianchi, has proposed that crime should be thought of as tort, a civil wrong, and criminal law replaced by reparative law. Reparation would be negotiated. For cases involving violence Bianchi proposes the revival of the concept of sanctuary, as used in England, France and The Netherlands until the seventeenth or eighteenth century: a place of refuge, often a church (Beverly Minster was one), where the perpetrator of a serious offence could live until negotiations could take place. If no agreement was reached within three months the offender would be extradited, or given a safe conduct to another sanctuary – or would remain and work there for life. There are parallels in recent times in the use of embassies by dissidents in oppressive countries, and of churches in America by refugees at risk of ill-treatment by the state. This would protect the offender against public anger and violence (which as we have seen is one of the objectives of the criminal law); in the small number of cases where there is a major risk that the offender will commit further serious and violent acts, there would be places of compulsory 'quarantine', but controlled by strict rules to avoid the abuse that could readily creep in (Bianchi, 1986, 1994).

To sum up: The aims of punishment are confused, and there is an unwarranted assumption that conflicting aims can be balanced or combined. General deterrence, the exemplary punishment of one person to frighten others, is unjust and of doubtful effectiveness. Punishment, especially imprisonment, has different effects on different offenders, and undesirable side-effects. There is no basis for deciding how much punishment is needed to deter, and even if there were, it would almost always be different from the amount required for retribution.

The amount of harm or pain suffered by the victim is no less difficult to quantify, and even if this were possible, it would introduce still more inconsistency if used to influence sentencing. Sentences based on rehabilitative principles, on the other hand, take no account of the harm, and there are other problems in determining their duration. There is no basis for equating a particular offence to a particular level of punishment. But more important than talk of levels is the very concept: punishment is either justifiable on certain conditions which the existing system is never likely to meet, or it is not justifiable at all.

A BASIS FOR THE FUTURE

What we have done so far is to start from where we are now. The whole system is riddled with illogicalities and contradictions, but judges, probation officers and prison officers, victim support workers and others do their best to make sense of it because it is all we have got. There is, it seems to me, not much hope of reforming such a flawed paradigm: we need a new one.

The basic questions need re-framing: how do we set about reducing crime, and how do we respond when it occurs? In this context, who are 'we'? Should it be left to agents of the state or local government, or should everyone be involved? How could we spend more effectively the vast sums allocated to law enforcement (which the Civil Servant summarised after the Politician's talk)?

Preventive policies seem as obviously desirable as they do in public health, and I will come back to them later; but first let us look at the response to crimes when they occur. If we go back to first principles, what should happen when a crime is committed? Two Australians, John Braithwaite and Philip Pettit, a criminologist and a philosopher respectively, have suggested the parameters which might define such a system.

In a communitarian concept of society, citizens have as much autonomy as possible, and the state intervenes as little as possible ('As much State as necessary, as little State as possible.'). They describe this view as 'republican', by which they mean that it maximises not merely individual freedom (*libertas*) but freedom within society (*civitas*, citizenship). State power should be kept in check; there should be no excessive policing or surveillance, no punishments which maim people. Crime is wrong because it deprives other people of autonomy. This view of society leads to certain conclusions about society's response to crime. We should try to restore the victim's autonomy by repairing the harm done, but in doing so we should not deprive the offender of more autonomy than necessary. The response should also express reprimand (which, unlike punishment, shows *why* measures are imposed on the offender); having done so, it should assist the reintegration of both victims and offenders into society. The response should be 'satiable', unlike conventional punishments which can be 'insatiable' because there is always pressure to do more, to more people, in the belief that this will reduce crime and satisfy people, but it never does.

The goal of autonomy (for which, for some reason, these authors use the word 'dominion') means freedom from the use of arbitrary power or interference. The burden of fear for ordinary citizens should be lessened, but as few activities as possible should therefore be defined as criminal, or prosecuted: as the Psychologist suggested in discussion, prosecution should be kept in reserve as a lever to secure compensation, as is normally done in Inland Revenue cases. Braithwaite and Pettit give the example of a nursing home, where illegal restraint of patients could be dealt with as a crime of violence, but the normal procedure of state inspectors is through adopting a diagnostic and catalytic role to promote good practice rather than by immediately threatening punishment. (But I am sure they would agree that this needs to be energetically done, and not used by governments as an excuse for cutting enforcement costs, still less for avoiding confrontation with employers.) Punishments should be kept to a minimum, and should preferably involve the transfer of property to the victim or the victim's family, or a payment to a victims compensation fund.

Professor Braithwaite says that there is a 'deterrence trap'. Assuming a rational person calculating whether a crime is worth the risk, if the chances of detection are small, the penalty has to be huge — so large that either if someone does commit the crime and is caught, he will be prepared to go to great lengths to escape conviction and punishment, or the state will shrink back from imposing it, as with the death penalty in eighteenth-century and nineteenth-century England. Braithwaite argues instead for 'the strength of weak sanctions'. The more serious the abuse, the more likely it is that many people will be involved. In some cases there may be a boss who can stop the misconduct. More commonly, there are subordinates, one or two of whom disapprove of the abuse and will take up the offer of an opportunity to stop it by revealing it; this works because it is in the long-term interest of the company to be seen to be reputable. In Canberra, Australia, it has been found that conferences of family and friends of drink-drivers can come up with plans to prevent a recurrence; for example drinking mates sign a designated driver agreement, or bar staff at the drinker's pub undertake to call a taxi when the offender has drunk too much. Whole-school action to prevent bullying works on this principle (Robinson and Maines, 1997); and the Psychologist has already referred to the 'soft' approach of the Truth and Reconciliation Commission in South Africa, and of the Canadian community which used similar methods to persuade its sex offenders to come into the open. Braithwaite concedes that there are some people who will not respond; it may then be necessary to restrain them by disqualification or physical containment (Braithwaite, 1998 III J).

Of the major industrial countries one which comes close to a restorative philosophy is Japan, according to Masters (1998b). The police are strongly community-based, providing services such as notification of lost property, directing people to addresses in Japan's un-named streets, and visiting local residents twice a year at home and at work, getting to know them and giving crime prevention advice. (This of course is a practice which could be regarded as benign or oppressive, depending on the context; and Japan is not short of gangsters and white-collar criminals.) Detectives treat the suspect as essentially a good person who made a mistake, in accordance with the Buddhist proverb 'Hate the sin and not the sinner' (which in the West is usually attributed to St Augustine, as the Psychologist mentioned, with the word 'not' replaced by 'love'). Police have considerable discretion not to send cases to the prosecutor; but the expectation is that the offender will make a sincere apology, and show his sincerity by offering reparation, and that the victim will accept it. Prosecutors then suspend prosecution in a further 30 per cent of cases, and when cases do go to court, judges feel able to impose short sentences, averaging less than one year, on repentant offenders. Moreover, a similar style of discipline is used in Japanese schools. The effect is conducive to reintegrating the offender into the community, and some criminologists regard it as the reason for Japan's unusually low rates of both crime and imprisonment, compared with other industrial nations (Haley, 1989; Masters, 1998b).

What can we learn from the theories and practices that have unfolded in such different parts of the world? I will leave the operational practicalities to the Mediator; but I will say something about the principles which underlie the practice. The theory has in fact evolved from practice. The first strand arose within the conventional system, when in 1974 a probation officer in Ontario, Canada, persuaded a judge to let two young offenders meet their victims and negotiate reparation for the damage caused (Peachey, 1989; Wright, 1996: ch.5). This developed into victim/offender mediation, which has spread from Canada and the United States to the United Kingdom and several other European countries. The second strand, known as 'conferencing', has grown from the interaction of Western and Indigenous peoples, in New Zealand and Canada. Here the typical pattern is not a one-to-one meeting of the victim and the offender; the extended families of victims and offenders are invited to take part in devising an action plan for the young person.

For the third strand we go back to theory, and back to Braithwaite; at the time when New Zealanders were developing conferencing, Braithwaite was independently working on his theory of 'reintegrative shaming'. He argued that shame is more effective than punishment in deterring people; but he distinguished between the stigma of a degradation ceremony, usually conducted by strangers, which tends to make the culprit feel more excluded than before, and 'reintegrative' shaming, in which people whose opinion matters to him condemn his behaviour while offering him the prospect of reacceptance into the law-abiding community. He then discovered that the New Zealanders were basing their judicial system on Maori practice called 'family group conferencing' using very similar processes. Although the Maori tradition is rural, the method has been applied in cities such as Wellington and Auckland. With some modifications they were adopted in the 'community accountability conferences' pioneered in the town of Wagga Wagga, New South Wales, since when all the Australian states have introduced varying forms of conferencing. A large research project is underway in the Australian capital Canberra (Sherman and Strang, 1997). The version used in some parts of Canada, in which a judge and other criminal justice officials also take part, is known as a 'sentencing circle'.

These practices developed at about the same time in three continents, North America, Europe and Australasia, and obviously there are differences relating to the cultures, legal systems and urban or rural locations. A family of theories is evolving. Different aspects and methods are emphasised, but there is a common underlying philosophy; the Restorative Justice Consortium (1999) has drawn up a definition and standards, and guidelines for good practice have been drawn up in Britain and Germany (Mediation UK, 1998; Servicebüro, 1998). An International Network for Research on Restorative Justice for Juveniles and a European Forum for Victim/Offender Mediation and Restorative Justice have been formed, both based in the Law Faculty of the Catholic University of Leuven, Belgium.

Putting theory into practice

One of the first theorists was Howard Zehr (1990), unusual because he was also a practitioner: he was the director of the first Victim/Offender Reconciliation Program in the United States, in the country town of Elkhart, Indiana. He listed a number of ways in which restorative justice differed from conventional justice (and perhaps exaggerated the dichotomy a bit to make the point); I will quote a few of them (*Table 1*).

I think you will get a better idea of the nature of the beast from the account which the Mediator is about to give; so I will finish with some thoughts on a strategy for putting this concept into practice, in a British context at least. Restorative justice is as different from conventional justice as Parliamentary democracy from the Divine Right of Kings; but there will still be a need for courts, just as there is still a place for a head of state. And we need a transition, not a revolution! As *Table 1* suggests, the conventional system says in effect to the offender 'You have broken the law, you must be punished, then we will try to give you some help in recovering from the effects of the punishment. In some cases, if the offence isn't too bad, we will offer the help without the punishment. This process doesn't usually involve victims, but we are trying to be more aware of them'.

Retributive justice	Restorative justice
Wrong as a violation of rules	Wrong as violation of people, relationships
Wrongs create guilt	Wrongs create liabilities and obligations
Crime seen as categorically different from other harms	Crime recognised as related to other harms and conflicts
Debt paid by taking punishment	Debt paid by making right
Focus on past	Focus on future
Imposition of pain to punish and deter	Reparation as a means of restoring both parties
Harm by offender balanced by harm to offender	Harm by offender balanced by making right
Offender denounced	Harmful act denounced
Justice serves to divide	Justice aims at bringing together
Victims' needs and rights ignored	Victims needs and rights central
Ignores social, economic and moral context of behaviour	Total context relevant
Process alienates	Process aims at reconciliation
State monopoly on response to wrongdoing	Victim, offender and community roles acknowledged
Community on sideline, represented abstractly by state (except for lay magistrates in England and Wales, and juries)	Community as facilitator in restorative process
	(Extracted from Zehr, 1995)

Table 1

Restorative justice begins by addressing the victim:

You have been harmed, and we will try to help you to recover; if we know who the offender is, we will require him to make amends. If you and the offender are willing, we will arrange for you to meet (or communicate indirectly), so that you can tell the offender the effects of what he has done to you, and work out with him what he will do to make up for it.

A corresponding message is given to the offender; some of these things are not pleasant for him or her to do, but that is not the reason why they are required: punishment for its own sake has no place in restorative justice. Where possible members of the community are involved in enabling healing and reintegration to take place, in a variety of ways summed up in the word 'reparation'.

The present and the future

How is restorative justice developing, and what is its future'? I will take England and Wales as an example; people with knowledge of other countries can make comparisons and contrasts.

Restorative justice is not a sudden innovation; its development has been gradual over many years. It began with ways of making things better for the offender and (much later) the victim, separately, as the Probation Officer and the Victim Assistance Worker have described. This might be described as 'unilateral' restorative justice.

Now we have in England two recent laws, mentioned by the Victim Assistance Worker, which have been described as restorative. The first is the Crime and Disorder Act 1998. This provides that local youth offending teams (YOTs) are created, with representatives of social services, police, education and other agencies. To take one of the new measures as an example, when a court is considering making a reparation order the YOT will arrange for a report to be written on the young offender suggesting suitable types of reparative activity, which are intended to relate closely to the type of offence, and to be proportionate to it. They may involve the victim, for example working for him or her or taking part in victim/offender mediation; in that case the victim is to be consulted first.

This does not appear to incorporate the idea of giving the conflict back to its owners, described by Christie (1977), not the respect for autonomy of Braithwaite and Pettit (1990). Decisions, or at least recommendations, are made mainly by officials and courts, even if there is some consultation. With regard to the process, victim/offender mediation seems to be regarded as an optional extra; as for the outcome, a narrow and somewhat punitive view is taken of reparation. There is pressure for speed, as the Victim Assistance Worker pointed out; the agenda is that of the government, not the participants, and the rhetoric is about being tough, punitive and controlling, and confronting the offender. I would describe this as 'authoritarian' restorative justice. In England 'nanny state' is a pejorative term for a government which is too protective of its citizens: but nannies can be authoritarian as well as caring, and this is a tendency of some politicians and officials.

It is fair to say, however, that some of the guidance issued by the Home Office and the Youth Justice Board (responsible for implementing the youth justice provisions of the Act), gives a more restorative interpretation, pointing out for example that a criterion for successful completion of a reparation order should be that it helps victims to come to terms with what they have suffered and that they feel the process to be of benefit (Home Office 1998c; Youth Justice Board 1999). Early signs are that the pilot programmes in London, Hampshire and elsewhere are trying to apply these principles, as far as the Act permits.

The second piece of new English legislation is the Youth Justice and Criminal Evidence Act 1999. This provides that almost all first-time offenders under 18 years old who plead guilty are ordered by the court to attend a youth offender panel. The panel will consist of three people, including one member of a YOT; it is not yet clear who the others will be. There is nothing to prevent suitably trained lay members of the community, rather than professionals, from taking part in panels, but there is nothing which requires this to happen. The offender can be accompanied by one person of his or her choice aged over 18, with the agreement of the panel, and the panel may also allow the victim to attend, in addition to 'any person who appears . . . capable of having a good influence on the offender'. The aim is to reach agreement with the offender on a programme of behaviour intended to prevent his or her re-offending; it may include financial reparation to the victim, attending mediation sessions, unpaid work for the community, attending school, staying at home or staying away from certain places, or taking part in specified activities such as treatment or training.

This is moderately restorative as far as the offender is concerned, but the victim is only 'allowed' to attend; it is said to have been based on the idea of family group conferencing, but there is no provision for the offender's extended family or the victim's family or supporters to be present—a feature of the original New Zealand process which reportedly works well. But the aim is to reach agreement with the offender, so it could be described as less authoritarian than the reparation orders, although victims might feel that it was still somewhat unilateral, in the offender's favour.

Advocates of restorative justice believe that it should progress further along the spectrum towards what might be called 'democratic' restorative justice. The Mediator will be describing the procedure; I will just outline its distinguishing characteristics. The first would be the maximum involvement of members of the community in working out their own restorative solutions, including of course victims and offenders themselves, and often their families or other supporters. The procedure described above would be turned round, so that the central part would be to offer victims and offenders the chance to communicate, and to agree on how the offender could make amends; the court's role would be as a safeguard, to ensure that the process was carried out well, and that agreements were not unfair to either the victim or the offender. Courts would also decide contested cases, and impose restraints or custody where these were necessary for the protection of the public. Secondly, a broader view would be taken of reparation: actions of the kind envisaged by the Youth Justice and Criminal Evidence Act would be included, as an indication of the offender's earnest desire to make things right. The reparative tasks would be chosen not because they were unpleasant, but because, besides being useful, they showed what the offender could do.

Members of the community would also have an active role in the conferencing process; the most 'democratic' services would be those run by independent non-govermental organizations, whose management committees would include suitable representation of the statutory agencies such as police, probation, the Crown Prosecution Service and the judiciary, in addition to Victim Support. Members of the public would be trained to become lay mediators (and members of youth offending panels). A national organization would maintain standards of mediating, administration and training, by a system of accreditation — as Mediation UK is doing. Accredited services would be funded by national or local government — preferably with some funds from other sources, to ensure a degree of independence. Democratic restorative justice would be inclusive: there would be no limits on the age of the offender or the type of the offence, subject only to screening to ensure the safety of the participants, because otherwise victims of other offenders or offences would be excluded.

In this way the community could contribute to the process, and learn from it what measures were needed to reduce the pressures which lead to similar crimes. This would form part of a crime reduction strategy, which would be disentangled from sentencing and would have much in common with a strategy for social reform. That is why, on the basis of my analysis of criminal justice, I propose that we should work towards replacing it with restorative justice.

DISCUSSION

Q. The Psychologist admitted that if punishment is severe enough, and certain enough, it does deter. Don't Islamic countries, with their low crime rates, bear this out? And if it works, isn't it ethically justified?

A. Statistics from those countries are not readily available here, so as far as we are concerned the evidence for the low crime rate is only anecdotal. As for cutting off the hand of a thief, which is what many westerners think of as the epitome of Islamic law, I would say first of all that we should be slow to condemn nations which use physical and capital punishments when we have used them ourselves in the not-sodistant past, and we still make large-scale use of imprisonment which is nothing to be proud of. Even if it prevented theft, would we really want to live in a country which cut off people's hands and feet? It could happen to a member of your family. As regards the alleged effectiveness of the punishment, in close-knit communities it may be another case where the certainty of detection, rather than the severity, is the crucial factor; and of course disabling the offender makes it much harder for him to earn an honest living.

I have been asked questions like this before, and I have done some research. At least one Islamic scholar questions whether 'cutting off hands' in the Quran is to be taken literally. Muhammad Zafrulla Khan, at one time Foreign Minister of Pakistan and later President of the International Court of Justice at The Hague, writes that the term *qat'a* (cutting off) could mean merely 'circumscribing the use of', and *aidee* (hands) can connote strength or capacity. 'Cutting off hands' could therefore be interpreted as 'prohibiting free movement', in other words imprisonment (Khan, 1967: 74-6), although some states have taken it all too literally, including Judge Khan's country Pakistan at a later date (Zia-ul-Haq, 1979). It should also be said that strict standards of proof are required, and that the need for mercy and generosity, both to one's family and to strangers, is stressed in the Quran (for example IV: 40); if this precept were followed, it could reduce the pressure to steal.

Q. Don't you think that offenders will quickly learn to play the system, so as to get off as lightly as possible?

A. No doubt they will try, but I am encouraged by the finding of early Home Office research that in one victim/offender mediation project 57 per cent of offenders said they had taken part in order to get their sentences reduced; but the prospect of the meeting focused their minds on 'What shall I say to the victim?' rather than 'What shall I get out of taking part?', and afterwards only 17 per cent gave a reduction of sentence as one of the benefits of meeting. Many were impressed by the understanding shown by victims (Marshall and Merry, 1990: 154-8). Seeing the harm suffered by victims may not change the attitudes of long-term professional criminals — though even that is possible — but the great majority will be able to realise that, unlike a punitive system which first hurts and stigmatises them and then, if they're lucky, provides after-care to re-integrate them into the community, restorative justice can reintegrate them from the outset.

SESSION 7

The Mediator

What mediators encourage people to do is to look for common ground, and that is what I shall try to do in a moment. We also help people to look for constructive ways forward, so I shall not dwell on the problems which other speakers have talked about, although there was much agreement about them; that is an essential first step, but now it is time to look to the future (and in many places the future is already here, as we shall see). May I just say at first that I have been described as a Mediator, and I am one, but it is a rather limited description of what I do. It would give a fuller picture of my work if I were called, say, a 'restorative justice development worker'; but for brevity I am happy to use the simpler title.

I will start from what I believe to be common ground as regards the way society should respond to crime. Secondly, in the light of the problems of punishment which we have heard about, we need to think what to put in its place, and I will propose a fourfold strategy. Then I will describe how restorative justice works in relation to the present justice system, and the participants' point of view. I will consider how it could be implemented, whether it 'works', and in conclusion, the effect it would have on existing institutions. I will ask the Civil Servant to give some detailed information, as before; and I have prepared a hand-out which tries to answer some common questions asked about restorative justice (see *Appendix* to report of Session 7).

Everyday responses

I think it would be fair to say, on the evidence that other speakers have put before this Symposium, that the following ideas would receive wide support. Firstly, the community's response when a crime is committed should begin with the individual victim of the crime (I am simplifying, of course; as we know, in many cases either there is no individual victim, or a person who is maltreated turns on their persecutor so that in a sense both are offenders and both are victims). Victims should be offered help and support, and be kept informed of the processes of justice. They want a process that does not add to their pain. They would like the harm that they have suffered to be acknowledged, both on behalf of the community and if possible by the offender himself. They would like some assurance that action will be taken to reduce the likelihood of others experiencing the same. Many of them would welcome the opportunity to speak to the offender, face-to-face or at least indirectly, to let him know what effect his actions have had on them (and often their families) to ask questions and many would like to be involved in working out what form the amends should take, which will be a question for us to look at later.

Secondly, what should happen to offenders? Many people, whether victims or not, would like them to be held accountable for what they have done, and to make some form of amends, either to the victim, or to the community, or by co-operation with any training or treatment that will help him or her to avoid similar behaviour in future. They want this to 'cost' the offender at least some effort, even if he has no money with which to pay compensation. Most would agree that those who are seriously likely to be seriously violent have to be restrained, but with the minimum necessary use of force.

There is a widespread feeling that punishment, however much some people clamour for it, doesn't achieve much, and is only used because 'something' should be done; many victims no longer want it if they feel they have been well supported, as the Victim Assistance Worker mentioned. Some want the offender to be punished, but others do not, or at least not by imprisonment; or they want acknowledgement and believe that punishment is the only way in which the system provides it—if it were available in a more constructive form, they would choose that. It does not appear that the majority of victims, in Britain at least, are more punitive than the rest of the population, nor do they want to be involved in deciding punishments. There are those who want to have a say in these decisions too, but it appears that most are content to leave it to the judges. Some people, let's face it, *are* punitive. All in all, this is a complex subject, as previous speakers have shown, and the question of punishment, whatever our own views, cannot be described as common ground.

As for what offenders themselves want, probably the only generalisation one can make is that they want to feel fairly dealt with. Most, naturally, want to avoid punishment, although there are some who accept it as the only available way of demonstrating regret (or as a way to show how tough they are). Others would like the victim to know that they regret what they have done: but few would spontaneously meet face-to-face to apologise—it is a daunting prospect.

Thirdly, what does the community want? Insofar as it has a collective voice, probably (like the victims themselves) it wants victims to be supported if they need it, for example through Victim Support and compensation for crimes of violence (compensation for property crimes probably has to be left to private insurance, except for those on the lowest incomes who can be helped through the state social security system in those countries where there is one). It wants offenders to make amends. There are other things which many people probably recognise as desirable, such as reintegrating offenders and enabling them to make reparation, for example by enabling them to do community service, or to undertake training or treatment programmes that will help them to avoid future offending. It must however be admitted that members of the community will sometimes have to be pushed into providing the necessary time and money to enable this to happen.

I also believe that most people, if asked, would also support the principle of prevention: that information should be fed back from the agencies that deal with crimes to those responsible for crime policy, to improve the way crime is tackled. It is often said that the 'criminal justice system' is not a system, because its parts do not interact with each other in a planned way. A further principle, then, is that it *should* be a system: that is, if the state is intervening in people's lives, it should study the cases that it deals with, providing feedback of information to the crime prevention agency both from the point of view of security (locks, alarms, Neighbourhood Watch, and so on) and of reducing pressures towards crime (for example by providing the right education, work, recreation and nurture for young people, persuading them to avoid drugs, and enabling them to make something of their lives). As one writer has put it, 'Instead of asking how effective our programmes are in controlling people and crime, we should be trying to find out what is so lacking in the lives of our neighbours that they see no alternative but a life of crime and violence' (Elias, 1993: 123). Policy-makers need to abandon their pre-conceived assumptions that the courts could prevent crime if they had more powers, as the Politician reminded us earlier when she spoke of King Canute.

That is the first part of what I believe to be common ground. The second is the political and philosophical approach which was summarised by the Philosopher, based (if I may grossly oversimplify) on maximising individual autonomy and community action and minimising the intervention of the state. You will notice what is *not* included in these aims. In the new society which he described, social agencies *other than* criminal justice are responsible for keeping down the total crime rate, and share responsibility for reducing re-offending, under the co-ordination of a government department for crime reduction. Together they would integrate children into society and its values from an early age, and reintegrate those who went astray; on the other hand, the crime reduction department would advise on ways of reducing pressures towards crimes and opportunities for committing them. Central government would, as a Home Office committee recommended in 1991, provide a 'community safety impact statement' for all new legislation and major policy initiatives (Home Office, 1991: 35) to see if they were likely to increase pressures and opportunities for crime, just as the Treasury considers financial implications. This approach is perhaps not common ground yet, but current thinking is moving on these lines, especially among those who follow the research (Gulbenkian, 1995; Utting, 1996; Goldblatt and Lewis, 1998) and I think that when people stop to think about it they will find it a relatively uncontroversial one. The British government has accepted a major recommendation of the 1991 Report in the Crime and Disorder Act 1998, which requires local authorities and police services to draw up crime and disorder strategies in co-operation with other agencies, and to consider the crime and disorder implications of their work. Certainly it is my experience that people nod in agreement when I say, for example, that it is a good idea to start in schools to show children ways of resolving conflict without violence and the advantages of treating each other (and adults) with respect.

Let me stress that a justice system cannot be just unless it is based on principles. It also has to be clear about aims, of course, otherwise it cannot know whether it 'works'; but without principles there will be a temptation to cut corners in achieving the aims, and these may themselves be flawed. There may not be unanimity about the principles, and they may vary in different times and cultures; but they provide a coherent structure without which law enforcement slips easily into inhumanity—and hence ineffectiveness.

The Philosopher has suggested a set of principles on which I believe there will be fairly wide agreement, and I will describe how a system based on such principles could work.

IN PLACE OF PUNISHMENT

My next point is more controversial. When liberal reformers are making a case for moderating the inhumane, illogical or ineffective aspects of the penal system, they often try to show that they are tough and realistic by saying something like 'Of course, nobody will deny that criminals must be punished, but . . . '. Well, I am this nobody! Before you accuse me of being soft and unrealistic, let me explain what I mean. If you will forgive all the negatives, not to punish does not have to mean doing nothing. Nor does it have to mean rehabilitation; as the Probation Officer pointed out, that does not satisfy the common feeling that offenders should 'pay back', which points to one aspect of an alternative to punishment: reparation. The second aspect is a new way of looking at shame. The third is to look not just at the outcome of any intervention, but at the process itself. Fourthly, there would be a new approach to crime prevention. Let us consider these one by one.

Reparation

The first distinguishing feature of restorative justice is that it is based on the idea that the response to crime should be to put right the harm, as far as possible, and not, as hitherto, to inflict further harm on the offender. As has been said, that achieves nothing except to add to the total amount of harm in the world (Wright, 1992). It is appropriate that as much as possible of the making good should be done by the wrongdoer, as far as he is able (provided, of course, that he is caught). This is in keeping with the feeling among people in general and victims in particular that some good should follow the harm, even if the harm itself cannot be undone.

The victim/offender dialogue itself, described below, is one aspect of the reparation. Often a symbolic act is the answer: the offender agrees to buy a token replacement for what he took, and perhaps to sell a valued possession (a stereo, a motor-bike) to pay for it. The victim may not want that, and ask instead that he perform some community service, for example to a charitable organization. The agreement may include measures such as not going out after a certain time, or not mixing with delinquent associates; this could be regarded as punishment, but in a restorative context is more appropriately thought of as preventive, and would have been agreed by the person concerned.

In many cases, especially with juvenile offenders, what the victim wants most is action to reduce the chances that they will re-offend — not only for the sake of potential victims, but from concern for the young person himself or herself. The offender will then agree to the proposed measures, such as remedial education, job training, or other forms of rehabilitation like drug therapy or alcohol therapy and the community (which may mean the local authority, employers, voluntary organizations, or specialist programmes) has a responsibility to make sure that the facilities exist. When the offender cannot repair the full extent of the damage (or is not caught), the community should do what it can to make up the shortfall.

This way of making things right is an acceptable form of reparation for many victims. The community has to play its part by making such programmes or work available. This is summed up by the Mediation UK *Guidelines On Starting a Service*:

> Reparation may include an apology, financial payment, practical work, return and/or repair of goods, an undertaking of future behaviour or voluntary participation in education, treatment or training programmes. (Mediation UK, 1994: 2)

Restoring respect

Meanwhile the concept of shame has been introduced into the discussion. It is argued that punishment, with all the drawbacks we have heard described, is an over-reaction; it is enough that the offender is genuinely remorseful, in addition to making reparation, and once he has done so, all efforts should be devoted to helping him to be reintegrated. But shame is a word that needs careful handling.

Its effects have been explored by the psychotherapist Don Nathanson (1992), who uses the word in a sense which seems to extend from 'embarrassment' to 'humiliation'. It is an emotion which can be brought on by the actions of others, by thinking about oneself or one's own actions, or by failing to achieve one's desires. It is normal, everyone experiences it; the key is the different ways in which we deal with it. Nathanson identifies five; four of them are comparable to the 'neutralisation techniques' (excuses) by which we persuade ourselves, often subconsciously, that our anti-social behaviour is justifiable ('Cheating the tax man isn't really a crime'):

- *withdrawal:* going silent, keeping away from people or places
- *attack self:* blaming oneself, being deferential to others in the hope of avoiding stigma
- *avoidance:* trying to make the feeling go away without tackling its source, for example through drink or drugs, being macho or changing the subject
- *attack other:* being aggressive, trying to diminish other people, taking revenge

When an individual (especially a child) repeatedly experiences shame and responds in one of these ways, it can become habitual and can mould a person's personality. The fifth path is

- to *reflect* on what has happened and learn from it.

One way of doing this is conferencing, which the Philosopher mentioned. It works like this (with local variations): The offender is asked to come to a conference with members of his family, and other significant people in his life, as well as the victim and his or her supporters. The offender is asked to say what he did, and then hears from the victim; this is highly likely to induce shame, especially in the presence of his family. When the victim's expression of hurt or anger leads to remorse or shame, as it usually does, this in turn leads to a response from the victim, who commonly expresses understanding and forgiveness, and a willingness to accept the offender's reparation and expiation, so that the victim can move on from his or her original negative feelings. All present can then help to work out an 'action plan' for reparation. This is what is meant by saying that shaming, conducted in this way, is 'reintegrative'. Clearly it requires mediators to be trained in the skills of encouraging this process; but it has been found that the method is so powerful that it can work even when carried out less-than-perfectly. (This account draws heavily on Masters, 1998b.)

Some advocates of restorative justice, however, point to a risk that as 'techniques of shame' develop, restorative justice will become dominated by the idea of changing the behaviour of the offender, rather than at aiming to provide both the victim and the offender with the opportunity to communicate. Others are uneasy with the idea of shaming precisely because the 'wrong kind' could so easily be inflicted; misunderstandings are all the more likely in English, because there is only one word for these different nuances, and in German, where *beschämen* implies unmasking someone, showing them up, and probably undermining their self-confidence (Hartmann, 1998). It is better in French, which distinguishes *honte*, disgrace, from *pudeur*, sense of decency, and especially, we are told, in Mandarin Chinese, which contains a number of shame/anger combinations (Retzinger and Scheff, 1996). Asian cultures, especially the Chinese, are very sensitive to the damaging effects of 'losing face'. Braithwaite himself has warned that 'for all types of crime, shaming runs the risk of counterproductivity when it shades into stigmatisation' (Braithwaite, 1989: 55). Perhaps we should avoid the word 'shame', with its potential for misunderstanding, and use words like 'embarrassment' or 'repentance' — the word generally used to convey the Hebrew *shûbh*, turning or returning, and the Greek *metanoia*, change of mind. This is surely what we are really aiming at, although of course it cannot be guaranteed to happen in every case; shame may be a step on the way to a change of direction, but it is not the aim; as we know, many offenders already suffer from having too little self-esteem. Children who feel abandoned or rejected (disrespected or 'dissed' in the current slang) can develop an inferiority complex, a chronic feeling of shame, or this shame may be unacknowledged and 'by-passed', to become destructive aggression (Scheff, 1994: 48). I suggest that it would be better to use a different term, such as 'restoring respect', which implies the shame but stresses the constructive outcome.

To achieve reintegration, then, the aim should be to draw out feelings of shame from within the offender, as the psychologist suggested, not to degrade or pillory him, and certainly not to inflict public humiliations such as those reported from America. Some American judges have exposed men on a cable TV show who were charged with soliciting, or required child molesters to put signs on their doors warning minors to enter at their own risk. The judges claim that this penalty is less destructive than imprisonment, and that it works as both an individual and a general deterrent (Wolff, 1998). One man convicted of assault was ordered to put up a sign by his gate saying 'Warning. A violent felon lives here. Travel at your own risk'—in addition to a year's curfew, paying his victim's medical bill, and a $7,500 fine (*Guardian*, 4 February 1997). Another, in Florida, was sentenced to place a newspaper advertisement announcing that he had solicited a prostitute; he challenged the order, and the local paper, the *Pensacola News Journal*, refused to accept the 'creative sentence' (all of which led the offender to become known nationally). Critics compared the practice with the branding of adulteresses in eighteenth-century New England; it was criticised for being too severe, because it could cost a person his livelihood, and for being too soft for middle-class offenders who could afford to 'buy their way out of a jail sentence' (*The Times*, 13 February 1991). The theory of restorative justice is that we must respect the individual while making him understand the results of his actions; this is not compatible with 'naming and shaming'.

Public humiliation met a stronger hostile reaction when it was tried in the Australian capital Canberra in March 1998: when a family group conference required a 12-year-old recidivist shoplifter to stand outside the store wearing a T-shirt stating 'I am a thief', there was a storm of criticism from the local media saying that this form of shaming was not reintegrative and the police should have vetoed it; but the criticism was not directed against the idea of conferencing. In that part of the world there is evidently respect for human dignity (Braithwaite, 1998b).

One study of ex-offenders distinguishes three kinds of shame which they experience (Leibrich, 1996). Public humiliation is experienced by many offenders in the courtroom, even without sanctions like the ones just described. It is stigmatising and tends to confirm a person as an outcast, in his own eyes and other people's. Personal disgrace is 'the experience of having their behavior exposed to people they . . . knew or loved and respected'; this often occurs in victim/offender conferences, and fits Braithwaite's description of 'reintegrative shaming', which maintains bonds of respect or love and enables the offender to be re-accepted. Thirdly, private remorse is the embarrassment of 'having offended one's own personal morality'. This cannot be imposed, but if it occurs it is a powerful pressure towards avoiding further offending. But, the study concludes, measures which humiliate offenders without encouraging reintegration are likely to alienate them and shift their personal morality still further from society's.

Process

This leads to the third part of the replacement of punishment. In conventional criminal justice the process is geared to producing a result, and the effect on the participants is merely incidental (and often painful, as the Victim Assistance Worker pointed out). Instead, restorative justice uses a process which is part of the solution. It provides an opportunity for the victim and the offender to communicate, and for the offender to recognise the effects of what he has done, and make reparation. The outcome of a conference may appear 'soft' compared with a conventional punishment, but taking part in a conference (in person, not represented by a lawyer) is in fact a difficult and demanding experience (Braithwaite, 1998a: III J 9). Acknowledging shame helps to build trust and connect the people concerned; but unacknowledged shame leads to a sequence in which it alternates with anger (Scheff, 1994: 61-62). Even if it were 'soft', remember that we already reduce punishment in return for co-operation with the police or a timely plea of guilty, so why not offer an incentive to take part in the restorative process.

The intention is that the offender will spontaneously feel what might be called 'the right kind of shame', which is closer to repentance than to humiliation. The process that has been found most likely to produce this result is victim/offender mediation or conferencing, in which offenders face not an officer of the law but people who have been harmed – and often also their own families. The process gives the victim the opportunity to express feelings and ask questions, and the offender to understand the hurt he has caused to the victim, his own family and the community; consequently, further punitive action is not needed or justified, because from then on it is a question of deciding how best the victim's loss can be at least partly made good, and what the offender can do towards that and towards achieving reintegration. This may require him or her to make some form of reparation, as an outward and visible sign of remorse and understanding.

But even if we use a more neutral term such as 'holding offenders accountable', it is an uncomfortable process for them. It means that they have to accept facts about themselves, their behaviour and their future which they preferred not to think about; but it is not punishment, as it has been defined in this Symposium, because the unpleasantness is not the aim, but a side-effect, and because the realisation and reparation are matched by what Professor Braithwaite calls 'public gestures of reacceptance' – or at least they should be if the community fulfils its side of the implied contract.

You will notice too that this account includes words like 'intention' and 'opportunity': it is not a cast-iron process. Conventional criminal justice could be compared to, say, a production line which exists mainly for the sake of an end product; but it uses human beings as its raw material, and they are made of resilient stuff which does not always stay in the shape into which the engineers thought they had compressed it. Restorative justice has perhaps more in common with agriculture: the farmer provides, as far as he can, the conditions in which he hopes the crops will grow, but seeds, soil, pests and weather are to varying degrees outside his control. He cannot be sure whether the seed will bear fruit a hundredfold, or sixtyfold, or thirtyfold, but he keeps trying. A more human analogy would be with old-style military discipline: the sergeant-major does not care what is in the soldiers' minds so long as they obey him unquestioningly, whereas the true leader works with colleagues using persuasion and two-way communication to create an effective strategy; he or she achieves results by encouraging loyalty, developing individual skills, and above all by setting an example. (The two are not entirely mutually exclusive—which perhaps makes the analogy all the more apposite.) In the same way, for lawyers the process is a means to a result, and is not designed to help the victim or the offender to gain deeper understanding. The restorative process, in contrast, aims to do just that, to heal, perhaps in some ways even to help people to be stronger.

A word often used to describe this process is 'transformative'. This may sound like a piece of jargon, but it means what it says: processes such as mediation and conferencing can actually help to transform people's attitudes and even their lives, in a way far removed from a formal apology or the legalistic table of compensation which says, for example, that a fractured heel bone with continuing disability is worth £5,000, and repetitive serious sexual abuse of a child £2,000 (examples from the British Criminal Injuries Compensation Authority, 1999: 23, 25, 27). I will give examples of this.

Crime prevention

The fourth part of the strategy is to focus directly on crime prevention. This is a huge subject, almost as complex and varied as crime itself, but it has two main aspects: making it harder to commit crime, known in the jargon as 'situational crime prevention', and tackling the pressures towards crime— 'social crime prevention'. The former includes physical security, supervision and other ways of making crime harder to commit; the latter aims at making people want to live without committing crimes or harming people, because they feel they have been fairly treated and want to treat others fairly. This is a great over-simplification, but I think it summarises an important part of the reason why most of us obey the law most of the time. It receives a very small part of the law enforcement budget, as we have been reminded, but there are measures which have been shown to be cost-effective (Graham, 1998). The more successful social crime prevention is, the less the situational kind will be necessary. It begins in childhood. The ideal, of course, is a stable family, with an adequate home, parents who are good role models, education in all its forms, adequately paid employment, and a supportive community; the difficult part is to find ways of making up deficits in those necessities. As the Probation Officer said, crime policy cannot be separated from social and economic policy.

In crime prevention the importance of starting young cannot be over-emphasised. One study after another has found that early upbringing is vital in relation to offending behaviour, and, more important, that effective action can be taken through home visits, personal development programmes for children and parents, especially for disadvantaged people (Junger-Tas, 1996). There are also increasing numbers of methods such as circle time and the support group approach to bullying in which children learn to treat each other with respect and consideration, and peer mediation, where they learn to help each other resolve conflicts (Robinson and Maines, 1997). The British Home Secretary has announced plans for a National Family and Planning Institute to promote good relationships within families, and the government, taking account of this research, has allocated £540 million to 'Sure Start' programmes for children under three, initially in 250 areas of greatest need (*Guardian*, 15, 24 July; *Independent*, 24 July; *Observer*, 18 July 1998). Psychologists have suggested that if we want a world with less violence and less dominating abuse of others, we need to take seriously rituals that encourage approval of caring behaviour so that citizens will acquire pride in being caring and non-dominating; restorative justice conferences, if well conducted, would contribute to this (Braithwaite, 1998a, summarising work by Retzinger and Scheff).

Such methods can begin as early as primary school. At Highfield Junior School Plymouth, in the south-west of England, for example, discipline had almost broken down; it was restored by first enforcing rules, but then encouraging the children to make, and enforce, their own. Children were shown how to treat each other with respect; anyone who behaved badly was not condemned, but helped to choose hehaviour that did not hurt other people (Alderson, 1997; Stewart, 1998: ch. 7). It is important, however, that these principles of mutual respect should be learnt by children from privileged backgrounds as well as disadvantaged ones, so that they do not result, later on, in a generation of the latter who understandingly and reasonably accept economic and social exploitation by the former.

HOW RESTORATIVE JUSTICE WORKS

Not long ago I would have headed this section 'How it would work'; but it is already in operation in 15 countries or more (Wright, 1996: 168-9). The

Philosopher referred to its origins; now in at least two countries (New Zealand and Austria) new juvenile justice laws based on restorative principles were introduced about ten years ago, and in others (including Australia, Germany and Poland) legislation has been amended to encourage the use of restorative processes. Inevitably the ways in which they have been put into practice vary, as do the legal systems themselves. Perhaps the best thing will be for me to outline a composite description; the Civil Servant will give details of some of the variants. I will use features of restorative justice as it is practised in various jurisdictions, so this model will not be applicable everywhere; for example, in some countries police do not have discretion to issue a warning instead of passing every case to the prosecutor. The meeting is usually called 'mediation' when only the victim and the offender, and perhaps one or two supporters on each side, attend, but it is also used to include 'conferencing', which brings in families, extended families, and others. For present purposes, except where I am making a specific distinction between the two, I will use 'conferencing' or 'mediation' as general terms to cover anything from one-to-one victim/offender mediation to group conferences at which quite a number of people may be present; the numbers will depend on the nature of individual cases.

I will tell two stories (in the boxes which follow). Other speakers used fables to make their points, but these stories are true; only some names and details have been changed to preserve confidentiality.

"Cathy", aged 12, was befriended by a local man in his thirties, and this led to sexual involvement which lasted nearly 20 years. By manipulation and deceit he maintained almost total control over her. At last she confronted him and reported him to the police. He pleaded guilty, and was sentenced to three years' imprisonment, but Cathy felt she had had no opportunity to be heard.

Although she was very fearful she desperately wanted to participate in a conference. This took place, with 29 participants from both families, and lasted five hours. Although the man accepted no responsibility and felt he was the victim (which no one else present agreed with) Cathy wrote afterwards that she felt free and validated, especially because it gave her a unique chance to face her parents and sister with the full truth, which gave them understanding and changed their behaviour towards her. She felt healed and "released from the prison I was forced to live in"—something the court had failed to offer her. The man's family also experienced a great sense of relief and have not given up on the possibility of changing his attitude.

"David", aged 17, had been involved in increasingly serious burglaries; cautions and court appearances had no effect. His father even took him to a psychiatrist. His sister was a police officer and suggested a conference just before he was due to go to court to be sentenced, but this was not intended to influence the sentence. The conference lasted three hours, and David began to realise that his family cared for him, although they were badly hurt by what he had done. His latest victims, whose house he had broken into twice, had since experienced separation and divorce, and described how they no longer felt safe. But towards the end of the conference they described him a "not a bad young bloke" and offered to help him. He was sentenced to six months in detention, and said later that he didn't think he could have coped with this but for the conference: "It was the most scary experience of my life. Up until I got into the conference, I had no idea how much damage I had caused . . . I just had to sit there and listen to the victims talk about how their lives had been affected [and] my family then talking about how I had hurt them . . . Nothing had made a difference for me until the conference".

He went to live with his sister and got a job; relationships had improved in his family, and the victims felt they were heard and validated.

Both examples summarised from cases described by Terry O'Connell, an Australian pioneer of conferencing: O'Connell, 1997: 7-13.

To give a more comprehensive picture, I will give a general description of the process as it affects the participants, the way it would be organized, and the way in which it fits into the rest of the justice system. I will try to answer the question 'Does it work?' and in discussion we can look at some of the questions which such a radical change raises, as regards both the day-to-day operation and the theoretical implications. Here is a new approach which makes a lot of sense on its own terms; but it raises some new questions. Could such a system co-exist alongside the conventional criminal justice system, and if so how would they fit in with each other? Or could a 'restorative justice system' (RJS) replace the criminal justice system (CJS)?

What do these stories tell us about the new response to crime? Two examples obviously cannot describe it fully, because there are different ways of doing it; but you can see how this process offers victims, offenders and their families the opportunity to transform their attitudes, their relationships and their behaviour. For David there was a real change of heart; and even though the offender in Cathy's case did not acquire insight in a blinding flash on the road to Damascus, there was hope that his family would help him to understand, and Cathy's relationships with her family were certainly transformed.

Restorative justice in practice

A crime is committed—a burglary or a bag-snatch, for example—and a suspect has been identified. He does not deny the act. Another common situation is that people have a dispute which leads to a crime—one assaults the other or damages his property. It is worth trying to help them to resolve the dispute, rather than deal with the criminal act without regard to its context. Of course, mediation at an earlier stage can sometimes forestall the crime altogether. These can be dealt with at various stages of the criminal justice process.

Diversion from the system

If the offence is not too serious, the police in some countries may decide to issue a warning. This informal diversion keeps the system from being inundated, but it requires safeguards and clear criteria for selection. In New Zealand conferences are reserved for the more serious cases: it is estimated that they are not used for 80 to 85 per cent of children and young persons who offend (McElrea, 1998: 5). There is a statutory presumption in favour of diversion: unless the public interest requires otherwise criminal proceedings should not be instituted against a child or young person if there is an alternative means of dealing with the matter (Children Young Persons and their Families Act 1989, section 208). Similarly in New South Wales, Australia: police have to make the lowest level of intervention or justify their decision not to (Young Offenders Bill (1998)). In other cases the police then propose a conference. In England, the Crime and Disorder Act 1998 restricts the police to not more than one reprimand and one final warning. Victims who knew the identity of the offender and preferred not to take the case to court would be able to go directly to mediation, just as they do with civil disputes.

More serious cases will go to the prosecutor, who in some jurisdictions such as Germany also has discretion to discontinue the case (with or without an official warning, a fine, a payment to a good cause, or community service) because prosecution is not necessary in the public interest; this may be because reparation has already been made, or provide an opportunity for it.

Restorative justice in courts

The most serious cases, where the accused is arrested, go to court; when the accused pleads guilty or is convicted, there is another opportunity for mediation before the sentence is passed. Courts frequently request a pre-sentence report from the probation service (in Germany and Austria the court assistance service); in the New Zealand juvenile system they refer it to a family group conference instead, in all cases except homicide. In this way the advantages of conferencing are made routinely available. The court will then consider the action plan that the conference puts forward, and will in most cases endorse it, but has the option of modifying it if it appears unfair to either party, for example if the offender appears to have agreed to an unreasonable amount of compensation, or if the victim has asked for very little and the court feels that the offender should do some community service in addition. The court also steps in if the mediation cannot reach agreement, or if the accused denies the act. Initially courts would often use existing punitive sanctions, but in time they would increasingly use restorative ones such as compensation and community service orders. They would retain the power to restrict liberty or impose custody, but only for the protection of the public, not as a punishment. There would have to be a complete change in the ethos and regime of prisons. The drastic reduction in their numbers, and the saving in the time of police, prosecutors and courts, would more than meet the costs of the service.

If the meeting takes place at any stage before the criminal justice process is complete, there is an incentive to fulfil the agreement because prosecution could be discontinued, or the court could 'adjourn in contemplation of dismissal' or defer the sentence to take account of it. This does however have implications for the voluntary nature of the mediation, but there are safeguards which we can talk about in the discussion. Clearly *mediation* should be voluntary, because it would be wrong to put pressure on the victim to take part; but I do not see any objection to putting pressure on the offender to make *reparation*, to the victim if he or she wants it, and otherwise to the community. In the last resort, however, enforcement is impossible, if for example a man will go to prison, or even the segregation unit of a prison, rather than comply (and the same is true of fines or prison labour).

If for any reason conferencing does not take place at an earlier stage, it can be arranged after sentence or before the offender's release from prison; this has the advantage that both parties know that the offender's participation is entirely voluntary.

The conferencing process
Preparation of both parties is important, to explain the process and what they can hope to get from it, so both should be visited (although some services make do with telephone calls). Where a very serious crime is involved, several visits will be necessary, to make sure they understand the process and are likely to find it beneficial.

The process itself may range from shuttle diplomacy, to one-to-one victim/offender mediation (V/OM), to V/OM with supporters present, to bringing in extended families. Collectively these methods are called restorative conferencing. Exponents of large conferences say that with a large number of people there is a better dynamic, with more people to contribute ideas towards a solution. The offender should hear his own family, as well as the victim's, talk about the effect of his actions, and this makes him ashamed; but when he expresses remorse, there is a large group of people ready to help him make amends. Others believe that some youngsters will be overwhelmed by a room which is full of people, and will open up better with half-a-dozen or fewer people present. Probably both are true in different cases, and in the course of time experience will show the best method for particular types of people and cases (Braithwaite, 1998: IV E note 1). There does seem to be agreement that those victims and offenders who are willing to meet find the process more rewarding, and that it works best when mediators keep in the background, providing a safe environment in which the participants can relate to each other.

There is a precedent for the idea of a discussion between child, parents and professionals, in the Scottish system of children's hearings, which has been in use for over 25 years; the new dimension is the involvement of the victim and (in the case of conferences) of the extended family.

If a meeting takes place, the mediators (who normally work in pairs, and are sometimes known as facilitators) will ask those present to agree to ground rules, and remind them that the process is voluntary. They are free to walk out; if the case has finished its progress through the justice system (for example with a final warning or a sentence) that is the end of the matter, but if not, the case goes to court. The procedure at the mediation or conference varies, but it will include asking the offender what happened, and inviting victims to describe the effects on them. In some cases this step towards understanding will be all the victim and offender want; but usually the offender apologises, and often the victim wants the offender to do something tangible to show that he means it, by making reparation as I described earlier.

New Zealand professionals recognise that FGCs cannot work on their own. Resources are crucial where, for example, an FGC agreement decides on an outcome that requires funding, such as a course of drug treatment or anger management; some of the money saved by closure of residential establishments should be allocated to this. The New Zealand researchers Gabrielle Maxwell and Jeremy Robertson (1995: 46) have suggested a ring-fenced budget for the 200 or so children with the greatest needs (in a population of about four million). But if conferencing is to fulfil its potential, the principle will have to be extended to adult offenders.

A further measure is needed in a fully restorative system, but not as yet much used: there are offenders who wish to express remorse but whose victims do not wish to hear from them, or could not be traced, and all too many victims whose offenders are never found. It has been found that group meetings where a guided discussion takes place between the victims and perpetrators of similar types of offence can be reassuring to victims and educative to offenders (Launay, 1987; Launay and Murray, 1989). A similar idea is Victim Impact Panels, started in America in 1982 by Mothers Against Drunk Driving to help offenders understand the impact of their crimes, and to provide victims with a structured, positive outlet to share their personal experiences, and Victim Impact Classes, operated in a similar way by the California Youth Authority. In both cases it is important to screen participants to ensure that they are suitable for this type of intervention, and to prepare them for it beforehand; it could make things worse for victims if they expected offenders to show understanding or regret for what they had done, but the offenders did not do so. Some work has been undertaken in English prisons, for example in the high-security Long Lartin prison, where the victim of a bank hold-up was able to meet men serving sentences for armed robbery, and to arrange for others to do so. As I speak this project is 'on hold' for lack of funding.

How will restorative justice be implemented?

Even where there is legislation, implementation would not be achieved all at once, and I will therefore describe it as a process. Victim/offender mediation services would be set up area by area, on the initiative of community mediation services, voluntary agencies such as NACRO, NCH Action for Children or Mediation UK, or statutory ones—the police, probation or youth justice services. A group has already been formed in Britain, the Restorative Justice Consortium, in which these agencies could work out which of them would take the lead in each area. The administrative structure of these services would be 'off-the-peg', with modifications if local circumstances made it necessary; their methods of working would be more varied, because there is not yet a consensus about the preferred model, but they would have to conform to standards of good practice in order to safeguard all concerned.

Who convenes the mediation or conference? In some places this is done by the police, although there is concern, shared by Judge McElrea (1998) among others, that this puts too much control of the process into the hands of one agency. Elsewhere it is done by a social worker or probation officer; some feel that there is a problem because the same agency (or even the same person) is acting in different roles at different times, but others claim that people can 'wear different hats' successfully provided they receive proper training. But the leader of the programme should be responsible for the conferencing service only, so that he or she does not have divided priorities. In New Zealand, FGCs are operated through the welfare arm of the state, which means that co-ordinators are not always seen as impartial, and money intended for youth justice becomes absorbed in the much larger welfare budget (Masters, 1998a).

These drawbacks are in my view best overcome by using a neutral agency, as the Philosopher described, whose aim would be not to assist offenders *or* victims, but to offer both of them a way to communicate if they wish, and to enable the offender to make reparation to the victim (if he or she wants it) or the community. Part of the reason for the success of out-of-court offence resolution in Austria is that mediation is seen as independent, and not as a service for offenders (Masters, 1998a). If a mediation service is managed by one agency, such as probation or the police, it could be vulnerable to changes in policy: a new chief officer could decide to change working practices in a way which watered down the restorative ideal, or even allocate resources elsewhere and close the programme.

An independent organization has to work that bit harder to build contacts and confidence among colleagues in the statutory agencies, but this can be done. Funding can cause headaches, but it can be a strength if you make the service a genuine partnership, supported by different agencies and the community as a whole, as well as local fund-raising efforts which give freedom of manoeuvre.

In Richard Adams's novel Watership Down, there are some very well-fed rabbits with glossy coats; but from time to time one of them disappears onto the farmer's dining table—but the subject is not spoken about. The rabbits in the woods are thinner and sometimes hungrier, but independent.

It goes without saying that funding must be adequate to the task; mediation services are never going to be fat cats (or rabbits!) but they do need enough staff if they are to succeed.

Mediators would be trained members of the public, either as volunteers or paid a sessional fee. Quality assurance of both the services and the mediators would be through accreditation by a national body—in Britain, Mediation UK, which would also provide advice and support where necessary, either nationally or through regional groups.

These ideas are being formulated in England, a country where there is a well-established tradition of voluntary social action, including a national voluntary organization, Victim Support, whose volunteers offer support to a substantial proportion of individual victims of crime. In other countries, mediators would probably take on some of this supportive role; the mediation service might encourage the development of work by trained, supervised volunteers, or the mediators could be paid for each session in which they took part. In either case the service should use members of the public from a wide range of social, occupational, ethnic and linguistic backgrounds.

Does restorative justice work?

The Politician asked about effectiveness. As always, before we can answer this question we have to define the aims. Perhaps I could begin by giving another case history.

"Danny" was 15 years old. Late one evening he left home with a can of spirits and a box of matches, and set fire to the school library. He had taken great care to see that no people would come to harm, but the damage amounted to £26,000, and the library was out of action for several weeks.

Six days later Danny walked into the police station, saying he wanted to "get something off my chest". His parents were invited to a formal interview where he confessed; he said that he had been worried about forthcoming exams and thought that disrupting the library might buy him more time. He said that he had confessed voluntarily because he realised the damage he had caused and the impact on other people, and was full of guilt and remorse.

Before his case came to the Crown Court, a psychiatrist reported that his behaviour could be attributed to acute adolescent depression. He was sentenced to two years in a young offenders institution—a shorter sentence than he would have received otherwise, because he had no previous convictions and had given himself up. Just afterwards, he commented: "Well, if I've learnt anything from all this, then it's not to tell anyone if I do something wrong!"

He wanted to give an explanation of what he had done, and he was being ridiculed and bullied in the prison for having confessed. Meanwhile the headmaster had unanswered questions, but also wanted to say directly to Danny that it was not the wish of the school that he should be sent to prison. Danny's parents, too, were struggling to come to terms and wanted to express a sense of shared responsibility.

After several visits to each of the parties, it was agreed that they should meet. The Conference took place at the school, and brought together Danny (who had been granted special leave from the prison), his parents, one of his friends, the headmaster, and the mediator. The librarian and a prison officer were invited but did not attend. The Conference lasted for over two hours:

they talked about how people had been affected by the crime, Danny answered questions and described his regret and remorse, forgiveness was expressed. The head was very moved by Danny's account; after the meeting he walked with his hand on Danny's shoulder to the library building which had been rebuilt, so that Danny could see the scars that had been healed, and said "Now we all have to make sure that you can heal from this experience". His father, walking behind them, said "To be honest with you I couldn't see that this would do any good, and have wondered if it might make things worse . . . but isn't it wonderful to see those two chatting away . . . like the best of friends".

(Summarised from notes of a case provided by Guy Masters)

Defining the aims
The aims and philosophy must be clarified before the mediators can be trained, and certainly before the service can be evaluated. They are different from what people are accustomed to. We have heard from other speakers that there is considerable doubt as to whether the crime rate is affected by what we do to offenders, so I don't think that should be a primary aim. Mediation services often say that reducing re-offending is not the criterion by which they want to be assessed, because they do not claim that a mediation session plus reparation, any more than a court hearing plus punishment, will be enough to turn a person's life around; but it is obviously a welcome by-product, a factor which people will inevitably ask about, if only for reassurance that the new method has not made things worse. One Home Office study even assessed the satisfaction of sentencers (May, 1995) — one would not have thought that keeping magistrates and judges happy was a top priority for the criminal justice system.

So what should the aims be? Bearing in mind the principle of autonomy, we should not be too prescriptive: we should not say, for example, that offenders should compensate victims unless victims have indicated that that is what they want. So we should define the aims in more general terms: to provide a space and time for victims and offenders to use in any *restorative* way they wish in order to help victims to feel better — which can be measured fairly easily, by asking them, although the conventional system seldom if ever does so. The process must serve the interests of the community, as well as of individuals; the offender should be held accountable for the harm done to the victim and hence to the safety and stability of the community. This is harder to assess, but perhaps indirect indicators are the number of apologies and agreements and the fulfilment of those agreements. Offenders should feel fairly dealt with; this may seem a surprising aim at first, but if it is accepted that the ideal, in a democracy, is for people to respect the law and not merely fear it, it is an appropriate criterion, which can also be measured by asking them. Offenders should be reintegrated into the community, which can be gauged indirectly by such factors as whether they have a home, obtain work, are part of a social or recreational network, and do not re-offend.

There have now been several research projects on victim/offender mediation—some of them, it has to be said, more rigorous than others (Mediation UK, 1997). But it can be said that all of them show that when restorative justice is carried out to high standards, the great majority of both victims and offenders are glad to have taken part and would do so again; as far as reconviction rates are concerned, no study has shown an increase, and some have shown a reduction, although the latter were not always conducted with comparison groups. The Civil Servant will summarise some of the findings, including a detailed research project in Canberra, Australia.

There have been warnings about possible misapplication of the idea of restorative justice. It will not be truly restorative if it is merely a programme 'bolted on' to an unreconstructed retributive system; this point is made by Gordon Bazemore and Kay Pranis (1997), and an ironic background is given to their article by the fact that it appears in the American journal *Corrections Today*, alongside advertisements for a private operator of prisons claiming that 'the programs at our juvenile facilities are based on a restorative justice model . . . ', as well as for reinforced windows, doors, locks, hinges, perimeter fences and other detention hardware. Bazemore and Pranis say that restorative justice should not be marginalised, or reserved for minor offences or juvenile offenders only (though it may have to begin there). There is a danger that the restorative ideal could be subverted by retributive attitudes. The same measure can be presented quite differently: reparation can be used as punishment if a court is so minded. But an offender is likely to respond in one way if he is told in effect 'You are a menace to society and you are ordered to do a really hard unpleasant job', and in quite another if he is given the same task, but told 'The old people's home is seriously understaffed, and we need you to help with the backlog of cleaning, which the residents would really appreciate'. So would you, I dare say? There is a need for a general change of attitudes, by explanation and education. Restorative justice should be explained on its own terms, not disguised as punishment. Talk of 'confronting offenders with their victims' is misguided for this reason, as well as because it would be quite unacceptable to put pressure on the victim to take part.

The whole system needs to be grounded in restorative principles, as has happened in New Zealand and in Austria; it needs both support from key professionals and decision-makers and the creative energy of the community, which in this context includes the offender's relatives and people who matter to him, and the victim's family and supporters, as well as those who make it possible for the offender to fulfil his reparative agreement, for example by obtaining work or learning skills.

Approaches to victims should be made by staff who are trained to be sensitive to their needs and feelings. It has to be accepted on its own merits, and not as a way of humiliating offenders, saving money, speeding up processes, or relieving court workloads. Criminal justice professionals should take part in the planning, but it should not be solely for their conventional purposes of punishing or rehabilitating offenders; it should also benefit victims, and they should be involved in designing the strategy. Job descriptions, performance measures, and incentives for staff such as criteria for promotion, should send a message that restorative justice goals are important.

Conclusion

In brief, what does this new approach provide? It recognises the needs and wishes of victims of crime, and offers them the opportunity to be involved in the process, without placing on them the responsibility for punishing the offender. It holds offenders accountable for what they have done to other people, so that they can repair the harm, actually or symbolically; but it does not compound the felony by inflicting further harm on the offenders. It acknowledges that many of them also have needs, and reintegrates them into society rather than stigmatising them. It respects the autonomy of both offenders and victims by offering them the opportunity to be involved in decisions (but not, of course, the use of their autonomy to harm others, by committing crimes against them or inflicting punishment on them, respectively). It also involves members of the community in several ways.

In a society based on restorative justice, courts would have a new role. Instead of using their 'hardness' as a virility symbol, they could at last let go of their long-standing fallacies: the notions that deterrent punishment is a fair or effective method of crime control, and that punishment inflicted on about two per cent of offenders plays a significant part in crime reduction. They would also accept what they have been uncomfortably aware of, that it is best to resolve matters outside the court if possible: people have the right to a 'day in court', but they also have the right to be spared the necessity of using it. Local services involving local people would offer out-of-court resolution. The courts would still have the important function of overseeing the operation of these services, and resolving matters which cannot be settled voluntarily. In particular, they would determine when a person has to be restrained for the protection of others, and above all the small number for whom the restraint must take the form of detention. In countries like

England, where the great majority of the courts of first instance rely on trained, unpaid magistrates, there would be less work for these public-spirited citizens to do, but their contribution could still be valued: many of them would be able to find a new role by re-training as mediators.

There would be changes for other actors in criminal justice, too. The police would move towards problem-solving policing, as some are already beginning to do: instead of 'How can we catch the offender so that he can be punished?' they would ask 'How can we catch him so that he can understand what he has done, and make up for it, and make better use of his life?' Prosecutors would have a third option, no longer having to choose between prosecuting and doing nothing; they could say 'It is not in the public interest to prosecute, but something ought to happen, so that the victim feels vindicated and the offender has to stop and think, and therefore this case should be referred for possible mediation'. The Probation Service would, as now, provide rehabilitative programmes and supervise the fulfilment of reparation agreements, and would take an active role in the establishment and management of mediation services. The few remaining prisons would be places of containment, not punishment; within them offenders would be able to make reparation, including participation in training and therapy if they needed it, in preparation for their eventual release.

But the most important changes would affect that hard-to-define entity, the community. In various contexts it means pretty well everybody: the 'active citizens' who do voluntary work such as mediation and sit on management committees; voluntary (non-governmental) organizations, local groups, and churches, which provide specialised social programmes, and the people who contribute time and money to them; statutory agencies which also provide services, including the Criminal Injuries Compensation Authority, and the taxpayers who pay for them; elected representatives who make the decisions, and the voters who elect them; and, not least, the families and supporters of victims and offenders who help to reintegrate them. Appropriate parts of the community would receive information from mediation services and courts, and use it to create a crime reduction strategy. This sounds like a huge social programme, and in a sense it is, because crime reduction and public order are vital to any society. But large parts of it exist already, although different countries have greater or lesser investment in statutory agencies, voluntary activity, compensation to victims of violence, and other services. I am not aware that any country has yet created a Ministry for Crime Reduction, but in Britain the seeds have been sown in the shape of government initiatives such as Safer Cities, which funds projects that could reduce crime, and the sections of the Crime and Disorder Act which give local authorities and chief police officers the duty of drawing up a strategy for the reduction of crime and disorder; a Crime Reduction Programme is now a central part of government policy.

I believe that restorative principles offer the basis of a practical response to criminal behaviour; but more than that, they contribute to the building of a fair and stable society. Courts still have a role dealing with the cases where the accused pleads not guilty, or where no agreement can be reached, and a more important one overseeing the restorative process in the interests of both victims and offenders. Their work will no longer be complicated by the attempt to combine it with crime reduction; that will be a likely by-product, but will mainly be the responsibility of a department of government specifically charged with reducing pressures and opportunities for crime. This leaves the justice system to deal with individual cases; its only concern with crime prevention is to pass information to local and national departments responsible for crime reduction, which in turn can convey it to the other departments which help to shape society.

Advocates of restorative justice do not offer a blueprint for an ideal system, but a compass which will guide us away from externally imposed control, which leads towards repression, and towards a society which encourages self-control and mutual help.

FACTS AND STATISTICS

The Civil Servant
The Mediator pointed out that there is no single model for putting restorative justice into practice; new non-adversarial, community-based methods are evolving, for which the umbrella term 'community justice' is sometimes used, and practitioners and researchers are in the process of finding out which work best in which circumstances. I will outline four of them.

In *Victim/offender mediation* meetings are usually arranged between one victim and one offender; some victims and offenders prefer to communicate indirectly, through go-betweens (so-called 'shuttle diplomacy'). Cases can be referred for mediation at any stage of the criminal justice process and may lead to reparation, in the broad sense outlined by the mediator.

Conferences are similar, except that both parties are encouraged to bring members of their extended families, and perhaps other supporters such as a teacher or youth club leader, as the Mediator has described.

Circle sentencing has developed in some parts of Canada, especially in Indigenous communities. The conference is attended not only by the families but by members of the local community and by the judge, prosecutor, social worker and others. Because the judge is present, the circle can handle any type of case that the judge can deal with, including quite serious repeat offenders; sentences may include punitive sanctions.

Reparative boards come from the American state of Vermont. So far they have handled only relatively minor, non-violent cases for which the offender has been sentenced to 'restorative probation'. A board of five members of the local community hears the case and draws up an action plan by which the offender can make reparation; there is less emphasis on involvement of offenders and victims than in the other models.

All of these are concerned to (re-)establish social peace and right relationships, rather than conduct a divisive 'war on crime'. They are likely to be flexible as regards the times and places where they are held. When offenders' families are involved, they may take on the role of making sure that the offender complies. In the first three methods, the victims and offenders receive preparation for the meeting; in cases where the crime has arisen from a dispute, they may help the parties to resolve it. In all the processes that involve victims, there is emphasis on offering them the chance to express feelings and ask questions, which may be at least as important as any other outcome. All are designed to deal with offenders who admit the act with which they are charged (though they may deny legal guilt); if they deny the act altogether, the case must be decided in court.

Further details are given by Bazemore (1997); Bazemore and Griffiths (1997); and Bazemore and Umbreit (1998).

Research

One of the early effects of victim/offender mediation was to introduce a new criterion for evaluating the criminal justice process: the satisfaction of victims and offenders with the process. An early study of an American Victim/Offender Reconciliation Program (VORP) found that 83 per cent of offenders and 59 per cent of victims were satisfied with the experience; only 11 per cent of victims expressed dissatisfaction, and all but one said they would participate again if the occasion arose. The primary motivation for victims to take part was to obtain restitution, but the most satisfying part was meeting the offender; they were also satisfied with the opportunity to obtain a better understanding of the crime and an expression of remorse from the offender. Offenders disliked the stress of preparing for the meeting with the victim, but were generally satisfied with the meeting itself and the discovery that the victim was willing to listen to them. They also welcomed working out a schedule to 'make things right' and, in some cases, keeping out of jail (Coates and Gehm, 1989).

British research also indicates high success rates. Marshall and Merry (1990) for example found that:

- Eighty-two per cent of victims who took part in mediation in Leeds, West Yorkshire, felt meeting the offender was valuable, including 22 per cent whom it helped to relieve their worries about the offence, and others who hoped it might help to reform the offender. Nearly all were glad to have taken part, although some were apprehensive beforehand.
- In Wolverhampton, West Midlands, 57 per cent of offenders said they agreed to take part so as to get a reduced sentence, but by the end of the meeting only 17 per cent gave this as one of the benefits; almost all were glad they had met their victims, and many were surprised at the sympathy and understanding offered by their victims—which could add to their embarrassment (Marshall and Merry, 1990: 153-165).

In Northamptonshire, where the service operates at cautioning stage, in 1991:

- Compensation totalling £47,500 was ordered; £37,800 paid, £1,400 (about three per cent) written off. The remainder was remitted for specific reasons, such as a change in the offender's circumstances. An earlier study (Newburn, 1988) found that when compensation was *ordered* by magistrates, 12 per cent had to be written off.
- Corporate victims: 71 per cent satisfied with handling of case
- Individual victims: 62 per cent satisfied (of a sample of 45), but three were opposed in principle, two dissatisfied with their offender's response, two felt the offender was not punished enough, and two were unhappy about enforcement of the agreement. Another survey found 90 per cent of victims, 96 per cent of offenders felt fairly treated by the Reparation Bureau.
- Reconvictions: a survey when 90 per cent had been at risk for at least one year found 81.5 per cent not reconvicted in the Adult Reparation Project in Kettering, 79.5 per cent in a matched sample from Wellingborough (not statistically significant). Results were slightly better for face-to-face mediation than with a go-between, but also not significant. (Dignan, 1990; Northamptonshire, 1992).

What most victims wanted when they took part in two English programmes (in Coventry, West Midlands, and Leeds, West Yorkshire) was to tell the offender the impact the crime had on them (90 per cent) and to receive answers from their offenders about what happened (80 per cent). An apology was wanted by 73 per cent, and only 65 per cent said it was important to negotiate restitution.

- 46 per cent of cases referred went to mediation in 1993.
- 79 per cent of victims who took part were satisfied with the outcome of mediation (the proportion was slightly higher among those who took part in direct (face-to-face) mediation).
- 90 per cent of offenders were satisfied (100 per cent of those who took part in direct mediation, but this was a small sample).
- 82 per cent of victims and 87 per cent of offenders felt they had participated voluntarily.
- 93 per cent of offenders said it was important to them to be able to tell the victim what happened, 62 per cent said it was important to negotiate restitution, and 90 per cent to apologise to the victim.
- 80 per cent of the offenders who took part did apologise.
- Victims who took part in mediation were only half as likely to fear re-victimisation (16 per cent as against 33 per cent).

It should be noted that in some of these cases there could be a self-selection effect, for example there may be a high proportion of victims who said it was important to them to tell the offender about the impact of the crime because those are the people who are likely to choose mediation (Umbreit and Roberts, 1996).

A study of four centres in the United States found that in line with the Northamptonshire findings, where there was mediation 81 per cent of offenders completed restitution, without mediation only 58 per cent. The centres were at Albuquerque, NM, Austin, TX, Minneapolis, MN, and Oakland, CA (Umbreit, 1994).

- 36 per cent of cases referred went to mediation in 1990-91. There were successfully negotiated agreements in 95 per cent of these cases. Agreements were 58 per cent financial, 13 per cent personal service, 29 per cent community service. The average financial restitution was US $219, the average personal service 18 hours, average community service 25 hours.
- Before mediation, 67 per cent of victims were upset about crime, after mediation 49 per cent. Before, 23 per cent were afraid of being revictimised by the offender, afterwards ten per cent. Both these results are statistically significant.
- 90 per cent of victims, and 91 per cent of offenders, were satisfied with the outcome of mediation.
- In the mediation group, 83 per cent of victims perceived the juvenile justice system as fair, compared with 62 per cent of those not referred

to mediation. Among the juvenile offenders, 89 per cent of those in mediation said they experienced fairness, as against 78 per cent of those not referred.

Although in restorative justice the above-mentioned factors are considered to be the primary criteria for 'success', the question is often asked, whether the process influenced the percentage reconvicted. In these four sites, 18 per cent of offenders were convicted for new criminal offences within one year after mediation, but where there was no mediation 27 per cent (but this difference fell short of statistical significance). Of those who re-offended, 41 per cent of those in the mediation group committed less serious crimes than before, compared with 12 per cent in a matched comparison group (Umbreit, 1994).

The research method used in the Leeds, England, Victim/Offender Unit was to compare predicted and actual outcomes. Of 73 offenders referred in 1993/4. 54.2 per cent reconvictions for Standard List offences within two years were predicted, but the actual rate was 49.3 per cent, despite increased substance abuse in the sample. The rates were better for violent offences than for burglary.

In New Zealand, after almost ten years' operation of the Children, Young Persons and their Families Act 1989, the proportion of 17 to 20-year-olds has gone down from 29.7 to 24.3 per cent of all arrests. Since 1989 the number of all arrests has increased by 35 per cent, but among 17 to 20-year-olds by only 9.8 per cent (Masters, 1998a).

The first large-scale study to compare restorative justice (in the form of conferencing) with courts is being carried out in Canberra, Australia, by Lawrence W Sherman and Heather Strang at the Australian National University. Cases were randomly allocated to court or conference; the sample included 111 young offenders (juveniles for property offences ranging from shoplifting to car theft, and offenders up to age 29 involved in violent crimes excluding sexual assault and domestic violence), and 437 drink-drivers. In both groups, more of those offenders who attended a conference said they had increased respect for the police, felt ashamed of what they had done, and said their case allowed them to clear their conscience. Many more victims received an apology and/or restitution, and fewer expected the offender to repeat the offence. After a conference, half as many victims as before it felt angry with offenders, and the proportion who felt sympathy for them almost doubled. There were many more findings, all pointing in the same directions, and almost all were statistically significant to at least the five per cent level (that is, there is less than a five per cent probability that these figures would have occurred by chance). Examples of comments by victims are:

I was able to say all the things I'd been thinking about for all those weeks and explain how angry I was . . . to put him in the picture of how it affected us made me feel so much better . . . I felt a great sense of relief getting it off my chest.

You realise they aren't the monsters you'd made them out to be . . . I don't have to feel conscious of people walking past and thinking, are they the ones? Are they the enemy?

In one example among many, Sherman and Strang describe how the family of one young victim felt transformed by the conference experience; the two boys became friends, and so did their parents (Sherman and Strang, 1997).

Further findings are summarised by Mediation UK (1997).

Aylesbury findings
The Restorative Cautioning Unit of Thames Valley police, in Aylesbury, operates a version of conferencing. It claims a recidivism rate of only four per cent (over an unspecified time-scale). Most victims said they preferred a conference to a court. The method is also intended to 'heal communities' and strengthen families, but these factors are more difficult to measure. The statistical basis of this claim has however been questioned, and further research is underway.

DISCUSSION

Chair: Because there are so many strands to this debate, I think it will be helpful to group the questions; first I will invite questions on the relation of restorative justice to conventional justice.

Q. Speakers at this Symposium have been dismissive of deterrence; so how do you propose to achieve crime reduction and the other aims of the conventional system? To put it another way, if we take a 'pacifist' position ('disarmament'), what happens to the things we have previously claimed to be achieving through punishment?

A. Let's take them one by one. As you heard from the Judge, the conventional aims include deterrence of the individual offender, deterrence of potential offenders, rehabilitation of the individual offender, containment of anti-social people, and denunciation of the seriousness of the crime. The first four are consequentialist or utilitarian, the last ('denunciation') is symbolic, and comes close to retribution for its own sake. There are other subsidiary aims, such as discouraging members of the public from taking the law into their own hands in a vindictive way. Most conventional methods have not been shown to be very effective in their professed aims, and several are incompatible with each other.

Individual deterrence is often counter-productive, because you don't get people to behave well by treating them badly, and it conflicts with the aim of rehabilitation; I believe that a policy based on changing offenders' attitudes and reintegrating them into the community is more likely to be effective than one based on fear, coercion and stigma.

General deterrence will, as now, depend much more on the likelihood of being caught than on the severity of the punishment, which most offenders think they will avoid—if they think about it at all—and in a restorative system offenders would be more likely to accept responsibility for their acts. Instead of the blunt instrument of fear, there will be two further strategies for crime reduction: research, monitoring and feedback from the justice process to the crime prevention agency; and, in accordance with psychological findings, a social policy based on rewarding good behaviour rather than on punishing deviance.

Rehabilitative measures can work if their aims are specific enough, but they fail to denounce the crime because they are based on the offender's needs rather than on his actions. But if the victim requests them, and the offender agrees, they become a way of making reparation.

Containment will still be available, for protection only; it will be achieved through non-custodial supervision and control wherever possible, but by coercion (including detention) if that is unavoidable. Opportunities for reparation will be available within the institutions.

As regards denunciation, the reparation will serve that purpose as well, although it will be based on what each victim and offender agree, rather than on an attempt to make everything consistent and proportionate to each offence. Denunciation is inconsistent with both deterrence and rehabilitation, because the seriousness of the crime is completely unrelated to the amount of fear, or help, that might prevent the individual from repeating it. And if a punitive sanction is supposed to express the impact on the victim as well as the criminality of the offender, the tangled skein begins to look more like a Gordian knot.

Retribution is closely allied to denunciation; in a restorative system it will be interpreted as 'paying back', in the sense explained by the Judge. There could be attempts to make it proportionate to the seriousness of the offence, although this would meet some of the same problems as the proportionality of punishment. But in restorative justice the *process* is as important as the *outcome*, and it is for the parties themselves to reach an agreement satisfactory for them; they should not be subject to the preconceptions of other people, such as lawyers or even victim/offender mediation services. Retributive justice is supposed to prevent people taking the law into their own hands (a euphemism for vigilantism or lynching); but as I have mentioned it creates an expectation that retribution should be the response to crime, and it may make vigilantism more, not less, likely.

The criminal justice system (or rather, restorative justice system) will deal with individual cases only; it will not be distorted by attempts to influence (through deterrence) the behaviour of people who have nothing to do with the crime being processed. If properly implemented, this is likely to reduce crime; but that will be a side-effect, a bonus, not a primary goal. And to answer the second part of your question, after what we have heard about punishment, I think that excluding it from the system will be a great step forward.

Q. It sounds as if the main aims of the conventional system are still there, but have become secondary ones?

A. You could say that, but they are still important. The main point is that I wouldn't define restorative justice merely in terms of conventional justice, because its essential qualities do not have much place in the existing system. Restorative justice regards the satisfaction of victims' needs as a primary criterion of success, it makes the offender an active, not a passive participant, and it involves the community. It also takes account of the fact that many offenders are also victims—literally, of crimes, but also disadvantaged, without adequate parenting, failed by schools, and 'victims of the system'. Its ethos is non-adversarial and problem-solving. Society should assist the victim and aid reintegration of the offender, and should act on crime-reduction implications which become evident from cases brought to mediation or court.

Q. How could restorative justice be linked to the new measures in the Crime and Disorder Act 1998?

A. That depends on how the Act is implemented. The basic principle should be to try voluntary measures, worked out through victim/offender mediation or conferencing, first, and to use compulsion only as a last resort. There is evidence, as the Civil Servant has said, that people pay compensation more reliably if they have agreed to it than if it is imposed by a court. What troubles me, like the Probation Officer, is that the Act is full of 'orders'—for reparation, action plans, and so on; I shall be reassured if, in practice, there is an opportunity for victims and offenders to agree on them first; and in the case of parenting orders, a family conference would be a good place for a family to accept that a parenting order would help them, before it was imposed on them. This is in the spirit of 'democratic' restorative justice, as the Philosopher described it. The Act also contains the controversial anti-social behaviour order, which is a civil order, but to breach it is a criminal offence; here again, there should be the possibility of resolving matters by mediation before the big stick is wielded—and similarly with other recent legislation such as the Noise Act 1996, the Housing Act 1996 and the Prevention of Harassment Act 1997.

Q. Is there a problem with the co-existence of restorative measures and the retributive system?

A. There is a difficulty, although we naturally hope it is temporary. Sometimes a restorative measure can replace a conventional one; and it should be remembered that some existing measures are at least partly restorative, such as compensation orders and community service orders. In other cases one can envisage the two side-by-side: the court can impose the official sanction, while on a personal level the restorative process takes place voluntarily, as in 'Danny's' case. Until it is more widely accepted, the sanctions for the most serious offences will be punitive ones, with an opportunity for post-sentence reparation or mediation for those who want it.

Chair: *I realise that there is much more to be said, but we need to move on. There are probably some questions about the practicalities of restorative justice, especially as regards victim/offender mediation and conferencing?*

Q. Who does the actual mediating?

A. It varies. In some places it is done entirely by paid staff, and there is a tendency (especially in Germany) towards creating a new profession. In Austria, full-time mediators are each expected to complete between 110 and 130 cases per year. In Britain, Norway and North America, much use is made of trained volunteers, which has the advantage that the service is close to the community, and as volunteers move on to other activities and new ones are trained, a growing number of the population has understanding of restorative justice. Volunteers also cost less, but—funding agencies please note—they do not cost nothing: they have to be recruited, trained, supported and supervised. (Victim Support uses volunteers similarly.) Another variant, in England at least, is that people start, after initial training, as volunteer mediators; when they have some experience they receive extra training so that they can undertake more complex cases, and are paid for each session. They can acquire an NVQ (national vocational qualification) in mediation skills, and are then eligible for the (still rather few) paid jobs in mediation.

Q. You say that you saw voluntary organizations as one way of involving the public in restorative justice; how would this work?

A. Voluntary organizations are non-governmental, not-for-profit organizations with independent management; as service providers they may be largely government-funded and operate according to standards negotiated with the (local and/or national) government, but ideally they obtain some of their funding from philanthropic sources so as to preserve their independence. This model can involve the community at several levels. The management committee may include officials or elected representatives of the local authority, police, probation, prosecutors, members of other voluntary organizations (for example, working with victims or offenders), churches, and active individual citizens. The second way of involving members of the community is as mediators. They may be trained volunteers who come from all sections and ethnic/linguistic groups of society; or a similar cross-section of people may be paid for each session, and/or there can be paid staff in mediation services. (Mediators should also be represented on the committee.) In some countries there is not so much of a tradition of voluntary activity as in others, but it is possible for this to develop, especially if social and economic conditions are favourable. Thirdly, conferencing involves those members of the community most directly affected: the families of the victim and the offender.

I should point out that victim/offender mediation is only one form of mediation; it is being used in other parts of society, such as in neighbour disputes, and especially in schools, where children have shown great aptitude for the principles of resolving conflict in everybody's interest (Alderson, 1997; Cohen, 1995). If that spreads, it could, in time, make a huge difference to social attitudes.

Q. Is it necessary for the offender to show remorse before mediation can be undertaken?

A. In some cases where the victim is an adult, the opportunity to express their feelings may be enough, as in 'Cathy's' case which I described; but where the victim is a child, they may not be able to handle it if the offender fails to express regret.

Chair: *Finally, I would like to give an opportunity for any questions on theoretical aspects, such as the implications for social justice.*

Q. Two related questions have been raised about the social philosophy underlying restorative justice. One is that responding to a crime by requiring the offender to make amends implies that the blame is put on the offender, just as in a punitive system, and fails to acknowledge the shortcomings of society which contributed to the pressures on him.

A. I don't think it is helpful to talk about blame in either/or terms: we know that many offenders come from deprived backgrounds, and we should offer them any help and support they need, but the fact remains that they have caused harm to other people, and it is appropriate that they should recognise this and make up for it.

Q. May I put a follow-up question? If, to put it crudely, a poor person steals from a rich one and is required to pay back, social inequality remains as great as before. Isn't the requirement to make reparation reinforcing the unjust status quo?

A. Theft and robbery are not acceptable ways of achieving redistribution of wealth (and in any case poor people often steal from poor people). The reparation which affluent victims ask for is often symbolic, and mediation has potential for increasing insight among all concerned—victims, offenders, families if present, and mediators.

Q. Is the process visible enough, as it is not held in open court?

A. Mediation uses the civil-law principle that efforts in good faith to reach a settlement are 'privileged', that is, the discussion cannot be used in a court later, so that the participants can speak freely without fear of self-incrimination. Mediation sessions are not open to the general public, nor reported in the press, but in the model which I prefer, one or both of the mediators are trained members of the public, and the service is managed by a voluntary organization with its own independent committee including members of the public as well as professionals. It could be argued that the *outcome*, but not the proceedings, should be reported in the press. The victim and the offender may be accompanied by family and friends, who are the members of the public most closely associated with the crime and its effects; in the case of conferencing, up to 20 or 30 people may be present (more than there are in the public seats of many court rooms). Finally there are the safeguards I have mentioned, including resolving the case in open court. So the community is involved in several ways.

Appendix: Handout for Session 7

Some Common Questions About Restorative Justice

(A) In relation to current legal concepts

It is claimed that reparation can be proportionate to the seriousness of the offence, just as punishment can; but does this not run into the same sorts of problems which the Philosopher raised? In the case of stolen or damaged goods, there is a clear cash value, but isn't it arbitrary to put a particular price on pain and suffering? Different people will suffer differently from outwardly similar crimes, and will feel differently about how much they want to demand from the offender; in any case, most offenders who come before the courts do not have the money to pay.

This question can be answered in two ways. One is to say that the problems are much the same as those encountered by the conventional justice system, except that here the inequality only affects the amount of good the offender is required to do (in the form of reparation), and not the amount of harm inflicted on him. As the Philosopher pointed out, consistency can even be unfair, because people are different, and the same measure has different impacts. The second is that restorative justice is concerned with a solution acceptable to individuals, and is not encumbered by the effort to include deterrence or retribution, to take account of such matters as the offender's previous convictions, nor to be comparable with the outcome of other cases; so if the individuals feel the process and outcome are fair, the objective has been achieved. Other individuals in apparently similar circumstances are free to come to different agreements if they wish. If unreasonable reparation is demanded of the offender, the safeguards just mentioned are available; if the amount appears much too little, it may be considered that the community has also been harmed, and the court can require some additional reparation on its behalf. In either case, restorative justice stresses the importance of the process of communication for its own sake, rather than the outcome.

There is inconsistency in sentencing under existing conditions; but wouldn't it be far more inconsistent, and hence unfair, if every victim and offender worked out their own sentence?

There are two essential differences. This is not punishment, but a way of making things better for the people concerned; so what is right for them does not have to be, in fact can't be, the same as what is right for others. We will no longer be aiming at an equality of misery, nor even of reparation: the aim is to find a solution acceptable to this victim and this offender. Another victim and another offender are entitled to make different choices. What's more, the conventional system imposes orders, or at best obtains the offender's consent; in a restorative process, both the offender and the victim not only agree, but help to work out the action plan. If there is no agreement, they can ask the court to decide.

Do prisons have any place in a restorative system? If so, and if the prison sentence is not proportionate to the seriousness of the crime because it is no longer based on punishment, how do you decide how long to restrain someone for the protection of the public?

There would be some restriction of liberty in restorative justice; the difference would be that any restraint, including custody, would be imposed only for public protection, not for punishment and wherever possible it would consist of non-custodial restraints, such as withdrawal of the right to drive a car or run a business. This would still require difficult decisions about release, similar to the decisions about paroling life sentence prisoners at present: how can behaviour outside be predicted on the basis of behaviour inside, what support do prisoners need after release to make them less likely to re-offend, and to what extent is it fair to lock up all people with certain characteristics when there is a statistical probability that, say, only 20 or ten or five per cent of them will commit another serious offence?

Assessing people's fitness for release is always a problem, especially on the basis of their behaviour in prison. But this is the same under any system. So is the fact that people's behaviour depends on their surroundings and their reception by the community. But in a restorative system it is expected that the offender will have spent his time in prison making reparation or working on any problems he had (illiteracy, lack of skills, quick temper, and so on); so the community should find it easier to accept him than if he just came out with the label 'dangerous offender'. We have to accept that zero risk is unattainable. Many more people are killed on the roads or in industrial accidents than through homicide: if we really wanted even to come close to achieving it we should have to begin by banning cars, which car owners would regard as an intolerable restriction of their autonomy; we should also have to lock up large numbers of people who in fact posed no risk, which is an even greater restriction.

If we continue to lock people away, we owe it to ourselves, let alone to them and their families, to ensure that prison regimes are constructive and humane—otherwise people will come out angry and unemployable.

How can someone make reparation where there is no actual harm: where the crime is an attempted one, or someone throws a stone from a motorway bridge but no one is injured, or (as in shoplifting or receiving stolen goods) the goods are recovered in the act of detecting the crime?

An attempt can still cause harm, because the victim and other members of the community are left fearing that the offender or someone else will make a successful attempt. So it can be treated as harm to the victim if he or she is aware of the attempt, or else to the community, and reparation made accordingly. In your second example (to which you might add drunken driving where no one is injured), the offender might be asked to meet motorway users, or ambulance officers, or victims who *were* injured in similar incidents. For some shoplifters, a meeting with the proprietor or manager may be enough; others might be required to pay a contribution to enforcement costs.

What happens if the offender cannot possibly repay the value of the goods he has stolen, or the amount of compensation which a victim should receive for his or her injury?

This is the sort of question which the victim and the offender are best placed to decide between themselves. In many cases the offender will only be able to pay a symbolic amount, and if the damage is irreparable, no cash value can be placed on it, for example if an item of great sentimental value has been stolen or destroyed, or if the victim's face is scarred. The victim may want to feel that the offender will regret his act for the rest of his life; some may want substantial reparation, either in the form of money or community service for a long period. In one case a woman had been raped, and the offender said that he was genuinely sorry. He had saved up nearly enough to buy a motor bike, which he wanted more than anything else; he handed over the amount he had saved. The important thing for the victim was that this was a real sacrifice for him, and that he had made it voluntarily. The actual amount of money was almost irrelevant. Courts could not reach solutions of this kind. If the victim suffers severe financial hardship or physical injury as a result of the crime, for which the offender cannot possibly pay adequate compensation, the community should provide care and support, for example through the social welfare or health care system (or, in countries that do not have a national health service, by paying medical bills).

That is how restorative justice can work at its best, and results of this kind are more likely to be reached where communication between the victim and the offender is possible. But there will be three kinds of case in which this model will not fit. Where the offender denies the act, the case must be tested in court. Where he or she expresses no regret, the victim and people in general will want 'something' to be done, and if the offence was serious they will want the something to be a substantial sanction. This brings us up against the question of proportionality once again; but it could be argued that if the sanction is a reparative one (that is, the offender is ordered to do some good rather than merely suffer some pain), its precise relationship to the offence or to other sanctions is less important. Thirdly, the offender may fail to complete the agreed reparation; in that case a degree of coercion would be appropriate.

Where there is a substantial risk that the offender will commit a further grave crime, restraint may be necessary, as has been pointed out above.

What guarantee is there that the offender will fulfil the agreement?

Compliance is generally good: often offenders genuinely want to show that they are sorry, and take the opportunity to make a fresh start. When the mediation or conference comes after the criminal justice process, for example after a caution, discontinued prosecution, or sentence, there is no criminal sanction for non-compliance. In the case of compensation, the mediation service may hold a further mediation session or assist the victim in taking civil enforcement action, but this is not common. However, in a conference, members of the extended family may undertake to ensure that the offender attends school, does community service, or whatever he agreed to do.

The alternative is to keep the official process in reserve, as an inducement to comply. This can be done at several stages of the process: prosecution can be conditionally suspended (provided the offender admits the act), the court hearing can be conditionally adjourned, or, after the offender has been convicted, sentence can be deferred, or the agreement can be made part of the sentence and subject to conventional enforcement procedures. All of these are used in various countries. All except the last, however, are in danger of being prevented by the pressure in some countries, including Britain, for the whole process to be concluded ever more quickly. These measures should be used to obtain *reparation*, but not to apply pressure for *mediation*; that would put pressure on the victim, which is not acceptable.

(B) In relation to its own principles: Voluntariness, safeguards for victims and offenders

Given that mediators stress that participation is voluntary and that it depends on the accused admitting the act, what happens when victims or offenders refuse to take part, or the offender is not caught or protests innocence?

To take victims first: how can pressure on them to participate be avoided? According to the Victim Assistance Worker, Victim Support has suggested that even asking victims to decide whether to take part could cause anxiety to some: they could worry about whether, by refusing, they would feel responsible for the offender getting a worse punishment, or even more seriously, they could fear reprisals. The long-established victim/offender mediation services have already taken this on board. Firstly, although the victim will of course be consulted, it is the mediation service that makes the decision whether mediation is appropriate in a given case, and this is made clear to the offender. Secondly, conferencing can go ahead without the victim, although the great majority choose to take part.

Thirdly, if the offender regrets his act but the victim does not wish to receive his apology, the offender can perform reparation to the community, so both the victim and the offender know that the offender is no worse off as a result of the victim's preference for not taking part, or (as I suggested in my talk) he can take part in a victim/offender group, if there is one. Fourthly, when mediation or conferencing is part of the normal procedure, as it is for juveniles in New Zealand and Austria, and some parts of Australia, the decision is much less stark; taking part will be as normal as giving evidence is now, but the safeguards just mentioned will enable victims to opt out if they want to. But it is likely that as the system becomes better known, more victims will wish to participate.

As for offenders, there are three levels of consent. When something is voluntary, you are no worse off if you don't do it. If it requires consent, you can choose, but you might get something worse if you refuse. The third level is compulsion. For mediation, there is some discussion as to whether to insist on the first level, or whether the second is acceptable and does not put too much pressure on the victim; for reparation, the offender should be given the opportunity to comply willingly, but compulsion may be used if he does not.

What will be the position of offenders? What procedural safeguards will they have? Will they have proper access to lawyers? How do you avoid pressure on them to admit guilt for the sake of what looks like a soft option?

A soft option it certainly is not: many victims have recognised that it took guts on the offender's part to come and face them. The risk of an innocent person pleading guilty to 'get it over with' would be no greater than it is now. What is more, if a person did admit something he didn't do, that would be likely to become clear in the mediation session; whereas court procedures are not adapted to testing guilty pleas. In the last resort, if someone is wrongly convicted, being compelled to do something constructive is less of an injustice than being wrongly punished (although obviously I am not belittling the importance of wrongful convictions, which are always a serious matter). As for lawyers, offenders have of course a right to be represented, but mediation is not based on legal concepts and it has not been found helpful for lawyers to be present. If the offender considers that the process was unfair in any way, he can use the complaints procedure, or he can walk out so that the case can be reviewed by the court.

It is important to distinguish two sorts of 'not guilty' plea. There is a difference between what Professor Nigel Walker calls the 'wrong person' and the 'blameless doer'. If the accused says 'It wasn't me, I have an alibi' or 'I never laid a finger on her', the case has to go to trial. But if he says 'I did the act, but I had a valid reason for doing it', there is something which can be cleared up between him and the victim. Admitting an act which is not disputed does not prejudice the right of the accused to plead not guilty on legal grounds.

It can be argued that decisions of this kind are seldom completely voluntary; even if the system exerts no pressure, other people such as family and friends may do so. Conversely, even if the system does exert pressure, parties may still take part willingly; they have the choice whether to 'engage' in the process, and this choice is empowering (S Wright, 1998: 34).

What happens when there are multiple offenders, or multiple victims? Or when the victim is an organization?

Multiple victims or offenders are not so much of a problem as you might think. The very first case which led to VORP's creation included 22 victims. If the numbers are very big, some sort of compromise will be necessary, just as prosecutors or courts often opt to proceed only on specimen charges.

When there is a corporate victim, such as a shop or a school, it can often be represented by the member of staff most affected—the night watchman or the assistant manager responsible for security, the school caretaker or a form teacher.

Does restorative justice draw people into the criminal justice process who might otherwise have been dealt with by informal measures?

Research in New Zealand suggests that on the contrary, since family group conferences were introduced in 1989, more cases have been diverted out of the system by the police, and conferences have been used in cases which would otherwise have gone to court (Maxwell and Morris, 1996). In Kettering, Northamptonshire, some experienced more intervention than they would have otherwise, some less. Braithwaite (1998) considers that restorative justice more often narrows the 'net' of formal state control, but tends to widen community control, and that this form of 'net-widening' can be a good thing, especially in such cases as white-collar crime and domestic violence.

Is it possible to deal with offences where there is very serious harm (such as rape or homicide) in a restorative system? Can the sanction be restorative in such cases? What if the victim is very forgiving, or very vengeful?

Firstly, bear in mind that the *process* as well as the outcome aims to be beneficial: many victims want to express their feelings and ask questions which only the offender can answer. The court can reduce reparation if it appears excessive, or impose an extra *reparative* sanction to make amends for harm done to the community. In the transitional period, victim/offender dialogue can be offered *after* the sentence: in parts of America, for example, there is a waiting list of relatives of murder victims who want to meet prisoners on death row, not to attack them but to find out about the death of their relative and complete their grieving—and sometimes to forgive. Judge McElrea advises strongly against the exclusion of serious crime: the deeper the hurt that has occurred the greater the need for healing (often on both sides) and the greater the potential benefit to the community from 'putting right the wrong'. It would not be suitable in every rape case, but in some it would have 'a huge amount to offer': he quotes a rape victim who said 'This is not a justice system. This is a legal system. My intention was never to have him sent to jail, because he is an elderly person and he is ill. My intention was only ever to get validation. It's important that you stop the eating away inside you of the big secret' (McElrea, 1998: 17).

These methods are very new. What is being done to ensure that both victims and offenders are dealt with properly?

What's right for particular people will be different in different cases, and we should respect that, but human rights safeguards are needed. The European Court of Human Rights has found, for example, that a mother has a right to see reports about her child at a Scottish children's hearing (in the case of McMichael: Kelly, 1996: 111-2).

Safeguards for all concerned are, or should be, provided by the usual methods of quality assurance. In Canberra and South Australia police or social workers present at a conference have a right and responsibility to veto outcomes that are seriously inappropriate; but they should not interfere with legitimate wishes of the parties. In New Zealand judges oversee the process, but in a restorative, not a legalistic, spirit. In Britain a *Victim & Offender Mediation Training Handbook* is available (Quill and Wynne, 1993), and *Practice Standards for Mediators and Management of Mediation Services* have been issued by Mediation UK (1998), covering such subjects as confidentiality and neutrality, but a more detailed code of practice is needed to provide for putting the standards into effect. Basic principles have been drawn up by the Restorative Justice Consortium (1999).

Mediation UK has introduced an accreditation procedure for mediation services, and is working on similar standards for individual mediators, and for trainers. Trainers should have experience of mediating themselves, and it will be some time before enough people have enough experience. There should be built-in supervision and in-service training. Preferably mediators should work in pairs, and evaluate their own and each other's performance after each session. There should be routine follow-up (with the parties' consent) to ask them whether they found the process fair and helpful, and periodic in-depth research. A further safeguard is a publicised complaints procedure, which should itself include an opportunity for independent mediation at an early stage.

UPDATE TO THE FIRST EDITION

Looking Back, Looking Forward

Is there more respect for justice since this 'Symposium' was first published? The answer appears to be 'Yes', when restorative methods are used. The word 'Respect' has been adopted by the British government as the slogan for a programme aiming to tackle bad behaviour and nurture good—and so help create a modern culture of respect. It is described on the official website[1] as being about working together to build a society in which we can respect one another; not about going back to the past or the days of 'knowing your place', but being considerate of the consequences of our behaviour for others. No one can take exception to that, but the examples given are selective: more about dumping litter and urinating in the street than, say, the behaviour of managers to employees, teachers to pupils or immigration officers to refugees from tyrannical governments. The message seems to be that respect is to be enforced by on-the-spot fines, anti-social behaviour orders and even prison, rather than that people will be treated with respect and fairness while the same is expected of them. There are signs, however, of progress towards the use of acceptable behaviour contracts, which require an element of consent, and there is scope for the use of mediation in drawing them up. Under the new government that took over under Gordon Brown in 2007, the Respect Taskforce was replaced that year by a 'Youth Taskforce' in the Department for Children, Schools and Families.

As regards criminal justice, there has been much emphasis on victims; for example the then Prime Minister, Tony Blair, said on 18 June 2002, 'The time has come to rebalance the system so that we restore the faith of victims and witnesses.' [2] Policies have however been focused on the existing criminal justice system; research showing that there is consistently high satisfaction with restorative processes, among both victims and offenders, has not been included in official rhetoric, where apparently little but reconviction rates are almost the only findings considered significant.

HOW FAR HAVE WE COME?

Both the practice and the theory of restorative justice have developed extensively in the first years of the new millennium. This postscript gives a short overview, and the list of references may likewise serve as a select bibliography. After this section—which reviews progress in schools, community mediation, victim-offender mediation and restorative justice, and research—it will consider problems faced by the restorative movement: reasons for the lack of progress, and also some theoretical concerns, political concerns, and professional resistance. It will then consider how the restorative movement could spread, contributing towards a restorative society. A comprehensive account of the development of restorative justice, with numerous case histories, is provided in Marian Liebmann's *Restorative Justice: How it Works*,[3] which also covers related issues, including its use in contexts such as domestic violence, sexual offences, and large-scale oppression.

Schools
More schools in England and Wales are beginning to realize the benefits of self-discipline based on mutual respect, as compared with imposed discipline based on authority. Older children are shown how to mediate between their younger peers; this can improve the atmosphere in playgrounds, reducing bullying and hence also the number of children excluded from school. A Peer Mediation Network is being established, with over 100 schools and individuals as members. Membership is growing, and it plans to encourage the further growth of peer mediation and other restorative practices in schools. In England and Wales, over 55 local authorities now run at least one 'restorative approaches in schools' project.[4] An example is Lewisham, in south-east London, which has pioneered the method since 2003 and uses it even for serious incidents such as a boy breaking another boy's nose; in such cases the parents are brought in as well. It has published an account of its experiences.[5] Mediation can also be used by adults: between staff in dispute, or between parents, teaching staff, and local education authorities. Parents can be shown how to use it at home. It is not a soft option: being accountable to fellow students, friends and family for the impact of one's behaviour can be an uncomfortable experience, but whereas a punitive

response alienates a person still more, a restorative one can re-integrate them into the school community.[6]

There has been considerable progress in Scotland. A study of the introduction of restorative practices in 18 schools found that 14 were assessed as having made significant progress, and a further three had some experience of success. In half of the schools there was strong evidence of improved relationships within the school community. In several there was a decrease in exclusions and school discipline referrals. There was clear evidence of children developing conflict resolution skills. Restorative practices have had a major impact on most of the schools involved in the evaluation. The report recommends continued support and training for the development of restorative practices in Scottish schools.[7]

Community mediation

Community mediation is continuing in many areas, some of which are developing in other fields such as schools and victim-offender work.[8] Development has been slowed by the difficulties of the national organization Mediation UK, leading to its closure through lack of funding in 2006, but moves are in train to fill the gap.

Victim-offender mediation and restorative justice

There was encouragement in 2003 when the Home Office published a consultation document on restorative justice strategy,[9], including 'a vision of restorative justice fully integrated into the criminal justice system and embedded in wider society' (p. 52). Soon afterwards, however, the Restorative Justice Unit in the Home Office was closed as part of a programme of civil service cuts ordered by the then Chancellor of the Exchequer. Also in 2003, the Criminal Justice Act introduced a number of measures in which restorative practice can be used, although it is not specifically mentioned. Two examples are deferment of sentence and conditional cautions for adult offenders, both of which provide opportunities for victim-offender mediation and possible reparation. The official guidance on conditional cautions[10] is sympathetic to the ideals of restorative justice, including, for example, references to the involvement of community-based organizations and volunteer facilitators; but only two of the six areas which piloted conditional cautions included a restorative dimension and there is little sign that this is happening widely now that the scheme is being rolled out nationwide. This is a challenge for the voluntary sector to provide a service; the Crown Prosecution Service, however, appears to be offering no funding for it.

The Criminal Justice and Immigration Bill 2007, in progress at the time of writing, replaces various sentences with 'youth rehabilitation orders', within which courts can order 'requirements'. One of these is an activity whose purpose is reparation, such as 'an activity involving contact between an offender and persons affected by the offences in respect of which the order was made', the first reference to victim-offender dialogue in English law; but it remains only a possibility until there are services to undertake the mediation, and the courts use them. It joins other measures, such as final warnings, deferred sentences and reparation orders, which allow the use of mediation but do not actively encourage it.

The most widespread application of something approaching restorative principles is the referral order. It is for juvenile offenders, aged ten to 17, who are pleading guilty and appearing in court for the first time.[11] For the great majority of these young people (unless their offences are too serious or too minor) the court must make a referral order, sending the case to a youth offender panel. Thus the panels do not suffer the difficulty in attracting cases experienced by some restorative projects: there are over 25,000 cases a year. The panels operate restoratively in that they can include the victim in the process; they seek to find a constructive rather than a punitive outcome, often including some form of reparation; and they involve members of the community as trained volunteer panel members. Little decision-making is entrusted to the victim and offender, however: the panel remains in control. In many places only a small percentage of victims take part. A relatively small part of the training of panel members is about restorative justice, but the Youth Justice Board has issued an action plan to 'broaden, develop and extend' the practice of restorative justice.[12]

The Government has introduced Community Justice Centres: the prototype, in Kirkdale, north Liverpool, was established in 2005, and about seven others have started or are due to open in 2007. There are preventive services for people with problems such as addictions, debts and accommodation difficulties, as well as activities for young people. They provide for reparative work in the community, such as cleaning up a canal or a churchyard, but this is part of a court order, not a restorative agreement. There is lack of clarity in the thinking: community service, introduced in 1972, is now given the less restorative name of unpaid work, and can be a requirement under a community order,[13] but it appears so similar to reparative work that the Home Office Crime Reduction website says that 'branding' will be required to distinguish them.[14] A restorative justice co-ordinator has been appointed, but not many conferences have taken place as yet. This seems a good opportunity to introduce community-based restorative justice; it remains to be seen how it will develop. Another innovation is the 'Police and peer panels' in Preston, Lancashire, in which teenagers conduct meetings with victims and perpetrators of anti-social behaviour. Unfortunately, although they have been called 'restorative justice centres' they have been presented as similar to a court, aiming to produce acceptable behaviour contracts; the advantages of the process for victims, and the difference from courts and punishment are not stressed, with the result that the media have ridiculed them.[15]

Perhaps closer to the restorative ideal is the Community Justice Panel in Chard and Ilminster, Somerset. This has similarities to the Preston project: it has a panel of trained volunteers and uses acceptable behaviour contracts, but it is mainly for adults, and emphasises the needs of victims and the restorative nature of the process. It will also use conditional cautions.[16]

Meanwhile the Restorative Justice Consortium has produced a statement of *Principles of Restorative Processes*[17] and is encouraging those who use restorative methods to adopt it. One application is to harmful behaviour which is not always thought of as 'crime': failure to comply with health and safety regulations which are easily mocked as bureaucratic or 'nannying', but which can be a matter of life and death. In 2006-7, for example, the number of deaths at work rose to a five-year high of 241, in a period when the number of staff and inspectors was cut by 1,000.[18] A report by the Better Regulation Executive on 'making sanctions effective' put changing the behaviour of the offender above punishment as a sanctioning principle, followed by aiming to restore the harm caused by regulatory non-compliance; accordingly it recommended the use of restorative justice techniques either as a pre-court diversion instead of a monetary penalty or within the criminal justice system, before or after sentence.[19] This principle and its applications in Australia and elsewhere have also been described by John Braithwaite.[20]

Scotland

Restorative justice is available in Scotland for juveniles. Provision for adult offenders or their victims is well established, although only in a few places.[21] For juveniles the services operate on the basis of diversion from prosecution; they are provided by the non-government organization Sacro (Safeguarding Communities, Reducing Offending). The facilitators include local volunteers recruited and trained by Sacro staff. A restorative intervention is also possible in combination with deferment of sentence, and in serious cases after sentence, but this is little used. The Scottish Executive has stated that it is politically committed to restorative justice processes.

Northern Ireland

Restorative justice has developed in an interesting way in Northern Ireland. Projects were started separately in the Republican and Loyalist communities, but drawing on the same philosophy. In a province where there was much hostility to the police, rough and violent justice had been enforced by paramilitary groups, but it was found to be ineffective, and Community Restorative Justice Ireland and Northern Ireland Alternatives were set up in the two communities, respectively. In Phase II of the programmes (2003-2005), 82 per cent and 71 per cent of potential paramilitary punishments were prevented in the two areas.[22] The Justice (Northern Ireland) Act 2002 brings restorative justice into the mainstream by providing that where the facts are not disputed, all but the least serious and most serious cases involving young offenders must be referred to a 'diversionary' conference (by the prosecutor) or a court-ordered one. Professional co-ordinators are used, but members of the community may be involved in the process. However, there is little co-operation with the community-based projects; official guidelines from the Northern Ireland Office imposed conditions to which both programmes objected, in particular because they would no longer allow self-referrals to the programmes.[23] The House of Commons Northern Ireland Affairs Committee recognised the work of Greater Shankill Alternatives (now part of Northern Ireland Alternatives) and the Republican-based Community Restorative Justice Ireland, and the former received the Queen's Award for Voluntary Service in 2007; but the committee wanted them both to be subject to requirements imposed by the formal criminal justice system.[24]

International

Restorative justice is developing internationally. In 1999 a European Forum for Victim-Offender Mediation and Restorative Justice was formed,[25] providing a network for those in all European countries to exchange experience and information. In addition to holding regular conferences[26] and workshops, publishing a newsletter and maintaining a website,[27] it has supported countries working to comply with the European Union Framework Decision of 2001, which calls on member states to promote mediation in criminal cases. Members of the Forum, and others, have contributed to 'Action A21', a project of COST (European Co-operation in the Field of Scientific and Technical Research), which is producing a series of seven books on restorative justice.[28] The Council of Europe meanwhile has produced recommendations on victim-offender mediation,[29] and commissioned the European Forum to write a book on establishing restorative justice programmes.[30] In parallel, the United Nations produced its own not dissimilar *Basic Principles*[31] followed by a *Handbook*.[32]

New Zealand is extending its restorative work to adults. The Sentencing Act 2002 lists eight purposes of sentencing: the first four are clearly oriented towards restorative justice:

- to hold the offender accountable for harm done to the victim and the community by the offending; or
- to promote in the offender a sense of responsibility for, and an acknowledgement of, that harm; or
- to provide for the interests of the victim of the offence; or
- to provide reparation for harm done by the offending.

The others are to denounce the offence, to deter the offender or others, to protect the community from the offender, to assist in the offender's rehabilitation and reintegration, or a combination of any of these.[33]

Different European countries follow restorative principles to different extents.[34] In Norway, mediation was introduced by law in 1991, for both civil and criminal conflicts (over half of them criminal, but limited to cases that do not qualify for immediate custody), and for adult and juvenile offenders. Local mediation services, financed by the Ministry of Justice, use volunteer mediators. In Austria, victim-offender mediation has had a legal basis since 2000; it can be used for offences punishable with not more than five years' imprisonment, for adults and juveniles. By 2002 nearly 9,000 cases per year were referred, the great majority of them ending without a prosecution. There is a very high degree of victim participation (96 per cent) and satisfaction (83 per cent); a substantial proportion of cases involve domestic violence, where it has been found that women feel that the process gives them an improved sense of control over their life. Professional mediators are used, however, and there is some feeling that the process is becoming routinized and over-regulated. Developments in 25 European countries have been summarized by the European Forum,[35] with updates in its newsletter and website.

Research

Research on restorative justice is a growing industry. To select just a few of the important reports published in this period:

All of the studies have shown a substantial proportion of both victims and offenders who are satisfied with the process, although it is important to provide support for those who are not, as Heather Strang has pointed out.[36] Gabrielle Maxwell and Allison Morris, who have researched family group conferences extensively in New Zealand, have made some findings which are not surprising but are important to remember.[37] The quality of the conferencing process makes a difference: there is less likelihood of re-offending if the offender feels remorse but is not made to feel a bad person, feels involved in the process, meets the victim and apologises, and agrees with the outcome. But these factors are outnumbered by the influences in early life, to which criminologists have drawn attention for years: being a victim of bullying, living in many places as a child, harsh punishment as a child, witnessing parental violence and similar factors. What happens after the conference is also important, such as not gaining employment, and not having close friends since the conference. Clearly the impact of restorative justice will be limited if these are not addressed.

Research has been carried out by Professor Joanna Shapland and colleagues in Sheffield into three projects for adults: Connect (a voluntary sector/probation partnership, offering mediation mainly after conviction and before sentence in South London); Justice Research Consortium (using conferencing in London, Thames Valley and Northumbria); and REMEDI (a voluntary sector mediation service in Sheffield). The research has shown: that the outcomes were better where victims were willing to meet offenders face-to-face rather than through 'indirect' mediation, pointing to the need to clarify the interaction with the criminal justice system[38]; and that the expectations of victims and offenders were generally met, although this was less likely in a minority of cases where the victim and offender strongly disagreed about what happened during the offence, where facilitators were too dominant or failed to intervene when things became too heated or one-sided, or where the mediation service did not follow up outcome agreements. Conferencing, with supporters present, tended to make agreements easier to achieve.[39]

Two other researchers, Professor Lawrence Sherman and Dr Heather Strang, after an extensive literature review (including their own research),[40] found that both victims and offenders were more satisfied with justice after a restorative process; victims who receive restorative justice do better, on average, than those who do not, and are less likely to express a desire for violent revenge (p. 63). Diversion from prosecution increases the odds of an offender being brought to justice, but there are legal obstacles to its use in England and Wales. Restorative justice does as well as, or better than, conventional criminal justice and short prison sentences as regards repeat offending, especially with violent crimes (p. 88). Sherman and Strang propose an official restorative justice board (p. 90), although others would recommend entrusting it to a non-governmental organization.

Other research meanwhile shows the importance of social factors; although individual incidents have to be responded to, crime reduction must be addressed through wider social policy. Richard Wilkinson, professor of social epidemiology at the University of Nottingham, has shown that there is now incontrovertible evidence, from many countries, that high inequality is more significant than poverty. It is regularly accompanied by more violence, including homicide; increased mental illness; lower trust; and poorer community relations. Inequality is a 'social pollution' which increases status competition and the stresses of early childhood, especially among poorer families. Its effects are particularly clear among young adults who lose out: rates of violence among young men and teenage pregnancies among women are reliable markers of the social breakdown caused by greater inequality.[41]

WHAT PROBLEMS DOES THE RESTORATIVE MOVEMENT FACE?

Lack of progress

The standard of debate on criminal policy is lamentable. Public concern about any particular form of crime is followed almost automatically by an increase in the maximum (or even the minimum) sentence: for example, the only action proposed by the then prime minister, Tony Blair, after an alarming number of gun crimes, was to lower the age at which a mandatory five-year sentence for carrying an illegal gun could be applied.[42] Politicians do not only 'talk tough', like the Politician in this Symposium, but act tough as well. In total, the Government has brought in 54 law-and-order measures[43] and created 3,023 new offences since May 1997. They include 1,169 which were debated in Parliament—and 1,854 which were not, being introduced by secondary legislation such as statutory instruments and orders in council.[44]

Even readers of the relatively liberal *Guardian* newspaper contribute to its website comments such as, 'We should lock up more of them in specialised schools. Public protection comes first,' and, 'I tend to think we might as well keep the damage they do to society to a minimum by keeping them away from everyone else,'[45] although there are also better-informed views. When the Lord Chief Justice, Lord Phillips, warned that our current long prison sentences may one day be seen as shocking, as the stocks and hanging are today, and called for more community punishments, he was branded as 'a poor judge' and pilloried in the popular press.[46] Despite an opinion poll finding more people agreeing that prison doesn't work and turns people into professional criminals, and that we should not build more prisons but look for other ways,[47] policy does not seem to be affected.

Television programmes have recently shown that disorganized young people can be inspired and trained to do remarkable things, such as learning catering skills, gardening or even ballet dancing, and other unpublicized projects are doing similar things, as varied as a bicycle repair shop at Wandsworth Youth Offending Team which refurbishes bikes and donates them to people whose bikes have been stolen, and the restoration of a public park in Middlesbrough by prisoners. Yet the idea that drawing out young people's abilities, rather than merely punishing their harmful behaviour, is slow to penetrate the public consciousness. A politician who dares to point out that offenders have skills that could be put to better use receives brickbats and little support.[48]

There are some moves in a more evidence-based (and humane) direction. The government has promoted Sure Start, a programme to give disadvantaged children a better start in life, and in the voluntary sector Home Start does similar work, while the children's charity Kids Company uses a combination of therapeutic techniques and loving care to provide practical and emotional support to 'lone children' who experience significant psychosocial difficulties because their parent is unable to function as a caring adult. Both, however, and many others, have a constant struggle to obtain adequate funding.

In another initiative, Circles of Support and Accountability bring together trained volunteers to support a sex offender with a low level of support and a high risk of re-offending, to befriend him and if necessary challenge signs of inappropriate behaviour. This may be considered a restorative programme, because among other things it encourages offenders to consider their victims' feelings, although in most cases direct communication between the victim and offender would be inappropriate.[49]

The government has forced Victim Support, the charity whose volunteers offer help to victims, to replace its locally managed services with centrally administered victim care units. These are being 'rolled out' nationally after three pilot schemes in 2006-07. The £5.6 million cost is intended to come from the Victim Surcharge Fund that was established on 1 April 2007. This requires that £15 of every fine imposed on offenders goes towards the Fund.[50] It is claimed that this will improve services to victims, but there is no connection between individual victims and offenders, and restorative interventions do not appear to be part of the plan.

The evidence shows, with very few exceptions, that schools benefit from the use of restorative methods; that in community mediation, parties who agree to mediate reach an agreement in eight or nine cases out of ten, and in criminal justice many more victims are satisfied with the process than with courts, while reconviction rates are no worse and usually better. In England and Wales it is growing, from the bottom up, but slowly; the encouraging statements by the Government have been followed by little action and still less funding. Similarly in schools, politicians often call for anti-bullying policies, but do not say that they should be restorative ones.

In many countries restorative practices are limited to juvenile offenders, and in almost all, serious offences are excluded, except that in some cases a restorative process can be added to a prison sentence rather than replace it. Similarly, government ministers in Britain are apt to make statements encouraging initiatives by volunteers; but voluntary organizations wishing to offer a service often find it difficult to obtain funds or even referrals, or to gain entry to the criminal justice system. There are also volunteers in the system, members of youth offender panels, but they are trained and managed by officials (although they have formed their own Association of Panel Members).

Clearly restorative justice has some answers (its advocates try to avoid excessive claims) but they have not yet been heard. Why is this? One mundane reason is that even if money were saved from the prison budget, we lack a mechanism for transferring the savings to pay the much lower costs of community-based sanctions. The Politician suggested a way of overcoming this, by 'cost transfer', in the first contribution to this Symposium (pp. 18-19), but we are still waiting for the penny to drop. However there may be deeper reasons than that. They fall into three broad groups: theoretical concerns about the nature of restorative justice; acceptability to politicians and the public; and professional resistance.

Theoretical concerns

In the literature which has been growing fast since this Symposium was first published, legitimate concerns have been raised about some aspects of restorative justice theory. One concerns the proportionality of the reparation agreement to the offence (see e.g. von Hirsch *et al.*, pp. 30-1[51]). The restorative answer is that if outcomes are right for the respective parties they are right, because they are proportionate to the victim's pain. Even if they are different to each other; to overrule them in the name of consistency would take away the autonomy and responsibility that the process is supposed to give them. In any case punishment is ineffective and sentencing cannot be both fair and consistent, as was explained by the Psychologist, the Judge and the Philosopher in the Symposium. As Judge McElrea has said, 'Consistency of outcome is not possible without some injustice'.[52] However, there are three concerns which restorativists have to address. Firstly, although there are few or no reports of its happening, the victim and offender might agree on a totally disproportionate outcome, or the mediation might be conducted in a grossly unfair way; some supervisory mechanism is needed as a safeguard.[53]

Secondly, there is a feeling among both theorists and 'ordinary' members of the public that the consequences should demonstrate the seriousness, as a way of 'norm-clarification' as it is called in the jargon. If there is to be a restorative outcome when a victim is very (too?) forgiving and demands very little reparation, either there has to be a way of adding some reparation on behalf of the community, or the community has to be persuaded that the process itself was enough to bring home to the offender the seriousness of the harm he or she had caused. This will be necessary anyway when victim-offender dialogue is for any reason not possible.

Thirdly, there is the question of public protection against a person who is considered very likely to inflict further serious harm. In some cases restrictions are enough, for example withdrawal of permission to drive a car or run a company; but even the most liberal reformers admit that some people are so uncontrollable that they have to be restrained. The Dutch criminologist John Blad has suggested 'restorative detention':[54] the individual would still be required to make amends, but in conditions which were not deliberately punitive. The seriousness of the crime would be expressed by the amount of reparation; the period of detention would be based only on an assessment of dangerousness. This would still come up against the familiar problem of how to decide the length of detention, but this would be no greater than at present. There is also the practical problem that prisons are constructed on a philosophy of punishment, and it would be hard to convert them to places of 'humane containment' where offenders made their reparation. This should not however be impossible, in view of the fact that the Inside-Out Trust in this country operates programmes in over 70 prisons where prisoners do valuable work for disadvantaged people here and abroad, from refurbishing wheelchairs and computers to producing large-print books, and that several prisons have been successfully converted into hotels (for example Malmaison in Oxford, the Four Seasons in Istanbul and the Liberty Hotel in the former Charles Street Jail in Boston, Mass.[55], as well as Långholmen in Stockholm).

These and other issues are under discussion by academics and practitioners. The most promising solution seems to be the model used in the New Zealand juvenile justice system, where considerable autonomy is left to the family and supporters of the victim and offender in a family group conference, but it is subject to the oversight of a judge who is generally in tune with restorative aims. In addition, questions of good practice and quality assurance need to be addressed by standard-setting,[56] training, support and supervision of mediators. It can be argued that if the involvement of the community is desirable, these functions can appropriately be undertaken by a non-governmental (but government-recognised) organization. It is also easier for an NGO to update a code of practice in the light of experience than it is for a government to amend legislation.

Political concerns

How can an enlightened but realistic politician make a credible case for restorative methods? The Politician in the Symposium attempted to do so. A few years later, there are still unthinking headlines, loaded with mistaken assumptions, such as 'Break an Asbo and still not be jailed'.[57] We live in a controlling society. Those who assume that increasing penalties is 'doing something about crime' have had the upper hand, but even they are worried about the record levels reached by the prison population as a result. In mid-1996, there were 55,256 prisoners in England and Wales; by November 2007 the figure had reached 81,454,[58] and it has continued to rise despite the early release of some prisoners with electronic tags. The average cost per prisoner in 2005-6 was £32,888.[59] This is despite the fall in the number of crimes, by 44 per cent from 1995 to 2005-6, according to the British Crime Survey.[60]

It has become obvious to more people that prison is not the solution but a large part of the problem. What could a well-informed and courageous politician do about it?

One challenge is the desire to symbolize wrongdoing and the task here is to show that we are using the wrong units of measurement. Just as the value of an individual or a company should not be measured in monetary terms but by what they contribute to society, the seriousness of a crime should not be represented by the amount of pain inflicted on the offender, but the effort to make amends. Related to this is the tendency to measure the wrong things, for example the number of anti-social behaviour orders rather than the reduction in anti-social behaviour. At present the number of arrests is counted as 'sanctioned detections' for statistical purposes, rather than incidents resolved without arrest; but it is hoped that this practice will be changed in the near future. Advocates of restorative justice often say that even if the reconviction rate were unchanged, the beneficial effect on victims would be reason enough to use it; yet politicians insist on making recidivism the main criterion.

Another challenge is to persuade politicians and the public that the most effective way to influence people's behaviour is to lead them rather than drive them; to encourage the best they can do rather than merely punish the worst. Our society is controlled by closed-circuit television, electronic tags, stigma ('naming and shaming'), the threat of punishment and ultimately force; a restorative one would keep force in reserve, relying first on the power of relationships, trust, generosity, and faith in everyone's ability to do better.

Professional resistance

Among professionals too there is a question of trust. Can victims and offenders be trusted to reach acceptable solutions? Volunteers to apply restorative principles rather than revert to punitive ones? Voluntary organizations to provide an efficient service? The answer to all of these has been shown to be 'Yes', at least as much as in the official system. Will this diminish the role of professionals? No, but it will change it: for example, prosecutors will have to consider which cases to divert to mediation, and judges to supervise the restorative process; both, however, will continue to deal with cases where the accused denies guilt. The Justice (Northern Ireland) Act 2002 goes further: prosecutors are expected to refer a young offender to the Youth Conferencing Service where they would otherwise have instituted court proceedings, unless he or she does not admit the offence or does not consent to engage in the process.[61]

SPREADING THE RESTORATIVE MOVEMENT

Towards a restorative society

Some governments have embraced restorative justice, both legislating for it and implementing it at least to a limited extent. Examples are Austria, Belgium, New Zealand, Northern Ireland, Norway and Slovenia. Norway is an example of how a statutory system can make use of volunteer mediators. That is one possible way forward. Another possibility is community-based, bottom-up growth until so many people have experienced it that it becomes politically acceptable. Similarly, as the results in pioneering schools become apparent, others may follow, and the same process may take place in families, communities and workplaces. The justice system could progress from the punishment of crime to the repair of harm. This would have to be accompanied by an extensive educative process, probably led by non-governmental organizations: just as over the last few years nearly everyone in Western societies has become aware of the importance of recycling and cutting CO_2 emissions, we would, from youth onwards, be shown skills such as listening and showing empathy, expressing our own feelings, asking how the other person is being affected, and looking for acceptable solutions to meet the needs of everyone involved.

One way of putting these ideas into practice is shown by the Peace Committee project in the South African township of Zwelethemba, and about 20 other communities in Western Cape.[62] A police station that had been closed was re-opened as a 'Community Peace Centre'. The idea of 'PeaceMaking' in South Africa is similar to conferencing; here it is taken further by 'PeaceBuilding'. A dispute or crime is referred to a PeaceMaking Gathering. The involvement of volunteer facilitators from a similar background to that of the participants is seen as an asset. Participants are safeguarded by a code of good practice. Self-referral is also possible, and the Peace Committee can convene a Gathering to address a potential dispute where there are worries that it could escalate into serious violence. They do not refer to 'offenders' or 'victims', because situations are often not as clear as that. Force is never used as a consequence of a Peace Gathering to resolve a problem; if coercion is required, the police are called in.

For each PeaceMaking Gathering, a sum is paid to the facilitators, but an additional amount is paid into a fund that is used for PeaceBuilding operations to approach generic community problems in many different areas like public health, education, crèches and playgrounds for children, youths' sporting activities, support for the elderly, security and environment, cleaning campaigns and so on. A Solutions Gathering may be called to address a long-term problem. These improvements are mainly at a local level; it is hoped that they are the beginning of a deliberative engagement between local values and the need for structural reforms in society.

What could we see in an optimistic crystal ball? The next generation of children would be educated in non-adversarial problem-solving, which would be modelled by their teachers. It would include respect for other people and the ability to express their feelings in a non-confrontational way. The task of teachers would be made easier by this form of self- and mutual discipline. There would be a drop in the number of exclusions and consequent delinquency.

The use of deliberative problem-solving would be a major step towards democracy-building at local level. It would not necessarily be used only for resolving disputes, but could be the method of making decisions in the first place. Methods of conducting consultations are being developed, using small groups, representative of different interests, in which everyone has a chance to contribute, rather than a large audience in which only a few assertive individuals can ask a question. One such approach is 'non-violent communication', expounded by Marshall Rosenberg, which can be used by individuals or mediators. It is based on empathy, statements of feelings and needs leading to understanding of the other's feelings and needs, and proposals for a solution, all combined with careful use of language which may be assertive but not aggressive or disrespectful.[63]

Community involvement, and indeed community building (as Judge McElrea has argued[64]), would be encouraged by the involvement of non-governmental organizations and volunteers wherever appropriate, or failing that, at least by including persons affected in a conferencing process. In most cases prosecution would be the last resort, and would in effect be the primary sanction applied where restorative measures were not suitable or possible. The approach would parallel that of 'better regulation', described above.

Crime reduction policy would be based on social policies and resources, in addition to security measures; individual offenders would be dealt with as individuals, not as vehicles for 'sending a message' to others who might or might not hear it. If there was a message it would not be, 'People who offend others will be made to suffer', but, 'People (including young people) will be treated fairly and are expected to treat others in the same way.' Punishment would be replaced not by leniency but by accountability, including an obligation to make up for the harm caused as far as possible. Judge McElrea points out that the importance of restorative justice is not its outcome but the fact that it is a *procedure* which can lead to vindication of the victim and discovery of the truth, whereas the adversarial procedure and the threat of punishment are an incentive to plead 'not guilty', denying all responsibility that the defendant or his lawyer thinks cannot be proved.[65] It could be said that punishment is the enemy of truth, and it appears that, faced with the choice, many victims would prefer to know the truth.[66]

Punishment also fails to educate: it merely tells people that an act was wrong, not *why* it was wrong, and does not give them a chance to put it right. This is why it is inappropriate to set the age of criminal responsibility low (10 in England and Wales at present). In trivial cases it also makes sense to respond educatively rather than invoke the criminal law: even the right-wing *Daily Mail* newspaper ridiculed the prosecution of cases such as a girl of 10 who was fingerprinted and fined £40 for crayoning on a neighbour's wall, or a boy of 12 who flicked a paper pellet at a classmate, accidentally hitting him in the eye, although he immediately looked after the boy and apologized.[67]

Perhaps the way ahead is to return to the teachings of peoples whose values have survived despite the 'developed' culture of the modern Western world.[68]. First Nations in North America emphasise processes and relationships rather than codes and lists of prohibitions. They tell their children stories showing them how to behave, rather than make lists of do's and don'ts. They do not need to make precise definitions of crimes in advance, because much less hinges on establishing exactly what took place. Instead they concentrate on acknowledging that they cannot continue in this fashion without life becoming worse; the antagonism between them affects others among their families and friends, and for the sake of all concerned they have a responsibility to agree to a new way to deal with each other in future, whether or not they agree on exactly what took place (p. 97). When a person has caused harm, they do not say that he 'is' a bad person, but someone whose mistakes require teaching (p. 123). Some of their languages do not have words such as 'stupid', 'waste', 'pest' or 'guilt'. In one tribe, on the other hand, verbs had a form indicating that 'this event has been concluded to the satisfaction of all' – the forgiveness tense (pp. 54, 88-9). The metaphor of balance is not used as in the scales of justice, which try (vainly, as the Philosopher showed) to balance crime with punishment. Instead 'People who offend against another … are to be viewed and related to as people who are out of balance [with themselves and others]. A return to balance can best be accomplished through a process of accountability that includes support from the community through teaching and healing. The use of judgement and punishment actually works against the healing process' (p. 171). Prison moves an already unbalanced person further out of balance (p. 38).

Lest this seem remote in time and place, it should be noted that these values have inspired the Community Holistic Circle Healing of Hollow Water, Lake Winnipeg. By using a restorative process, this community encouraged many long-standing sexual abusers to come forward and take part in the process; almost none re-offended.[69] Their experience also inspired the idea of community sentencing circles, as Howard Zehr mentions in his book *Changing Lenses*,[70] and the circles of support and accountability mentioned above.

The aim of restorative methods is to repair the harm, rather than merely to punish, even if the only repair possible is to acknowledge the truth and this makes the offender more likely to admit what he or she has done, as truth and reconciliation commissions have found. In addition, the involvement of a number of people, usually seated in a circle rather than a formal court setting, helps to consider what reparation, if any, is appropriate and possible, and to go further and explore social factors that contribute to undesirable behaviour. So far this has only happened in a few places such as Zwelethemba, but the involvement of local citizens, as in the New Zealand family group conferences, Norwegian mediation services or the English young offender panels, gives an opportunity for people to become aware of social shortcomings and do something about them. Without this, the restorative movement is missing a trick.

If patterns emerge indicating pressures towards offending, there should be a channel for passing this to the authorities responsible for crime reduction policy. At first they could operate on a local level, but they have the potential to identify structural flaws and inequalities in the society as a whole, and create pressure for change. For example, supposing 'community safety impact statements' were introduced (a recommendation of a Home Office committee mentioned by the Mediator), such a statement might well have advised that if large-scale gambling were permitted, with permission to advertise on television, it would be a 'racing certainty' that a number of people would become addicted, and a proportion of them would commit crimes. If the government ignored this advice, but it was found that many offenders in areas served by a casino blamed their crimes on gambling, this would put pressure on the government to reconsider its policy.

It is not just a matter of methods, however, but of values. If we return to the North American tradition we find the Navajo ideal of *k'e*, described as 'compassion, cooperation, friendliness, unselfishness,

peacefulness and all the other positive values which create ... solidarity'.
[71] In another continent, a similar tradition lives on in South Africa: in the
Nguni group of languages *ubuntu* describes a person who is generous,
hospitable, friendly, caring and compassionate: one with a proper self-
assurance that comes from knowing that he or she belongs in a greater
whole and is diminished when others are humiliated, oppressed, or
treated as if they were less than who they are.[72]

The name Zwelethemba means 'a place of hope', and Restorative
Practices Scotland has pointed to hope as an essential quality. Restorative
justice, they say: recognises that no matter how severe the wrongdoing, it
is always possible for the community to respond in ways that lend
strength to those who are suffering and that promote healing and
change; does not penalise past actions, but instead addresses present
needs and equips people to move forward with their lives; and nurtures
hope: the hope of healing for persons harmed, the hope of change for
those responsible, and the hope of greater civility for society.[73]

ENDNOTES FOR *UPDATE*

[1] http://www.respect.gov.uk/article.aspx?id=9054 (updated 5.1.07).
[2] http://www.pm.gov.uk/output/page2430.asp (accessed 9.9.2007).

HOW FAR HAVE WE COME?

[3] Liebmann, M (2007) *Restorative justice: how it works.* London and Philadelphia: Jessica Kingsley Publishers.

Schools
[4] ' "There's no justice, just us...": young mediators resolve conflict in schools and the wider community.' *Resolution* (Restorative Justice Consortium), 2007 Summer (26), 8-9.
[5] Warren, C, and Williams S (2007) *Restoring the balance 2: changing culture through restorative approaches – the experience of Lewisham schools.* London: Lewisham Action on Mediation Project (fax +44(0)20 8690 1133).
[6] Hopkins, B (2004) *Just schools: a whole school approach to restorative justice.* London and New York: Jessica Kingsley Publishers.
[7] Kane, J., et al. (2007) Full report of evaluation of restorative practices in 3 Scottish councils. (Web only publication)
http://www.scotland.gov.uk/Publications/2007/08/24093135/0 (accessed 9.9.2007).

Community mediation
[8] See above, reference 3, pp. 117-37, 178-81.

Victim-offender mediation and restorative justice

9 Criminal Justice System (2003) *Restorative justice: the government's strategy*. London: Home Office Communications Directorate.
www.homeoffice.gov.uk/justice/victims/restorative/index.html

10 Criminal Justice System (2004) Conditional cautioning: Criminal Justice Act 2003, sections 22-27; code of practice and associated annexes.
http://www.restorativejustice.org.uk/Resources/pdf/conditional_cautioning_cp.pdf (accessed 10.9.2007)

11 Youth Justice and Criminal Evidence Act 1999.

12 Youth Justice Board (2006) *Developing restorative justice: an action plan*. London: Youth Justice Board. www.yjb.gov.uk

13 Criminal Justice Act 2003, sec. 177(1)(a).

14 www.crimereduction.gov.uk ,(accessed 1.10.2007).

15 Nacro news release 'Young people to deliver community justice in UK's first peer panels', 21 March 2007; S Doughty, ' "Child judges" aged 10 given the legal power to punish' *Daily Mail* 23.10.2007; M Phillips, 'Children as judges? The final proof morality's been turned on its head', *Daily Mail*, 24.10.2007.

16 Mirsky, L (2006) 'The Chard and Ilminster Community Justice Panels: restorative community justice.' http://www.realjustice.org/library/cicjp.html , accessed 29.10.2007.

17 Restorative Justice Consortium (2004) *Principles of restorative processes*. London: RJC.

18 Hencke, D 'Number of deaths at work rises to five-year high.' *Guardian Unlimited*, 26.7. 2007. http://www.guardian.co.uk/uk_news/story/0,,2135566,00.html

19 Macrory, R B (2006) *Regulatory justice: making sanctions effective*. London: Better Regulation Executive. www.cabinetoffice.gov.uk/regulation/penalties

20 Braithwaite, J (2002) *Restorative justice and responsive regulation*. New York: Oxford University Press.

Scotland

21 Kearney, N, S Kirkwood and L MacFarlane (2006) 'Restorative justice in Scotland: an overview.' *British Journal of Community Justice*, 4(3), special issue on restorative community justice.

Northern Ireland

22 Mika, H (2006) *Community-based restorative justice in Northern Ireland*. Belfast: Queen's University, Institute of Criminology and Criminal Justice.

23 O'Mahoney, D, and J Doak (2006) 'The enigma of "community" and the exigency of engagement: restorative youth conferencing in Northern Ireland.' *British Journal of Community Justice*, 4(3), special issue on restorative community justice; see also reference 3 above, chapter 7.

24 House of Commons. Northern Ireland Affairs Committee. *First report*, 18 January 2007.

International

25 It has since shortened its name to European Forum for Restorative Justice.

26 The proceedings of the first are published as *Victim-offender mediation in Europe: making restorative justice work*. Leuven, Belgium: Leuven University Press. 2000.

27 www.euforumrj.org

[28] Subjects include institutionalizing restorative justice, evaluative research projects, restorative justice legislation, restorative justice theory, restorative justice after large-scale violent conflicts, empirical research, and restorative justice in Europe. For details, see above, reference 27.

[29] Council of Europe. Committee of Ministers (1999) *Recommendation No. R(99) 19 of the Council of Ministers to member states concerning mediation in penal matters.* Strasbourg: Council of Europe.

[30] Aertsen, I, R Mackay, C Pelikan, J Willemsens and M Wright (2004) *Rebuilding community connections: mediation and restorative justice in Europe.* (Responses to violence in everyday life in a democratic society.) Strasbourg: Council of Europe.

[31] United Nations (2002) *Basic principles on the use of restorative justice programmes in criminal matters.* New York: UN Economic and Social Council. E/2002/INF/2/Add.2.

[32] United Nations. Office on Drugs and Crime (2006) *Handbook on restorative justice programmes.* (Criminal Justice Handbook Series.) Vienna: UN.

[33] McElrea, F.W.M. (2006) 'Restorative justice: a New Zealand perspective.' In: D J Cornwell, *Criminal punishment and restorative justice: past, present and future perspectives.* Winchester: Waterside Press, p. 120. But they are not necessarily listed in order of priority.

[34] This section is based on a publication of the European Forum: D Miers and J Willemsens, eds (2004) *Mapping restorative justice: developments in 25 European countries.* Leuven: European Forum for Restorative Justice .

[35] Miers, D, and J Willemsens (2004) *Mapping restorative justice: developments in 25 European countries.* Leuven: European Forum for Victim-Offender Mediation and Restorative Justice.

Research

[36] Strang. H (2002) *Repair or revenge: victims and restorative justice.* Oxford: Clarendon Press. See especially Chapter 6.

[37] Maxwell, G, and A Morris (2001) 'Family group conferences and re-offending.' In: A Morris and G Maxwell, eds. *Restorative justice for juveniles: conferencing, mediation and circles.* Oxford and Portland OR: Hart Publishing.

[38] Shapland, J, et al. (2006) *Restorative justice in practice: the second report from the evaluation of three schemes.* Sheffield: University of Sheffield Centre for Criminological Research.

[39] Shapland, J, et al. (2007) *Restorative justice: the views of victims and offenders. The third report from the evaluation of three schemes.* (Ministry of Justice Research Series 3/07.) London: Ministry of Justice. http://www.justice.gov.uk/publications/research90607.htm

[40] Sherman, L W, and H Strang (2007) *Restorative justice: the evidence.* London: Smith Institute. www.smith-institute.org.uk

[41] Wilkinson, R (2007) 'Dysfunctional societies: why inequality matters.' Paper to conference on 'Crime and social justice', Centre for Crime and Justice Studies, 5-6 July 2007.

WHAT PROBLEMS DOES THE RESTORATIVE MOVEMENT FACE?

Lack of progress

[42] Woodward, W, H Muir and D Ward , 'Blair pledges action on gun crime as toll rises: tougher sentences may be extended to 17-year-olds.' *Guardian*, 19.2.2007.

[43] Travis, A 'Blair's justice bill in trouble as prisons near bursting point; ministers fear plan will put 3,000 more in prison.' *Guardian*, 26.5.2007.

[44] Walker, K '3,000 new criminal offences created since Tony Blair came to power.' *Daily Mail*, 16.8.2006.
http://www.dailymail.co.uk/pages/live/articles/news/news.html?in_article_id=400939&in_page_id=1770

[45] http://societyguardian.co.uk , ' "Children should not be jailed" – utterly wrong.' Memo 183, 19.5.2007, #15, #19.

[46] *The Sun*, editorial, 11.10.2006; see also A Porter, 'Judge: we're too tough'. *Sun* 11.10.2006; C Dyer, 'Phillips urges more community penalties.' *Guardian*, 11.10.2006.

[47] Shaw, S (1982) *The people's justice: a major poll of public attitudes on crime and punishment*. London: Prison Reform Trust. See also Wright, M (1989) 'What the public wants.' In: M Wright and B Galaway, eds. *Mediation and criminal justice: victims, offenders and community*. London: Sage; Glover, J 'More prisons are not the answer to punishing criminals, says [Guardian/ICM] poll'. *Guardian*, 28.8.2007.

[48] Carlin, B. ' Tessa Jowell: Gangs are skilled entrepreneurs' *Daily Telegraph*, 26.9.2007.

[49] Quaker Peace and Social Witness (2005) *Circles of Support and Accountability: the first three years, April 2002 to March 2005*. London: Quaker Communications.

[50] Government News Network press release, 4.7.2007. Minstry of Justice (East Midlands). '£5.6 million to improve services for victims of crime: improved services piloted in Nottingham.'

Theoretical concerns

[51] von Hirsch, A, A Ashworth and C Shearing (2003) 'Specifying aims and limits for restorative justice: a "making amends" model.' In: A von Hirsch, J V Roberts and A Bottoms, eds, *Restorative justice and criminal justice: competing or reconcilable paradigms?* Oxford/Portland: Hart Publishing.

[52] See above, reference 33, p. 130.

[53] Roche, D (2003) *Accountability in restorative justice*. Oxford: Oxford University Press.

[54] Blad, J R (2006) 'The seductiveness of punishment and the case for restorative justice: The Netherlands.' In: D J Cornwell, *Criminal punishment and restorative justice: past, present and future perspectives*. Winchester: Waterside Press, pp. 144-6.

[55] Usborne,D (2007) 'The big sleep: soft cell for guests.' *Independent*, 10.9.2007, 32-3.

[56] See above, references 17, 29 and 31.

Political concerns

[57] *Metro*, 17.8.2007, p. 1

[58] Prison Reform Trust (2006) *Prison factfile*. (Bromley Briefings.) London: PRT. www.prisonreformtrust.org.uk

[59] Hansard (House of Commons), Parliamentary Answer 8.3.2007, Gerry Sutcliffe, col. 2162W.

[60] http://www.crimestatistics.org.uk/output/Page54.asp

[61] See O'Mahoney and Doak, above, reference 23.

SPREADING THE RESTORATIVE MOVEMENT

Towards a restorative society

[62] Froestad, J, and C Shearing (2007) 'Beyond restorative justice – Zwelethemba: a future-focused model using local capacity conflict resolution.' In: R Mackay, M Bošnjak, J Deklerck, C Pelikan, Bas van Stokkom and Martin Wright, eds. *Images of restorative justice theory*. Frankfurt am Main: Verlag für Polizeiwissenschaft. See also Roche, reference 53 above, pp. 264-6.

[63] Rosenberg, M B (1999) *Nonviolent communication: a language of compassion*. Del Mar, CA: PuddleDancer Press.

[64] See above, reference 33, p. 131.

[65] See above, reference 33, pp. 127-9.

[66] This assertion could be tested empirically.

[67] 'Girl of 10 fingerprinted and fined £40 for writing on neighbour's wall in crayon,' *Daily Mail*, 29.9 2007; Andrews, E, 'Charged with GBH, the boy, 12, who flicked paper at a classmate.' *Daily Mail*, 29.9.2007.

[68] Ross, R (1996) *Returning to the teachings: exploring Aboriginal justice*. Toronto: Penguin Books. See especially p. 97.

[69] Solicitor General, Canada. Aboriginal Peoples Collection (2001) *The four circles of Hollow Water*. [Ottawa]: Public Works and Government Services Canada.

[70] Zehr, H (1995) *Changing lenses: a new focus for criminal justice*. 2nd ed. Scottsdale, PA: Herald Press. Appendix 4.

[71] See above, reference 67, p. 264.

[72] Tutu, D (1999) *No future without forgiveness*. London: Rider, pp.34-5.

[73] www.restorativejusticescotland.org.uk (accessed12.9.2007).

References

Anon (1997) 'The punishment project', *Probation* (Inner London Probation Service) November, 4.

Adler, J R (1997) *Fear in prisons: its incidence and control.* Unpublished thesis, University of Kent at Canterbury.

Ainsworth, Peter B, and Ken Pease (1981) 'Incapacitation revisited'. *Howard Journal*, 20(3), 160-169.

Alderson, P (1997) *Changing our school: promoting positive behaviour.* Highfield Junior School, Torridge Way, Efford, Plymouth PL3 6JQ.

Ashworth, Andrew (1993) 'Victim impact statements and sentencing'. *Criminal Law Review*, 1993, 498-509.

Atkinson, Rita L, Richard C Atkinson, Edward E Smith and Ernest R Hilgard (1987) *Introduction to psychology.* 9th ed. San Diego: Harcourt Brace.

Azrin, N H, and W C Holz (1966) 'Punishment' in Werner K Honig, ed. *Operant behavior: areas of research and application.* New York: Appleton.

Baldry, Anna C, and David Farrington (1998) 'Parenting influences on bullying and victimization'. *Legal and Criminal Psychology*, 3, 237-254.

Bandura, Albert (1977) *Social learning theory.* Englewood Cliffs: Prentice-Hall

Bandura, Albert, and R H Walters (1963) *Social learning and personality development.* London: Holt, Rinehart and Winston.

Bar Council (1997) *Code of professional conduct* (as amended). General Council of the Bar, 3 Bedford Row, London WC1R 4 DB.

Baron, Robert A, Donn Byrne and William Griffith (1974), *Social psychology: understanding human interaction.* Boston MA: Allyn and Bacon

Bazemore, Gordon (1997) 'The "community" in community justice: issues, themes, and questions for the new neighborhood sanctioning models'. *Justice System Journal*, 19(2), 193-228.

Bazemore, Gordon, and Curt Taylor Griffiths (1997) 'Conferences, circles, boards, and mediations: the "new wave" of community justice decisionmaking'. *Federal Probation*, 61(2), June, 25-37

Bazemore, Gordon, and Kay Pranis (1997) 'Restorative justice: hazards along the way'. *Corrections Today*, December, 84, 86, 88, 89, 128.

Bazemore, Gordon and Mark Umbreit (1998), *Conferences, circles, boards and mediations: restorative justice and citizen involvement in response to youth crime.* Washington DC: Office of Juvenile Justice and Delinquency Prevention, Balanced and Restorative Justice Report.

Bianchi, Herman (1986) 'Abolition: assensus and sanctuary' in Herman Bianchi and René van Swaningen, eds. *Abolitionism: towards a non-repressive approach to crime.* Amsterdam: Free University Press.

Bianchi, Herman (1994) *Justice as sanctuary: toward a new system of crime control.* Bloomington, IN: Indiana UP.

Blackman, D E (1996) 'Punishment: an experimental and theoretical analysis' in James McGuire and Beverley Rowson, eds. *Does punishment work? Proceedings of a conference. London, 1-2 November 1995.* ISTD: Centre for Crime and Justice Studies, 8th floor, 75-79 York Road, London SE 1 7 AW.

Boswell, Gwyneth R (1996) *Young and dangerous: the backgrounds and careers of Section 53 offenders.* Aldershot: Avebury.

Boswell, Gwyneth R (1998) 'Criminal justice and violent young offenders'. *Howard Journal*, 37(2), 148-160.

Braithwaite, John (1989) *Crime, shame and reintegration.* Cambridge: Cambridge University Press.

Braithwaite, John (1998a) *Restorative justice: assessing an immodest theory and a pessimistic theory.* Canberra: Australian Institute of Criminology: webmaster@aic.gov.au

Braithwaite, John (1998b) 'Shame and the social movement politics of restorative justice'. Paper to seminar of Institute of Criminology, University of Sydney, April, unpublished.

Braithwaite, John, and Stephen Mugford (1994) 'Conditions of successful reintegration ceremonies: dealing with juvenile offenders'. *British Journal of Criminology*, 34(2), 139-171.

Braithwaite, John, and Philip Pettit (1990) *Not just deserts: a republican theory of justice.* Oxford: Clarendon.

Brown, Sir Stephen (1998) 'Justice for children'. *New Law Journal*, April 10, 510.

Buonatesta, Antonio (1998) 'Mediation and community service within the Belgian law on juvenile protection: a paradoxical approach to a restorative model' in Lode Walgrave, ed., *Restorative justice for juveniles: potentialities, risks and problems for research.* Leuven, Belgium: Leuven University Press.

Christie, Nils (1997), 'Conflicts as property', *British Journal of Criminology*, 17(1), 1-15

Christie, Nils (1982), *Limits to pain.* Oxford: Martin, Robertson

Church Council on Justice and Corrections (1996) *Satisfying justice: a compendium of initiatives, programs and legislative measures.* CCJC, 507 Bank Street, Ottawa ON K2P 1Z5, Canada.

Clements, L J (1994) *European human rights: taking a case under the convention*. London: Sweet and Maxwell.

Coates, Robert B, and John Gehm (1989) 'An empirical assessment' in Martin Wright and Burt Galaway, eds. *Mediation and criminal justice: victims, offenders and community*. London: Sage.

Cohen, Richard (1995), *Students resolving conflict: peer mediation in schools*. Glenview, IL: Good Year Books.

Conrad, J F, S Dinitz *et al.* (1978) *In fear of each other: studies of dangerousness in America*. Lexington.

Cooper, Paul, and Josie Cooper (1995) 'Victim information in sentencing reports: magistrates' reactions to an experimental model'. *Vista*, September, 2-13.

Cretney, Antonia, and Gwynn Davis (1995) *Punishing violence*. London: Routledge.

Criminal Injuries Compensation Authority (1999), *The Criminal Injuries Compensation Scheme* (Issue No.2, 4/99), CICA, 300 Bath Street, Glasgow G2 4JR.

Current law statutes annotated (1991) Vol. 3. Ed. by Sarah Andrews *et al.* London: Sweet and Maxwell.

Darwish, Adel (1998) 'Brutal childhood paved way for Godfather's killing games'. *The Times*, 16 February.

Davidson, Angus ([1938] 1950) *Edward Lear*. Harmondsworth: Penguin.

Dember, W N, and J J Jenkins (1970) *General psychology: modeling behavior and experience*. Englewood Cliffs, NJ: Prentice-Hall.

Dignan, Jim (1990) *Repairing the damage: an evaluation of an experimental adult reparation scheme in Kettering, Northamptonshire*. University of Sheffield, Centre for Criminological and Legal Research.

Dobash, Russell, Rebecca Emerson Dobash, Kate Cavanagh and Ruth Lewis (1996) *Re-education programmes for violent men: an evaluation*. (Research findings No. 46.) London: Home Office Research and Statistics Directorate.

Dodd, Tricia and Paul Hunter (1992), *The National Prison Survey 1991*, London: Office of Population Census and Surveys.

Doob, Anthony N, Voula Marinos and Kimberly N Varma (1995) *Youth crime and the youth justice system in Canada: a research perspective*. Toronto: Centre for Criminology, University of Toronto.

Dunning, E, P Murphy and J Williams (1988) *The roots of football hooliganism: an historical and sociological study*. London: Routledge.

Elias, Robert (1993) *Victims still: the political manipulation of crime victims*. Newbury Park, CA: Sage.

EPOCH (1990) *Child abuse and physical punishment*. APPROACH [Association for the Protection of All Children], 77 Holloway Road, London N7 8JZ.

EPOCH Worldwide and Rädda Barnen ([1996]) *Hitting people is wrong – and children are people too*. EPOCH Worldwide [End Physical Punishment of Children], 77 Holloway Road, London N7 8JZ, and Rädda Barnen, 107 88 Stockholm, Sweden.

Erez, Edna (1991) 'Victim participation in sentencing, sentence outcome and victim's welfare' in G Kaiser, H Kury and H-J Albrecht, eds. *Victims and criminal justice: legal protection, restitution and support*. (Criminological Research Report 51). Freiburg: Max-Planck-Institute for Foreign and International Penal Law.

Erez, Edna (1994) 'Victim participation in sentencing: and the debate goes on . . .'. *International Review of Victimology*, 3(1/2), 17-32.

Erez, Edna (1999), 'Who's afraid of the big bad victim? Victim Impact Statements as victim empowerment and enhancement of justice', *Criminal Law Review*, 545-556.

Findlay, Jim, Jon Bright and Kevin Gill (1990) *Youth crime prevention: a handbook of good practice*. Swindon: Crime Concern.

Fitzgibbons, Richard P (1986) 'The cognitive and emotive uses of forgiveness in the treatment of anger'. *Psychotherapy*, 23(4), 629-633.

Folkard, M S, D E Smith and D D Smith (1976) *IMPACT volume II*. (Home Office Research Study 36). London: HMSO.

Fry, Margery (1951) *Arms of the law*. London: Gollancz.

Gesch, Bernard (1998) Personal communication.

Glover, Elizabeth (1949) *Probation and re-education*. London: Routledge.

Godwin, William (1793), *Enquiry concerning political justice, and its influence on modern morals and happiness*. Harmondsworth: Penguin

Goldblatt, Peter and Chris Lewis, eds. *Reducing offending: an assessment of research evidence on ways of dealing with offending behaviour*. (Home Office Research Study 187.) London: Home Office.

Graham, John (1998) 'What works in criminality prevention' in Peter Goldblatt and Chris Lewis, eds. *Reducing offending: an assessment of research evidence on ways of dealing with offending behaviour*. (Home Office Research Study 187). London: Home Office.

Griffiths, J (1970), 'Ideology in criminal procedure, or, a third "model" of the criminal process'. *Yale Law Journal*, 79(3), 359-417.

Gross, Hyman (1979) *A theory of criminal justice*. New York: Oxford University Press.

Gulbenkian Foundation Commission (1995) *Children and violence: report of the . . . Commission*. (Chair: Sir William Utting). Calouste Gulbenmkian Foundation, 98 Portland Place, London W1N 4 ET.

Haley, John O (1989) 'Confession, repentance and absolution' in Martin Wright and Burt Galaway, eds. *Mediation and criminal justice: victims, offenders and community*. London: Sage.

Hartmann, Arthur (1998) Personal communication.

Hedderman, Carol, and Darren Sugg (1996) *Does treating sex offenders reduce re-offending?* (Research Findings no. 45). London: Home Office Research and Statistics Directorate.

Hodgkinson, Peter (1996) 'A shameful human rights record: capital punishment in the USA'. *Criminal Justice Matters* (ISTD), (25), 18-19.

Home Office (1974) *Working party on vagrancy and street offences: working paper*. London: HMSO.

Home Office (1990) *Crime, justice and protecting the public*. London: HMSO.

Home Office (1991) *Safer communities: the local delivery of crime prevention through the partnership approach*. (Standing Conference on Crime Prevention. Chair: James Morgan). London: Home Office.

Home Office (1995) *Information on the criminal justice system in England and Wales: Digest 3*. Home Office Research and Statistics Department, Room 1308, 36 Wellesley Road, Croydon CR 9 3 RR.

Home Office (1996a) *Prison statistics England and Wales 1994*. Cm 3087. London: HMSO.

Home Office (1996b) *The victim's charter: a statement of service standards for victims of crime*. London: Home Office.

Home Office (1997) *Criminal statistics England and Wales 1996*. Cm 3764. London: Stationery Office.

Home Office (1998a) *Annual report 1988: the government's expenditure plans 1998-99*. Cm 3908. London: Stationery Office.

Home Office (1998b) *Prisons-probation review: final report*. London: Home Office.

Home Office (1998c) *The reparation order: draft guidance document*, London: Home Office Juvenile Offender Unit. See also similar documents for other orders such as action plan orders.

Home Office, Department of Health and Welsh Office (1995) *National standards for the supervision of offenders in the community*. London: Home Office Probation Division.

Home Office. Chief Inspector of Prisons (1997) *Young prisoners: a thematic review*. London: Home Office.

Hough, Mike, David Moxon and Helen Lewis (1987) 'Attitudes to punishment: findings from the British Crime Survey' in Donald C Pennington and Sally Lloyd-Bostock, eds. *The psychology of sentencing: approaches to consistency and disparity*. Oxford: Centre for Socio-legal Studies.

Hough, Mike, and Julian Roberts (1998) *Attitudes to punishment: findings from the 1996 British Crime Survey*. (Home Office Research Study 179, and Research findings 64). London: Home Office Research and Statistics Directorate.

Howard Journal (1996, 35(2)) Penal policy file 61.3.

Howard League for Penal Reform (1976) *No brief for the dock*. London: Barry Rose and HLPR.

Howard League for Penal Reform (1998a) '436 people committed suicide in prisons'. Press release 26 January.

Howard League for Penal Reform (1998b) *Sentenced to fail – Out of sight, out of mind: compounding the problems of children in prison*. London: Howard League.

Howard League for Penal Reform (1998c) *The big prison squeeze: prison overcrowding*. London: Howard League.

Hoyle, Carolyn, Ed Cape, Rod Morgan and Andrew Sanders (1998), *Evaluation of the 'One Stop Shop' and victim statement pilot projects*. London: Home Office Research Development and Statistics Directorate.

Hudson, Joe, Alison Morris, Gabrielle Maxwell and Burt Galaway, eds. (1996) *Family group conferences: perspectives on policy and practice*. Annandale, NSW, Australia: Federation Press, and Monsey, NY, USA: Criminal Justice Press.

Interdepartmental Working Group (1998) *Speaking up for justice: report . . . on the treatment of vulnerable or intimidated witnesses in the criminal justice system*. London: Home Office.

Johnston, Peter (1994) *The Victim's Charter (1990) and the release of life sentence prisoners: implications for probation service practice, values and management*. Institute of Criminology, University of Cambridge.

Junger-Tas, Josine (1996) *Youth and family: crime prevention from a judicial perspective*. The Hague: Ministry of Justice, Policy Directorate.

Justice (1998) *Victims in criminal justice: report of the Justice Committee*. (Chair: Joanna Shapland). Justice, 59 Carter Lane, London EC4V 5AQ.

Justice Department (n.d., ca. 1980) *Can you bring up children successfully without spanking?* Justice Department, Fack, 103 10 Stockholm, Sweden.

Karsh, Efrain and Inari Rautsi (1991), *Saddam Hussein: a political biography*, London: Brassey.

Kelly, Alistair (1996) *Introduction to the Scottish children's panel.* Winchester: Waterside Press.

Kendler, H H (1963) *Basic psychology.* New York: Appleton Century Crofts.

Khan, Muhammad Zafrulla (1967) *Islam and human rights.* The London Mosque, 16 Gressenhall Road, London SW 18.

Kraus, J (1976) 'Juvenile delinquency and the psychology of general deterrence'. *International Journal of Social Psychiatry*, 22 (2) Summer, 112-119.

Kubizek, August (1954) *Young Hitler: the story of our friendship.* London: Allan Wingate.

Launay, Gilles (1987) 'Victim/offender conciliation' in Barry J McGurk, David M Thornton and Mark Williams, eds. *Applying psychology to imprisonment: theory and practice.* London: HMSO.

Launay, Gilles, and Peter Murray (1989) 'Victim/offender groups' in Martin Wright and Burt Galaway, eds. *Mediation and criminal justice: victims, offenders and community.* London: Sage.

Lee, Angela (1996) 'Public attitudes towards restorative justice' in Burt Galaway and Joe Hudson, eds. *Restorative justice: international perspectives.* Monsey: Criminal Justice Press, and Amsterdam: Kugler.

Lee, Angela, and Wendy Searle (1993) *Victims' needs: an issue paper.* Policy and Research Division, Department of Justice, Private Box 180, Wellington, New Zealand.

Leeds Victim/Offender Unit (1996) *Annual report 1995/6.* West Yorkshire Probation Service, The Basement, Oxford Place Centre, Leeds LS1 3AX.

Leibrich, Julie (1996) 'The role of shame in going straight: a study of former offenders' in Burt Galaway and Joe Hudson, eds. *Restorative justice: international perspectives.* Monsey: Criminal Justice Press, and Amsterdam: Kugler.

Light, Roy, Claire Nee and Helen Ingham (1993) *Car theft: the offender's perspective.* (Home Office Research Study 130). London: HMSO.

Lloyd, Charles (1995) *To scare straight or educate? The British experience of day visits to prison for young people.* (Home Office Research Study 149). London: Home Office.

Lloyd, Charles, George Mair and Mike Hough (1994) *Explaining reconviction rates: a critical analysis.* (HORS 136). London: HMSO.

Lomax, Eric (1995) *The railway man.* London: Cape. Extract reprinted in *Sunday Times Review*, 13 August 1995.

McElrea, F W M (1998) 'The New Zealand model of family group conferences'. Paper to conference 'Beyond prisons: best practices along the criminal justice process', Kingston, Ontario, March.

McGuire, James, and Philip Priestley (1995) 'Reviewing "what works": past, present and future' in James McGuire, ed. *What works: reducing re-offending. Guidelines from research and practice.* Chichester: Wiley.

McIvor, Gill (1992) *Sentenced to serve.* Aldershot: Avebury.

MacKenna, Sir Brian (1978) 'A plea for shorter prison sentences' in P R Glazebrook, ed. *Reshaping the criminal law: essays in honour of Glanville Williams.* London: Stevens.

McLennan-Murray, Eoin (1997) 'Cognitive skills and sex offenders' in Claire Holden and Stephanie Hayman, eds. *Treating sex offenders in a custodial setting.* [Now: Centre for Crime and Justice Studies, 8th floor, 75-79 York Road, London SE 1 7 AW].

MacLeod, M D, *et al.* (1996) *Listening to victims of crime: victimisation episodes and the criminal justice system in Scotland.* Edinburgh: Scottish Office Central Research Unit.

McShane, Marilyn D, and Frank P Williams III (1992) 'Radical victimology: a critique of the concept of victim in traditional victimology'. *Crime & Delinquency*, 38 (2), 258-271.

Maguire, Mike (1982) *Burglary in a dwelling: the offence, the offender and the victim.* London: Heinemann.

Maguire, Mike, and Claire Corbett (1987) *The effects of crime and the work of Victims Support Schemes.* Aldershot: Gower.

Marshall, Tony, and Susan Merry (1990) *Crime and accountability: victim/offender mediation in practice.* London: HMSO.

Martin, G, and J Pear (1992) *Behavior modification: what it is and how to do it.* Englewood Cliffs NJ: Prentice-Hall.

Masters, Guy (1998a) Personal communication.

Masters, Guy (1998b) *Reintegrative shaming in theory and practice: thinking about feeling in criminology.* Unpublished thesis, Lancaster University.

Mawby, Rob, and Sandra Walklate (1994) *Critical victimology.* London: Sage.

Maxwell, Gabrielle, and Allison Morris (1993) *Families, victims and culture: youth justice in New Zealand.* Wellington, NZ: Social Policy Agency and Institute of Criminology.

Maxwell, Gabrielle, and Allison Morris (1996) 'Research on family group conferences with young offenders in New Zealand' in Joe Hudson, Allison Morris, Gabrielle Maxwell and Burt Galaway, eds. *Family group conferences: perspectives on policy and practice.* Leichhardt, NSW: Federation Press; Monsey NY: Willow Tree Press.

Maxwell, Gabrielle, and Jeremy Robertson (1995) *Child offenders: a report to the Ministry of Justice, Police and Social Welfare*. Wellington, NZ: Office of the Commissioner for Children.

May, Chris (1995) *Measuring the satisfaction of courts with the probation service*. (Home Office Research Study No. 144). London: Home Office.

Mediation UK (1994) *Victim/offender mediation: guidelines for starting a service*. Mediation UK, Alexander House, Telephone Avenue, Bristol BS1 4BS.

Mediation UK (1997), *Restorative justice – Does it work? Digest of current research on victim/offender mediation and conferencing*. Mediation UK, as above.

Mediation UK (1998) *Practice standards for mediators and the management of mediation services*. Rev. ed. Mediation UK, as above.

Menninger, Karl (1968) *The crime of punishment*. New York: Viking Press.

Moberly, Sir Walter (1968) *The ethics of punishment*. London: Faber.

Minnesota Sentencing Guidelines Commission (1982) *Preliminary report on the development and impact of the Minnesota Sentencing Guidelines*. St Paul MN: the Commission.

Mirrlees-Black, Catriona, *et al.* (1998) 'The 1998 British Crime Survey England and Wales'. *Home Office Statistical Bulletin*, (21).

Morgan, C T, and R A King (1971) *Introduction to psychology*. 4th ed. New York: McGraw-Hill.

Moxon, David, J M Corkery and C Hedderman (1992) *Developments in the use of compensation orders in magistrates'courts since October 1988*. (Home Office Research Study 126). London: HMSO.

Munn, N L, L D Fernald and P S Fernald (1969) *Introduction to psychology*. 3rd ed. Boston: Houghton-Mifflin.

NACRO (1997) *Criminal Justice Digest*, July.

NACRO (1998a) *Criminal Justice Digest*, January.

NACRO (1998b) *Criminal Justice Digest*, July, 8.

Nathanson, Don (1992), *Shame and pride: affect, sex and the birth of the self*, New York: W W Norton.

Newburn, Tim (1988) *The use and enforcement of compensation orders in magistrates'courts*. (Home Office Research Study 102). London: HMSO.

Newman, G R (1983) *Just and painful: a case for corporal punishment*. New York: Macmillan.

Nixon, Allen J (1974) *A child's guide to crime*. Sydney: Angus and Robertson.

Northamptonshire Adult Reparation Bureau (1992) *Annual report 1992*. Diversion Unit, 198 Kettering Road, Northampton NN1 4BL.

O'Connell, Terry (1997) 'Conferencing and community empowerment: rediscovering the human face of justice'. Paper to conference 'Dawn or dusk in sentencing', Quebec, April.

Parker, T, and R Allerton (1962) *The courage of his convictions*. London: Hutchinson.

PAPPAG (1999), *Changing offending behaviour: some things work*. Parliamentary All-Party Penal Affairs Group, c/o 169 Clapham Road, London SW9 0PU.

Peachey, Dean E (1989) 'The Kitchener experiment' in Martin Wright and Burt Galaway, eds. *Mediation and criminal justice: victims, offenders and community*. London: Sage.

Pearson, Geoffrey (1983) *Hooligan: a history of respectable fears*. London: Macmillan.

Pease, Ken, and Joyce Wolfson (1979) 'Incapacitation studies: a review and commentary'. *Howard Journal, 18(3), 160-167.*

Penal Affairs Consortium (1996) *The Crime (Sentences) Bill: a briefing on the Bill's proposals for mandatory and minimum sentences and 'honesty in sentencing'*. Penal Affairs Consortium, 169 Clapham Road, London SW9 0PU.

Penal Affairs Consortium (1997) *The prison system: some current trends*. The Consortium, as above.

Penal Reform International and International Centre for Prison Studies (1998) *Penal Reform Project in Eastern Europe and Central Asia: Newsletter*, No. 1, July. PRI, 169 Clapham Road, London SW9 0PU.

Plotnikoff, Joyce, and Richard Woolfson (1998) *Witness care in magistrates'courts and the youth court*. (Research findings No. 68). London: Home Office Research and Statistice Directorate.

Powers, Edwin (1982) *Constitutional rights of prisoners*. Boston, MA: Crime and Justice Foundation.

Pranis, Kay, and Mark Umbreit (1992) *Public opinion research challenges perception of widespread demand for harsher punishment*. Citizens Council, 822 South 3rd Street, Minneapolis MN 55415.

Prison Reform Trust (1997a) *The prison population in Britain, Europe and the rest of the world*. PRT, 14 Northburgh Street, London EC1V 0AH.

Prison Reform Trust (1997b) *Sentencing: a geographical lottery*. PRT, as above.

Prison Service (1997) *Annual report and accounts 1995-96*. [HC 247] London: Stationery Office.

Quill, Deirdre, and Jean Wynne, eds. (1993) *Victim and offender mediation handbook*. Available from Mediation UK, Alexander House, Telephone Avenue, Bristol BS1 4BS.

Reeves, Helen (1993) 'Victim impact statements: against'. Speech to National Conference of Victim Support, Warwick, England, 1993.

Renshaw, Judy (1998) 'Misspent youth: update '98'. *On track*, Newsletter for youth justice practitioners (Home Office), (2), 1.

Restorative Justice Consortium (1999) *Standards for restorative justice*. RJC, c/o Social Concern, Montague Chambers, Montague Close, London SE1 9DA.

Retzinger, Suzanne M (1991) *Violent emotions: shame and rage in marital quarrels*. London: Sage.

Retzinger, Suzanne M, and Thomas J Scheff (1996) 'Strategy for community conferences: emotions and social bonds' in Burt Galaway and Joe Hudson, eds. *Restorative justice: international perspectives*. Monsey: Criminal Justice Press, and Amsterdam: Kugler.

Reynolds, Teresa (1997) Speech to ISTD conference 'Repairing the damage', Bristol, 20 March 1997.

Robinson, George, and Barbara Maines (1997) *Crying for help: the No Blame approach to bullying*. Bristol: Lucky Duck Publishing.

Robinson, Paul H (1987) *Dissenting view of Commissioner Paul H Robinson on the promulgation of sentencing guidelines by the United States Sentencing Commission*. Washington DC: US GPO.

Rolph, C H (1974) *Living twice: an autobiography*. London: Gollancz.

Royal Commission on Criminal Justice (1993) *Report*. (Chair: Viscount Runciman). Cm 2263. London: HMSO.

Schafer, Stephen (1968) *The victim and his criminal: a study in functional responsibility*. New York: Random House.

Scheff, Thomas J (1994) *Bloody revenge: emotions, nationalism and war*. Boulder, CO: Westview Press.

Schofield, Helen (1997) 'Probation officer recruitment and training'. *NAPO News* (National Association of Probation Officers), (92), September, 5.

Servicebüro für Täter-Opfer-Ausgleich und Konfliktschlichtung (1998) *Standards: ein Handbuch für die Praxis des Täter-Opfer-Ausgleichs*. Servicebüro, Aachener Strasse 1064, D-50858 Köln, Germany.

Sessar, Klaus (1995) 'Restitution or punishment: an empirical study on attitudes of the public and the justice system in Hamburg'. *EuroCriminology*, 8-9, 199-214.

Shapland, Joanna (1983) 'Victim assistance and the criminal justice system: the victim's perspective'. Paper to 33rd International Course in Criminology, Vancouver.

Shapland, Joanna, and Emma Bell (1998) 'Victims in the magistrates' courts and Crown Court'. *Criminal Law Review*, August, 537-546.

Sherman, Lawrence W, and Heather Strang (1997) *RISE working papers: the reintegrative shaming experiments for restorative community policing*. Research School of Social Sciences, Australian National University, Canberra.

Smith, David, and John Stewart (1997) 'Probation and social exclusion'. *Social Policy and Administration*, 31(5), 96-115.

Sprott, W J H, A P Jephcott and M P Carter (1954) *The social background of delinquency*. Nottingham: University of Nottingham.

Stern, Vivien (1998) *A sin against the future: imprisonment in the world*. London: Penguin.

Stewart, Susan (1998) *Conflict resolution: a foundation guide*. Winchester: Waterside Press.

Sweden. Department of Justice (ca. 1980) *Can you bring up children successfully without smacking and spanking?* Justitiedepartmentet, Fack, 103 10 Stockholm.

Tarling, R (1979) *Sentencing practice in magistrates' courts*. (Home Office Research Study 56). London: HMSO.

Taylor of Gosforth, Lord (1996) *Witnesses, victims and the criminal trial*. London: Victim Support.

Taylor, L (1984) *In the underworld*. Oxford: Blackwells.

Temple, William (1934) *Ethics of penal action*. London: Clarke Hall Fellowship.

Thomas, David A (1984-) *Current sentencing practice*. London: Sweet and Maxwell.

Thorvaldson, A B (1980) 'Does community service affect offenders?' in J Hudson and B Galaway, eds. *Victims, offenders and alternative sanctions*. Lexington, MA: D C Heath.

Tonry, Michael (1996) *Sentencing matters*. New York: Oxford University Press.

Tonry, Michael H, and Norval Morris (1978) 'Sentencing reform in America' in P R Glazebrook, ed. *Reshaping the criminal law: essays in honour of Glanville Williams*. London: Stevens.

Umbreit, Mark (1994) *Victim meets offender: the impact of restorative justice and mediation*. Monsey, NY: Criminal Justice Press.

Umbreit, Mark (1995) *VSOD model: victim sensitive offender dialogue through mediation*. School of Social Work, University of Minnesota (see below).

Umbreit, Mark, and Robert B Coates (1992) *Victim/offender mediation: an analysis of programs in four states of the US*. School of Social Work, University of Minnesota (see below).

Umbreit, Mark S, and Ann Warner Roberts (1996) *Mediation of criminal conflict in England: an assessment of services in Coventry and Leeds*. Centre for Restorative Justice and Mediation, School of Social Work, University of Minnesota, 1386 McNeal Hall, 1985 Buford Avenue, St Paul MN 55108, USA.

United Nations. Commission on Crime Prevention and Criminal Justice (1998) *Handbook on justice for victims on the use and application of the United Nations Declaration of Basic Principles of Justice for Victims of Crime and Abuse of Power.* (E/CN.15/1998/CRP.4/ Add.1). Vienna: the Commission.

United States. Department of Justice (ca.1997) *Examples of restorative justice practices.* Washington DC: Office of Justice Programs *et al.*

United States Sentencing Commission (1987a) *Sentencing guidelines and policy statements.* Washington DC: US GPO. (See also Robinson 1987).

United States Sentencing Commission (1987b) *Supplementary report on the initial sentencing guidelines and policy statements.* Washington DC: US GPO.

Utting, David (1996) *Reducing criminality among young people: a sample of relevant programmes in the United Kingdom.* (Research study 161). London: Home Office.

Varela, Jacobo A (1971) *Psychological solutions to social problems.* New York: Academic Press.

Vass, Antony A (1986) 'Community service: areas of concern and suggestions for change'. *Howard Journal*, 25(2), 100-111.

Vennard, Julie, Carol Hedderman and Darren Sugg (1997) *Changing offenders' attitudes and behaviour: what works?* (Home Office Research Study 171). London: HMSO. (Summarised in Research findings No. 61. London: Home Office Research and Statistics Directorate.)

Victim Support (1994) *Support for the families of road death victims: report of an independent working party.* Victim Support, 39 Brixton Road, London SW9 6DZ.

Victim Support (1995) *The rights of victims of crime: a policy paper by Victim Support.* London: Victim Support, as above.

Victim Support (1996a) *Victims of crime and the media.* London: Victim Support, as above.

Victim Support (1996b) *Women, rape and the criminal justice system.* London: Victim Support, as above.

Victim Support (1997) [Annual] *Report 1997.* London: Victim Support.

Victim Support (1998) *Restorative justice and the Crime and Disorder Act.* (National conference edition). London: Victim Support.

Von Hirsch, Andrew, and Nils Jareborg (1991) 'Gauging criminal harm: a living-standard analysis'. *Oxford Journal of Legal Studies*, 11(1), 1-38.

Waite, Robert G L (1977) *The psychopathic god: Adolf Hitler.* New York: Basic Books.

Walker, Nigel (1969) *Sentencing in a rational society.* London: Allen Lane and Harmondsworth: Penguin.

Walker, Nigel (1978) 'Punishing, denouncing or reducing crime?' in P R Glazebrook, ed. *Reshaping the criminal law: essays in honour of Glanville Williams.* London: Stevens.

Walker, Nigel (1980) *Punishment, danger and stigma: the morality of criminal justice.* Oxford: Blackwell.

Walker, Nigel (1991) *Why punish?* Oxford: Oxford University Press.

Walker, Nigel (1995) 'The quiddity of mercy'. *Philosophy*, 70, 27-37.

Walmsley, Roy, E Howard and S White (1992) *The National Prison Survey 1991: main findings.* London: HMSO

Waterville Projects (1997) *Projects for children and young people.* Waterville Projects, The Vicarage, St John's Terrace, Percy Main, North Shields, Tyne and Wear NE 29 6 HL.

West Yorkshire Probation Service. Leeds Victim/Offender Unit. *Annual report 1995/6.* The Basement, Oxford Place Centre, Leeds LS1 3AX.

Wilczynski, Ania (1997) *Child homicide.* London: Greenwich Medical Media.

Wilson, Margaret (1931) *The crime of punishment.* London: Cape.

Wolff, Jennifer (1998) 'Named and shamed'. *Marie-Claire* (Australian edition), May, 50-54.

Wright, Martin (1982) *Making good: prisons, punishment and beyond.* London: Burnett/ Unwin Hyman.

Wright, Martin (1983) *Victim/offender reparation agreements: a feasibility study in Coventry.* West Midlands Probation Service, 1 Printing House Street, Birmingham B4 6DE

Wright, Martin (1989) 'What the public wants' in Martin Wright and Burt Galaway, eds. *Mediation and criminal justice: victims, offenders and community.* London: Sage.

Wright, Martin (1992) 'Victim/offender mediation as a step towards a restorative system of justice' in Heinz Messmer and Hans-Uwe Otto, eds. *Restorative justice on trial: pitfalls and potentials of victim/offender mediation – international research perspectives.* Dordrecht: Kluwer.

Wright, Martin (1995) 'Victims, mediation and criminal justice'. *Criminal Law Review*, March, 187-199.

Wright, Martin (1996) *Justice for victims and offenders: a restorative response to crime.* 2nd ed. Winchester: Waterside Press.

Wright, Susan (1998) *A consideration of two key mediation concepts and their relevance to restorative justice processes: approaching restorative justice from a mediation perspective.* Unpublished dissertation, Massey University, New Zealand.

Wynne, Jean (1998) 'Can mediation cut re-offending?' *Probation Journal*, 45(1), 21-6.

Youth Justice Board (1999) *Guidance for the development of effective restorative practice with young offenders.* London: Youth Justice Board.

Zehr, Howard (1990) *Changing lenses: a new focus for crime and justice.* Second edn. Scottdale, PA: Herald Press and London: Metanoia Book Service.

Zia-ul-Haq, Mohammad (1979) 'Enforcement of Nizam-i Islam'. *Hamdard Islamicus*, 2(2), 3–60 (including Annexe 6, Offences against property (Enforcement of Hudood) Ordinance, February 1979).

Index

The New Ministry of Justice
An Introduction ~ Bryan Gibson

' Gibson is to be applauded for having produced the first word on these new departments ' **Jamie Bennett, HMPS,** *Prison Service Journal*

' Bryan Gibson and Waterside Press are to be congratulated on producing these stimulating books so soon after such a fundamental change was effected. ' *Justice of the Peace*

This is the first and as of now only book to describe the **post 2007 UK systems of justice and law enforcement.** It is also dynamic and ahead of any criminology text in assessing the type and impact of key institutional changes. Anyone purporting to write or research on UK or comparative matters of crime and punishment cannot really afford to be without it without appearing to be out of date. It also contains a full historical and developmental context.

160 pages | September 2007 | ISBN 978-1-904380-35-1

The New Home Office
An Introduction ~ Bryan Gibson

' Bryan Gibson is well placed to explain the new system to us, having been associated with the criminal justice system for some considerable time. This is a book that should be read by everybody involved in the Criminal Justice System ' **Rob Jerrard**, Internet Law Book Reviews.

' These two guides will prove invaluable for anyone trying to get their head around the 21st century new world of criminal justice. ' *Thames View*

172 pages | September 2007 | ISBN 978-1-904380-36-8

Buy the set now

Criminal Punishment and Restorative Justice
Past, Present and Future Perspectives
~ David J Cornwell

If the voice of restorative justice is to resonate more widely RJ must demonstrate that it will deliver better justice in a modern-day context. This book sets out to establish the credentials of RJ for this - as a **force for change at criminological, penal and everyday, practical levels**. The book provides a refreshing analysis of the inherent divide between punitive and restorative approaches to questions of criminal justice.

Looks at matters that serve to restrict more **active and enthusiastic adoption** of principles of restorative justice so that RJ tends to be constrained to a secondary role on the margins of criminal justice development. It examines claims to mainstream consideration against the backdrop of traditional justifications for punishment - and, in an era when increasing use of custodial and other punitive methods is a growing worldwide, questions communities would not be far better served by a more emphatic and early shift in favour of restorative methods.

The book provides an international perspective re the potential of restorative justice to deliver an altogether more enlightened approach towards dealing with offenders and victims. It argues that the use of custody can be reduced by challenging offenders to take responsibility for their offences and to make reparation for their wrong-doing. It seeks to consign to history the fallacies and false horizons of traditional thinking in favour of a principled, more purposeful use of sanctions.

Criminal Punishment and Restorative Justice **pulls no punches** in its criticism of traditional approaches and their failure to achieve crime prevention.

David Cornwell appraises the potential of restorative justice to make 'corrections' more effective, civilised, humane, pragmatic and non-fanciful - by looking at 'bedrock issues' in contemporary criminology and penology and demonstrate that RJ offers no 'soft options', rather the demands of remorse, acceptance of responsibility, and the repairing of harm done. It makes the case for the radical overhaul of existing approaches on the basis of principle not political expediency.

186 pages | 2006 | ISBN 978-1-904380-20-7

☯ WATERSIDE PRESS

Restorative Justice in Prisons
A Guide to Making It Happen
~ Tim Newell and Kimmett Edgar

This is the best leading edge information and ideas from two of the UK's most respected practitioners and authorties. It is for people who want to make a difference, suggests the tools for this and offering guidance - wholly up to speed with what is happening in UK prisons.

PART OF A MAJOR INITIATIVE ACROSS UK PRISONS THAT IS KEY READING FOR EVERY RJ PRACTITIONER AND STUDENT

Prison as an institution is sometimes taken to represent the opposite of restorative justice. The culture of prisons includes coercion, highly structured and controlled regimes, banishment achieved through physical separation, and blame and punishment – whereas restorative justice values **empowerment, voluntarism, respect, and treating people as individuals.**

Recent developments in some prisons demonstrate a far more welcoming environment for restorative work. Examples such as reaching out to victims of crime, providing prisoners with a range of opportunities to make amends and experimenting with mediation in response to conflicts within prisons show that it is possible to implement restorative justice principles in everyday prison activities.

Guided by restorative justice, prisons can become **places of healing and personal transformation**, serving the community as well as those directly affected by crime: victims and offenders. This new book advocates the further expansion of restorative justice in prisons.

Building on a widespread interest in the concept and its potential, the authors have produced a guide to enable prisons and the practitioners who work in and with them to translate the theory into action.

> 'What strikes you as you read through this text is the sheer simplicity with which Edgar and Newell have captured the changes that are so apparently needed in the prison system today'.
> **Andy Bain, Institute of Criminal Justice Studies, University of Portsmouth**

One of the most important penal reform books for years

134 pages | 2006 | ISBN 978-1-904380-25-2

≋ WATERSIDE PRESS

Doing Justice Better
The Politics of Restorative Justice
~ David J Cornwell

An **uncompromising appraisal** of the unique
penal crisis affecting Britain and other Western-style
democracies. Escalating resort to prisons, longer
sentences, overcrowded and ineffective regimes,
high rates of re-offending and eclectic penal policy
all combine to fuel this crisis, whilst failing to reduce
offending.

In *Doing Justice Better*, **David J Cornwell** argues that
the symptoms of this penal malaise are grounded
in media sensationalism of crime and the need of politicians (and their advisers)
to retain electoral credibility. Change is long overdue, but it requires a fresh,
contemporary penology based on Restorative Justice. The book challenges the
status quo, asks 'different questions' and places victims of crime at the centre of
the criminal justice process.

> ' David Cornwell seeks to drill down into [the key] issues. This book identifies
> the organizational stresses and strains, the target-setting, the policy "blips"
> and all the problems of trying to bring radical change to our criminal justice
> system ' **Sir Charles Pollard QPM** Director, Restorative Solutions, former
> Chief Constable, Thames Valley Police Service

> ' An important and timely contribution to the literature ' **Mark S Umbreit**

> ' One of the leading writers in the [restorative justice] campaign... intelligent
> and helpful... an urgent call to action particularly about the penal crisis
> which hangs permanently over this country's head ' *Justice of the Peace*

David Cornwell is a criminologist and former prison governor with extensive
experience of operational practice and consultancy within both state and
privately managed sectors of correctional administration in a number of countries
worldwide. His first book, Criminal Punishment and Restorative Justice, was
published by Waterside Press in 2006

200 pages | August 2007 | ISBN 978-1-904380-34-4

☙ WATERSIDE PRESS

Law, Justice and Mediation
The Legend of St Yves
~ Bryan Gibson

NEW

The Legend of St Yves is not widely known in Britain, even though he is the patron saint of lawyers (among other things). In this informative account, **Bryan Gibson** places St Yves - born Erwan Helouri - on a par with Robin Hood, Jessie James and Ned Kelly in terms of their appeal to various national psyches - and up there alongside Joan of Arc and Bernadette of Lourdes as regards his native France.

But whilst conventional outlaws used bows, arrows, six-guns and bullets to 'rob the rich to help the poor', St Yves challenged the **poverty and social inequality** which he saw as the root of many a prosecution or claim via **argument, debate, reason and consensus**. At a time when bribery and corruption was rife, St Yves waged an historic struggle to enhance the fairness of proceedings and their outcomes.

Hailing St Yves as an **icon of justice, counselling, mediation and reform**, Gibson explains why Erwan Helouri deserves to be better known, including for the values of **decency, integrity and ethics** that his approach to resolving conflict imparts.

The result is not just a fascinating portrayal of the man but a work that will serve as an encouragement to anyone who believes that there are better ways of doing justice. Building on connections across time, place and elements of the supernatural, *Law, Justice and Mediation: The Legend of St Yves* also stands in its own right as an enlightening and compelling tale.

As *Guardian* columnist and legal commentator **Marcel Berlins** writes in the Foreword:

> 'St Yves deserves to be far better known than he is, especially in the English-speaking world, and in Bryan Gibson he has found a worthy champion'.

96 pages | February 2008 | ISBN 978-1-904380-40-5

☰ WATERSIDE PRESS